Holy wells were once widespread throughout Britain. They were often dedicated to local saints and were important features in the medieval sacred landscape. Over many centuries, pilgrims sought the healing powers of their waters, and many left votive offerings in the form of bent pins, coins and rags.

Interest in this aspect of our sacred heritage has been growing since the publication of Janet Bord's first book on holy wells over twenty years ago. Many holy wells have now been restored, and the modern visitor may still experience a quiet communion with the spirit of the place, and come away spiritually uplifted.

For this book Janet Bord has sought out three hundred of the surviving holy wells of England, Wales and Scotland that are most rewarding to visit, and she recounts their histories and traditions in the light of current historical research.

Holy Wells in Britain is the first guidebook to British holy wells to draw upon the extensive research of recent decades. Up-to-date practical information for visitors is also provided to inspire readers to seek out these evocative sacred sites for themselves.

This guide is a companion to Janet Bord's recent book, *Cures and Curses: Ritual and Cult at Holy Wells* (2006) and Jeremy Harte's *The Holy Wells of England: A Sourcebook* (2008).

By the same author

Cures and Curses: Ritual and Cult at Holy Wells

Footprints in Stone: Imprints of Giants, Heroes, Holy People, Devils, Monsters and Supernatural Beings

Mazes and Labyrinths of the World

Fairies: Real Encounters with Little People

The Traveller's Guide to Fairy Sites

With Colin Bord

Mysterious Britain

The Secret Country: An Interpretation of the Folklore of Ancient Sites in the British Isles

A Guide to Ancient Sites in Britain

Earth Rites: Fertility Practices in Pre-Industrial Britain

Sacred Waters: Holy Wells and Water Lore in Britain and Ireland

Ancient Mysteries of Britain

Atlas of Magical Britain

Dictionary of Earth Mysteries

The Enchanted Land: Myths and Legends of Britain's Landscape

Holy Wells in Britain

A Guide

Janet Bord

Heart of Albion

Holy Wells in Britain: A Guide
Janet Bord

Cover: St Queran's Well, Dumfries.
Photograph by Janet Bord

ISBN 978-1-905646-09-8

Published by
Heart of Albion Press
113 High Street, Avebury
Marlborough, SN8 1RF

albion@indigogroup.co.uk

Visit our Web site: www.hoap.co.uk

Printed in England by Booksprint

Contents

Acknowledgements   xii

Introduction   1

England: South-West

Cornwall   3
St Anne's Well, Whitstone – St Cleer's Well, St Cleer – St Clether's Well,
St Clether – St Cuby's Well, Duloe – Dupath Well, Callington –
St Guron's Well, Bodmin – Jordan Well, Laneast – St Keyne's Well,
St Keyne – Madron Well – St Michael's Well, Michaelstow – St Neot's Well,
St Neot – St Sampson's Well, Golant – St Swithin's Well, Launcells

Devon   15
St Brannoc's Well, Braunton – Fice's Well, Princetown – Fitz's Well,
Okehampton – St Gudula's Well, Ashburton – Ladywell, Pilton –
Lady Well, Sticklepath – Leechwell, Totnes – St Leonard's Well,
Sheepstor – St Nectan's Well, Stoke – St Nectan's Well, Welcombe –
St Urith's Well, Chittlehampton

Isles of Scilly   21
St Warna's Well, St Agnes

Somerset   22
St Agnes' Well, Cothelstone – St Aldhelm's Well, Doulting –
St Andrew's Well, Stogursey – St Andrew's Well, Wells – St Anne's Well,
Brislington – Chalice Well, Glastonbury – St Decuman's Well, Watchet –
Holy Well, Edington – St Joseph's Well, Glastonbury – King Arthur's Well
and Queen Anne's Well, South Cadbury – St Mary's Well, Charlcombe –
Sacred Spring, Bath

England: South

Berkshire   29
St Anne's Well, Caversham – Ladywell, Speen

Dorset   31
St Augustine's Well, Cerne Abbas – Holy Well, Hazelbury Bryan –
Holy Well, Holwell – Lady's Well, Hermitage – St Wite's Well,
Morcombelake – Wishing Well, Upwey

Hampshire   36
Holy or Wishing Well, Binsted – Holy Well, Sopley – Holybourne
Springs – Iron's Well (Lepers' Well), Fritham

Isle of Wight   38
St Lawrence Well, St Lawrence – White Well, Whitwell

Wiltshire   39
Cat's Well, Bratton – Daniel's Well, Malmesbury – Ladywell,
Bradford on Avon – Monkswell, Edington

England: South-East

Greater London   42
Caesar's Well, Keston – Caesar's Well, Wimbledon Common –
St Eloy's Well, Tottenham – St Mary's Well, Willesden

Kent   43
The Black Prince's Well, Harbledown – St Edith's Well, Kemsing –
St Ethelburga's Well, Lyminge – St Leonard's Well, West Malling –
St Margaret's Well, Broomfield

Surrey   47
St Anne's Well (Nun's Well), Chertsey – St Anne's Well, Stanwell –
Anne Boleyn's Well, Carshalton – St Catherine's Spring, Artington –
St Edward's Well, Sutton Park, Guildford – St John the Baptist's Well,
Bisley – Mag's Well, Mugswell – St Mary the Virgin's Well, Dunsfold

East and West Sussex   50
Bone Well, Willingdon – Ludwell Spring, Horsted Keynes –
St Peter's Well, Lodsworth – Spring at Fulking

England: South Midlands

Bedfordshire   52
Holy Well, Stevington

Buckinghamshire   53
St Osyth's Well, Bierton – St Rumbold's Well, Buckingham –
Schorne Well, North Marston

Gloucestershire   55
St Anthony's Well, Forest of Dean – St Bride's Well, St Briavels –
Calmsden Cross Well – St Kenelm's Well, Winchcombe –
Our Lady's Well, Hempsted – Our Lady's Well, Lower Swell –
Seven Wells, Bisley

Herefordshire   63
St Ann's Well and Lady Well, Aconbury – St Clodock's Well, Clodock –
St Edith's Well, Stoke Edith – St Ethelbert's Well, Hereford – Holy Well,
Garway – Holy Well, Luston – St Peter's Wells, Peterchurch

Hertfordshire   67
Amwell, Great Amwell – Chadwell Spring, Ware – Holy Well, St Albans

Northamptonshire   68
Becket's Well, Northampton – St John's Spring, Boughton Green –
St Rumbold's Well, King's Sutton

Oxfordshire   72
Fair Rosamond's Well, Woodstock – Lady Well, Wilcote –
St Margaret's Well, Binsey

Warwickshire   76
Berks Well, Berkswell – Holy Well, Burton Dassett – Holy Well,
Southam – Rowton's Well, Sutton Park

Worcestershire   79
St Ann's Well, and Holy Well, Malvern Hills – St Katherine's Well,
Bredon Hill – St Kenelm's Well, Romsley

England: East

Cambridgeshire   83
Holy Well, Holywell – Holy Well, Longstanton – Holy Well
(St Cloud's Well), Longthorpe – Red Well, Knapwell

Essex   85
St Cedd's Well, North Ockendon – St Peter's Well, West Mersea –
The Running Well, Runwell

Lincolnshire   86
Holy Well, Sempringham – St John's Well, Bottesford – Kell Well,
Alkborough – Lud's Well, Stainton-le-Vale – Spring Wells, Billingborough

Norfolk   88
Walsingham Wells – St Walstan's Well, Bawburgh – St Withburga's Well,
Dereham

Suffolk   94
The Lady's Well, Blythburgh

England: North Midlands

Cheshire   95
Three Wells on Alderley Edge – St Chad's Well, Chadkirk, Romiley –
St Patrick's Well, Bromborough – St Plegmund's Well, Plemstall –
Whistlebitch Well, Utkinton

Derbyshire   100
St Alkmund's Well, Derby – St Anne's Well, Buxton – Holy Well,
King's Newton - Mompesson's Well, Eyam – Roman Baths,
Stoney Middleton – Tissington Wells

Leicestershire   105
Holy Well, Ab Kettleby – Holy Well, Beeby – King Richard's Well,
Bosworth Battlefield

Nottinghamshire   106
St Catherine's Well, Newark – St Catherine's Well, Westhorpe, Southwell

Rutland   107
Wishing Well, Ashwell

Shropshire   108
St Cuthbert's Well, Donington – St Julian's Well, Ludlow – St Milburga's
Well and St Owen's Well, Much Wenlock – St Milburga's Well,
Stoke St Milborough – St Oswald's Well, Oswestry – St Winifred's Well,
Woolston

Staffordshire   112
St Bertram's Wells, Ilam – St Chad's Well, Stowe – Egg Well, Bradnop –
St Helen's Well, Rushton Spencer – Holy Well, Sandwell Valley –
Wulfruna's Well, Wolverhampton

England: North

Cumbria   116
St Andrew's Well, Kirkandrews-on-Eden – St Cuthbert's Well, Colton –
St Helen's Well, Great Asby – St Kentigern's Well, Aspatria –
St Kentigern's Well, Caldbeck –St Mungo's Well, Bromfield –
St Ninian's Well, Brisco – St Oswald's Well, Kirkoswald –
St Patrick's Well, Patterdale – Stanger Well, Embleton

Durham   121
St Cuthbert's Well, Durham – Holy Well, Wolsingham – St Mary's Well,
Gainford – St Oswald's Well, Durham

Isle of Man   122
Well of the Baptism (Chibbyr y Vashtee), Patrick – St Catherine's Well
(Chibbyr Catreeney), Port Erin – St Mary's Well (Chibbyr y Woirrey),
Ramsey – St Maughold's Well, Maughold – St Patrick's Well
(Chibbyr Pherick), Lonan – St Patrick's Well (Chibbyr Pherick), Peel

Lancashire   125
Holy Well, Hollinshead Hall, Tockholes – Ladyewell, Fernyhalgh Lane,
Fulwood – St Oswald's Well, Winwick – St Patrick's Well, Heysham –
St Thomas's Well, Windle

Northumberland   129
St Cuthbert's Well, Bellingham – Lady Well, Holystone – Pin Well,
Wooler – St Mary's Well, Jesmond Dene, Newcastle – St Mungo's Well,
Holystone

Yorkshire: East   132
Drummer's Well, Harpham – St Helen's Well, Goodmanham –
St John's Well, Harpham

Yorkshire: North   134
St Cedd's, St Chad's and St Ovin's Wells, Lastingham – Dropping Well
and Wishing Well, Knaresborough – Ebbing and Flowing Well
(and Bank Well), Giggleswick – St Helen's Well, Farnhill – St Helen's Well,
Kirkby Overblow – St Hilda's Well, Hinderwell – Our Lady's Well,
Threshfield – Mary Magdalene Well, Spaunton – Old Wives' Well, Stape

Yorkshire: South and West   139
St James's Well, Midhopestones – Lady Well, Hartshead – Peace Well,
Dore – Town's Well, Hampole – White Wells, Ilkley

Wales

Anglesey   141
Ffynnon Cerrigceinwen – Ffynnon Seiriol (St Seiriol's Well), Penmon –
Ffynnon Wenfaen (St Gwenfaen's Well), Rhoscolyn

Carmarthenshire   143
St Anthony's Well and Ffynnon Fair (St Mary's Well), Llansteffan
(Llanstephan) – Ffynnon Deilo (St Teilo's Well), Llandeilo –
Ffynnon Gwyddfaen, Llandyfan

Ceredigion   146
Ffynnon Gybi (St Cybi's Well), Llangybi – Ffynnon Llawddog, Cenarth

Conwy   147
Ffynnon Gelynin (St Celynin's Well), Llangelynin – Ffynnon Drillo
(St Trillo's Well), Llandrillo-yn-Rhos (Rhos-on-Sea)

Denbighshire   149
Ffynnon Beuno, Tremeirchion – Ffynnon Ddyfnog, Llanrhaeadr-yng-
Nghinmeirch – Ffynnon Degla (St Tegla's Well), Llandegla – Ffynnon Fair
(St Mary's Well), Cefn Meiriadog – Ffynnon Sara, Derwen

Flintshire   152
Ffynnon Wenfrewy (St Winefride's Well), Treffynnon (Holywell)

Gwynedd   153
Ffynnon Beuno (St Beuno's Well), Clynnog Fawr – Ffynnon Beris
(St Peris's Well), Nant Peris – Ffynnon Fair (St Mary's Well),
Bryncroes – Ffynnon Gybi (St Cybi's Well), Llangybi

Monmouthshire   156
St Anne's Well (Virtuous Well), Trellech – St Tewdic's Well, Mathern

Pembrokeshire   157
Bletherston Holy Well – Burton Church Well – St Govan's Well,
Bosherston – Gumfreston Church Wells – Llanllawer Holy Well –
St Justinian's Well, St Justinian – Margaret's Well, Templeton –
St Non's Well, St Davids

Powys   161
Ffynnon Fair (St Mary's Well), Llanfair Caereinion – Ffynnon Fair
(St Mary's Well), Pilleth – Ffynnon Gynydd (St Cynidr's Well), Glasbury –
St Issui's (Isho's/Ishow's) Well, Partrishow/Patrisio/Patricio –
Ffynnon Myllin (St Myllin's Well), Llanfyllin

South Wales   165
St Cenydd's Well, Llangennith, Gower, Swansea – St David's Well and
St John's Well, Newton Nottage, Porthcawl – Ffynnon Deilo
(St Teilo's Well), Llandaff, Cardiff – Ffynnon Fair (St Mary's Well),
Penrhys, Rhondda – Trinity Well, Illston, Gower, Swansea

Scotland

Aberdeenshire   169
St Drostan's Well, New Aberdour

Angus   169
St Fergus's Well (Lady Well), Glamis

Argyll and Bute   170
St Columba's Well, Keil Point, Southend, Kintyre – Holy Well,
Kilmory Oib, Tayvallich – St Ninian's Well (Tobar Ninian), Dervaig,
Isle of Mull

Borders   170
Cheese Well, Minchmoor – St Ronan's Well, Innerleithen –
Tamlane's Well, Carterhaugh

Dumfries and Galloway   172
Brow Well, Ruthwell – Chipperdingan Well, near Port Logan –
St Finnan's Well, Chapel Finian, Mochrum – St Medan's Well, Monreith –
St Queran's Well, Islesteps, Dumfries

East Lothian   174
St Baldred's Well, East Linton – St Bay's Well, Dunbar – Rood Well, Stenton

Edinburgh   174
St Anthony's Well, Holyrood Park – Balm Well, Liberton –
St Margaret's Well, Holyrood Park – St Mungo's Well, Currie –
St Triduana's Well, Restalrig

Fife   177
St Fillan's Well, Pittenweem

Highland   178
St Boniface's Well (Cloutie Well), Munlochy – St Bennet's Well
(Craigie Well), Avoch – St Ignatius's Well, Glassburn –
St John the Baptist's Well, Fodderty – St John the Baptist's Well,
Helmsdale – St Mary's Well, Culloden – St Ninian's Well, Drumnadrochit –
Well of the Dead, Culloden – Well of the Heads, Loch Oich

Isle of Skye   182
Tobar Ashik (St Maelrubha's Well), Broadford

Moray   182
St Fumac's Well, Botriphnie – St Mary's Well (Well of Grace), Orton –
Pictish Well, Burghead

North Lanarkshire   184
Holy Well, Carfin Lourdes Grotto

Perth and Kinross   185
St David's Well, Weem – Well at Scotlandwell

Stirling   185
St Fillan's Well, Strathfillan

Sources   187

Bibliography   206

Index   215

Acknowledgements

I wish to thank the following people, all of whom have helped in my quest to make these wells accessible to more interested people. In alphabetical order they are: Lionel Beer, John Billingsley, Andy Burnham, Graeme Chappell, Pam and Maurice Day, Clive Fewins, Jenny Frith, Betsy Gray, Peter Griffin, Jeremy Harte, J.A. Hilton, Tristan Gray Hulse, Katy Jordan, Brendan O'Malley, Richard Pederick, Tim Prevett, Nona Rees, Iain and Carol Reid, Susan and Peris Sinnett-Jones, Julie Trier, Bob Trubshaw, Paula Veen-Voskuijl, Edna Whelan, Rosemary and Edwin Wilson, David C. Woods. Thanks also to everyone who supplied photographs: they are credited by name beside their pictures.

I also wish to thank all those anonymous people who have been involved in preserving and restoring the rich heritage of holy wells in Britain – long may they continue to do so!

Introduction

There were once hundreds, if not thousands, of holy wells in England, Wales and Scotland, a surprising number of which still survive, though not always in good condition. Some have been in existence for hundreds of years, once being the focus of devout cults and visited by thousands of pilgrims: they are the genuine holy wells, dedicated to a local saint and often being part of a wider sacred landscape. However, not all so-called 'holy wells' are genuine, some being no more than village water sources, or eccentric garden ornaments, or modern wishing wells, and so are, strictly speaking, outside the scope of this book. Nor have I included wells that were developed as spas and never attracted a religious following – though sometimes a genuine holy well would later be turned into a healing spa, and some examples of these have been included.

Sorting out the genuine holy wells from the rest is not always easy, as the surviving evidence can sometimes be ambiguous. Anyone wishing to know more about what defines a genuine holy well will find further discussion in my earlier book *Cures and Curses: Ritual and Cult at Holy Wells.* In this book I have tried to concentrate on genuine holy wells – but a few non-holy wells with interesting accretions have crept in, especially if visiting them is a rewarding experience. Therefore the selection of wells in this guidebook is somewhat idiosyncratic. It is a personal choice, consisting mainly of wells that I have visited and consider to be worth revisiting – but I have not been able to visit all of them, and so the selection includes some interesting wells that other people have visited fairly recently and which therefore have a good chance of still existing today. (I indicate in the Sources which wells I have visited personally, and when.) The listings on The Megalithic Portal website (www.megalithic.co.uk) have proved especially useful in confirming the condition and accessibility of wells I have not been able to visit, and I wish to express my thanks to all the well-hunters who have contributed to those listings of more than 600 wells.

Because of the interest shown in them by local people and by visitors, many holy wells that were in danger of being lost have been restored in recent years and are now being maintained: it is greatly to be hoped that this will continue. However, judging by the number of well names found on maps and in old texts, but with no further information available, there are probably literally hundreds of lost holy wells, something amply confirmed by the listings in Jeremy Harte's magnificent compilation *The Holy Wells of England: A Sourcebook.* So it is even more important to preserve what we still have.

I have tried to provide sufficient information to enable visitors to find the wells I have included, and I hope that the location information will prove adequate. Ordnance Survey map references are given, but they are approximate and for guidance only, not having been obtained using GPS. I have selected the names of counties and administrative areas to suit my purpose of making the wells easy to locate, so the divisions contain a mixture of old and new. All the wells in this book are reasonably accessible and I have included very few wells that are on private land or in people's gardens. Where those are included, I have checked (or am aware) that the landowner does not object to people visiting their well. It goes without saying that all visits to holy wells should be undertaken quietly and unobtrusively, leaving no trace of one's presence other than a small offering of a coin or something organic that will decay over time.

The entries for the English wells are categorised as 'major' and 'minor', the latter having less space devoted to them. In the section for Wales no such differentiation is made: a shortage of space has meant that some information has had to be omitted, though most of the best wells are included, and I am hoping to write a much fuller guide to the holy wells of Wales in the not-too-distant future. My descriptions of the Scottish wells are also brief, mainly because my knowledge of those wells is decidedly patchy and I have had to rely much more on information from others, therefore the Scottish wells are no more than a sample of what that country has to offer. My original intention was to include all the wells in Britain that I could find that were worth visiting, but this proved an over-optimistic aim which did not find favour with my long-suffering publisher, and so I have had to restrict the selection to some degree. This means that there are still plenty of surviving wells that do not appear in these pages – and certainly there are some that I do not know about – leaving plenty of scope for well-hunters to continue their research.

Janet Bord

North Wales
October 2007

England: South-West

Cornwall, Devon, Isles of Scilly, Somerset

CORNWALL

There are so many fine holy wells in Cornwall that I have restricted this list to those that resonated the strongest when I visited. Anyone wishing to find out more about Cornwall's wells should consult a modern guide such as Cheryl Straffon's *Fentynyow Kernow: In Search of Cornwall's Holy Wells* which gives directions to 125 of them, or check the Megalithic Portal website (www.megalithic.co.uk) where more than 130 are listed.

St Anne's Well, Whitstone

This is an archetypal holy well in an evocative churchyard setting. A well-preserved stone building topped by a stone cross stands over the well, which still contains

St Anne's Well in Whitstone churchyard in 2001.

water. The well appears to have little recorded history, but it has clearly been of local importance in the past, and it was restored in the 1880s, at which time 'Saint Anna' was carved round the archway, and bits of stone including the cross were brought in from elsewhere to make up the structure that we see today. There is an empty niche above the archway; and even more intriguingly, there is a strange carved head on the back wall inside the well, above another small niche. When I first visited this well in 1978, a gnarled old thorn tree grew on the bank immediately to the left, leaning protectively over the well. Even though that has now gone, the location still has a strong atmosphere.

Location: In the churchyard of Whitstone church, beside a lane on the north-west side of the village, which is twelve miles north-west of Launceston. SX263986

St Cleer's Well, St Cleer

The well building may date from the fifteenth century, though in 1850 when seen by Thomas Quiller-Couch it was ruinous and the only surviving wall may be the back wall today (the building was restored in 1864). Nothing is known of its history, and it was apparently in a poor state as far back as the early eighteenth century, when William Hals described it as 'a famous chappell well dedicated to St. Clare, a work of great skill, labour, and cost, though now much decayed.' St Cleer himself is equally shrouded in mystery. Cleer is the same as Clair, Clare and Clarus, and the first mention of him in connection with St Cleer church is in 1212. His name in Latin means 'clear', and it has been suggested that this saint was linked to wells whose water was good for the eyes. The 'halt and the blind' were said to have resorted to the well at St Cleer, and it has also been suggested that it was used as a bowssening

The holy well at St Cleer, photographed in 1978. More recent visits have confirmed that it has not changed noticeably.

pool (where the insane were pushed into the water as a cure), but I have not found any documentary confirmation of this. The construction of the well-chamber argues against this use, unless it was rebuilt on a smaller scale, or unless an adjacent pool has disappeared. (More information on bowssening can be found in my book *Cures and Curses*.)

Location: In the village of St Cleer, two miles north of Liskeard. The well building and seven-foot stone cross are easily found beside the road in the centre of the village, a few hundred yards north-east of the church. SX249683

St Clether's Well, St Clether

The well in its small stone building, and the large well chapel (about twenty feet long) beside it, are now in fine condition, thanks to the efforts of the Reverend Sabine Baring-Gould who brought about their restoration in 1899. The water flows from the well, and into the chapel through the wall close to the four-foot-long granite altar, leaving through a niche in the south wall. The peaceful rural location makes this one of the most atmospheric of well sites. The early history of the site is unknown, but the chapel may date from the fifteenth century. The relative grandeur of the chapel indicates that this was once an important and much-visited well. Clether or Cleder is said to have been one of the twelve sons of the Welsh king Brychan, and Baring-Gould was convinced that St Clether had his baptistery at this site, 'for the traditional usage of fetching water from it for baptisms in the parish church has lingered on there'.

The ceremony of rededication in 1899 was described by an unnamed Cornishman.

> The rededication service of the restored well-chapel of St Clether...was a very interesting function. The chapel, which had long been in ruins, was situated in a bog, and last year...suddenly the water resumed its old course and flowed by a subterranean channel under the east wall and bubbled up beneath the altar, and then was carried away by a second subterranean conduit into the second holy well. The chapel has been completely restored. Almost all the old stones were found, and its reconstruction was like the putting together of a puzzle. The situation is one of extraordinary beauty among prongs of volcanic rock rising above the Inney. Sunday was a fine day. There was a procession from the parish church, headed by a cross, consisting of masons and carpenters who had rebuilt the chapel, the Sunday school children, choir, and clergy singing 'O Word of God above' and the 'Exurgat Deus'. The effect of the many coloured banners borne by the procession winding among the rocks and tufts of gorse and heather under a brilliant sun was very striking. On arriving at the west door a collect was said, and the choir entered singing the 'Urbs Beata'. The procession passed round the chapel singing 'A living stream as crystal clear' when suddenly a striking incident occurred. A couple of poor people arrived, and asked for their

St Clether's Well and Chapel (1990). To the right is the holy well (or the upper well); in the centre is the east end of the chapel; and at bottom left is the lower well where the water emerges from the chapel.

> child to be baptised at the well; and this was done, the name given being 'Clether'. The Rev. Sabine Baring Gould gave an address on the saint's history. The 'Nunc Dimittis' concluded an interesting service...

Location: The well is a quarter-mile north-west of the church of St Clether, which is a hamlet seven miles west of Launceston. A footpath leads to the well from behind the church and along the valley of the River Inney. SX202846

St Cuby's Well, Duloe: The ancient font in Duloe church was originally sited at the well, and St Cuby may have used it for baptisms in the sixth century. (Illustrated under 'Baptism' in my *Cures and Curses*.) The well is beside the main road through Duloe village. SX241579

Dupath Well, Callington: The largest well-chapel in Cornwall after St Clether's, built of granite around 1510, though since restored. It may have functioned as a pilgrimage chapel rather than simply being a holy well. The water was believed to cure whooping cough – and the presence of a bathing tank suggests that at the time the well-chapel was built, cures were also sought for other ailments. Located close to Dupath Farm east of Callington. SX375692

St Guron's Well, Bodmin: The fifteenth-century well-house is in St Petroc's churchyard close to the church; the water flows out through two stone heads into a

Left: *St Cuby's Well as it was in 1978.*

Right: *The fine stone building housing Dupath Well in 2004.*

Below: *St Guron's Well, Bodmin: the two stone heads.*

trough lower down the hill. SX073670. There is also an Eye Well in the town (near car park off Dennison Road; SX070671).

Jordan Well, Laneast: The water was used for divining the future, for baptisms, and for making butter. The well in a late-medieval well-house is in the field opposite the church. SX229839

St Keyne's Well, St Keyne

The well is covered by a small stone building with a rounded arch and has been maintained in good condition since its restoration in the 1930s. When visited by the Quiller-Couches in 1891, it was 'in a very dilapidated state, the arch tumbling to pieces'. St Keyne (also Kayne, Kein, Keinwen) was another of the offspring of the Welsh king Brychan (see *St Clether's Well* above). She took a vow of chastity and shunned marriage – but is best remembered for her connection with a marriage custom. It has long been believed that after a marriage, the first one of the couple to drink the water of St Keyne's Well would for ever afterwards gain mastery in the marriage. This belief was first recorded in 1602 by Richard Carew:

> In name, in shape, in quality,
> This well is very quaint;
> The name, to lot of Keyne befell,
> No over-holy Saint.
> The shape, 4. trees of divers kinde,
> Withy, Oke, Elme and Ash,
> Make with their roots an arched roofe,
> Whose floore this spring doth wash.
> The quality, that man or wife,
> Whose chance, or choice attaines,
> First of this sacred streame to drinke,
> Thereby the mastry gaines.

Better known is the poem *The Well of St Keyne* by Robert Southey, written in the early nineteenth century, which tells how St Keyne often drank from the well and 'laid on the water a spell' that gave mastery of the marriage to whoever drank there first. It also tells of one sheepish Cornishman who, on rushing to the well immediately after the marriage service, found that he had been outwitted by his wife:

> 'I hasten'd as soon as the wedding was done,
> And left my Wife in the porch;
> But, i' faith, she had been wiser than me,
> For she took a bottle to Church.'

Location: Beside a lane half-a-mile south-east of St Keyne church (two-and-a-half miles south of Liskeard), at a minor junction. SX248603

St Keyne's Well in its rural setting, photographed in 1974. It is still maintained in good condition.

Madron Well

The location of Madron Well is most atmospheric and the history of the site is complex. The spring which is today known as the holy well is a hole in the ground, not exactly picturesque or easily accessible, in a thicket of trees and in boggy ground. The trees all around are hung with offerings in the form of pieces of cloth. (For the purpose of these, see 'Cloutie wells' and 'Rags' in my *Cures and Curses*.) There is a small ruined chapel not far away and inside can be found what was probably the original holy well. At the time of writing the chapel is being restored, an event sadly marred by mindless vandalism.

The well-chapel has been dated to the fourteenth/fifteenth century and this provides evidence of how long this place has been considered special. Reliable documentation only dates back to the early seventeenth century, when Nicholas Roscarrock wrote: 'I have heard there hath been sundrye miracles wrought [at the well], and especiallie on the feastes of Corpus Christie'. John Trelille's miraculous cure c.1638–40 was investigated by Joseph Hall, Bishop of Exeter, who wrote that Trelille was 'suddenly so restored to his limbs, that I saw him able both to walk, and to get his own maintenance; I found there was neither art nor collusion, the thing done, the Author invisible.' Trelille had been cripped for sixteen years since as a boy of twelve he had been hit on the spine with a stick, and afterwards he could only get

The interior of the ruined chapel at Madron Well in 1990, looking towards the altar stone; note the stone seats on either side. There is no longer any trace of St Maddern's Bed, which was beside the altar.

around by crawling. At the age of twenty-eight he dreamed he could recover his strength if he washed himself in the spring 'sacred to Maddernus', and so

> one Thursday in May... he crawled to this place out of the hope he had conceived through his dream and lay down before the altar, praying earnestly for health and for the recovery of the strength of his sinews, as he understood from the dream. He washed his whole body in the stream which penetrates the chapel and flows from the spring, and fell asleep for half an hour on St Maddern's bed, when he cried out with an intense pain, now in his nerves, now in his arteries. Being helped and raised up by his companion, he felt his legs and arms extend a little, so that he went out of the chapel somewhat stronger, and proceeding partly on his feet, partly on his hands, came home in a more erect manner than usual.

He returned to the well two times more, and each time he was able to walk better than before. The final time, after washing and sleeping, 'when he awoke [he] sprang up wholly sound', and four years later he enrolled for military service – though he sadly died in 1644 at the siege of Lyme. The fuller account I have quoted from was published by Francis Coventry in his *Paralipomena Philosophica* (1652). One hundred years later, the antiquarian William Borlase wrote that people were still frequenting the well:

> Here people who labour under pains, aches and stiffness of limbs, come and wash, and many cures are said to have been performed... Hither also upon much less justifiable errands come the uneasy, impatient, and superstitious, and by dropping pins or pebbles into the Water, and by shaking the ground round the Spring, so as to raise bubbles from the bottom, at a certain time of the year, Moon, and day, endeavour to settle such doubts and enquiries as will not let the idle and anxious rest.

Madron Well was also believed to be good for curing childhood ailments such as rickets, and sickly children were taken there on the first three Sunday mornings in

May. They were dipped into the water three times while naked, the person dipping them standing facing the sun, and then they would be passed round the well nine times, from east to west. Finally they were dressed and laid on St Maddern's Bed. If they slept, and the well water bubbled, these were encouraging signs – but complete silence had to be maintained throughout the procedure.

St Madron was also known as Madern, Maddern, Madernus and other similar names, and he was first recorded as the patron saint of Madron church in 1203, but nothing is known about him. He is now remembered only because of Madron Well, which has been active for more than seven hundred years. As mentioned earlier, there are actually two wells at this location, and it is probable that the well in the chapel was the original holy well. As the early descriptions show, the chapel played an integral part in the healing rituals, and several of its features are still identifiable, such as an altar stone nearly six feet long, stone seats along the sides, and in one corner the holy well which was used as an immersion tank, with an inlet to let water in and a drain to remove it afterwards. St Maddern's Bed was a grassy mound beside the altar, probably the traditional location of the saint's tomb or grave – it was also the custom at other wells for a person seeking a cure to lie in a place closely linked to the saint (see 'Incubation' in my *Cures and Curses*).

In addition to the healing rituals, there were other customs practised at Madron well from at least the 1700s, as noted by Borlase. The content of the Borlase quotation (above) suggests that some time between the mid-seventeenth century and Borlase's time, the original cult had degenerated, and moved from the chapel to the spring in the bushes. This in turn suggests that during this hundred years the chapel had become ruined, most probably under the Commonwealth. Later, the nineteenth-century writer Robert Hunt reported that 'here divination is performed on May mornings by rustic maidens anxious to know when they are to be married. Two pieces of straw about an inch long are crossed and transfixed with a pin. This, floated on the waters, elicits bubbles, the number of which, carefully counted, denotes the years before the happy day.' Thomas Quiller-Couch said that two pins or pebbles had to be thrown together into the water, and if they sank together, the person would soon be married. He also described seeing 'rags and bandages on the thorns which grew around' when he visited the well in 1845, a custom which continues to the present day.

Location: Madron village is about a mile to the north-west of Penzance; take the Morvah road from Madron and then shortly a lane heading north to Boswarthen. A short distance along the lane, a signposted path heads north to the well and chapel. SW446328

St Michael's Well, Michaelstow

The well is a pleasingly simple square structure in the churchyard. It may be on the site of the original baptistery; the water was still being used for baptisms late in the nineteenth century and perhaps more recently than that. SX081788

St Neot's Well, St Neot

Like most of the Cornish wells, this one fell into disrepair, but was thankfully restored by the vicar in 1852, a fact now emblazoned across its structure. The water is protected by a solid granite well-house with an arched doorway, and surmounted by a stone cross. This well is closely linked to St Neot, whose history is uncertain but who, according to the Lives written 800-1,000 years ago, may have been a Cornishman who died here at St Neot in the 870s. Some supposed events from his life are depicted in a fine medieval stained-glass window dating from 1530 in St Neot church. It shows him renouncing his claim to the throne of East Anglia, becoming a monk at Glastonbury, and saving a doe from a hunter.

One series of images tells the story of St Neot and the fishes. He found three small fishes in a 'copious fountain' (presumed to be his holy well) and an angel told him to take only one fish each day, leaving the other two, and that if he did this, each day there would be three there again. One day he was ill and unwilling to eat, so to tempt him his servant fetched two fishes from the well. He fried one and boiled the other, and took them to the saint. On learning what the servant had done, St Neot told him to take them back to the well, and he then prayed continuously until he was told that there were again three fishes swimming in the well, the two cooked fish having been resurrected. He asked for one to be brought to him, and on eating it he immediately regained good health. Other panels show him using stags to pull a plough after his oxen were stolen, receiving the pope's blessing in Rome; and there is one panel that shows St Neot sitting in the holy well reciting his psalter, something

St Neot's Well at St Neot in 1998.

he was wont to do regularly as an act of self-mortification. This is a very rare medieval depiction of ascetic immersion. (This use of holy wells is described more fully, and St Neot's window depicted, under the heading 'Immersion' in my book *Cures and Curses*; and the window telling the story of the fishes is shown under 'Fishes and frogs'.)

Location: On the southern edge of Bodmin Moor, about five miles north-west of Liskeard; the well is just outside the village of St Neot and reached by a pleasant walk along a lane leading north off the main street (west of the church) and along the valley of the St Neot River. SX183680

St Sampson's Well, Golant

The well is contained within a small building, unusually positioned very close to the church. It has an arched doorway, and is well maintained, having been restored in 1938. A rough stone figure inside at the back may have been intended to represent the saint. St Sampson is believed to have had Welsh ancestry, and to have been a sixth-century Welsh bishop, and he passed through Cornwall on his way to Brittany, where he built churches, and established a monastery at Dol, hence his more familiar name, Samson of Dol. Scholars have been unable to establish the precise link between St Sampson and Golant, but it may have been the place where, according to the saint's seventh-century Life, he vanquished 'a poisonous and most evil serpent' living in a 'horrible cave', and it may also have been the place where he had a cell – and he may have used this very well. St Sampson is depicted in stained-

The small well building is to the left of Golant church porch (2000). Its former intimate connection with the church is shown by the fact that it has its own little door in the west wall of the porch.

One of the St Sampson windows inside Golant church, showing the saint 'baptizing a heathen'.

glass windows inside the church, including 'baptizing a heathen' and as a bishop, surrounded by scenes from his life.

Location: The well is sited close to the church entrance at Golant, a village overlooking the river two miles north of Fowey. SX121551

St Swithin's Well, Launcells: The well is easily found close to the church entrance at Launcells east of Bude. SS244057.

DEVON

Like Cornwall, Devon has many holy wells, far too many to include in this guidebook, and again I have selected the ones that I have myself visited, plus others that are highly thought of by other well devotees. Terry Faull's 2004 book *Secrets of the Hidden Source* provides a useful guide to many more accessible wells in the county, as does his website www.holywells.com.

St Brannoc's Well, Braunton

This 'well' is a stone-edged pool, standing in a wooded dell beside St Brannoc's Roman Catholic church. Brannoc or Brannock may (or may not) have been the same as the Welsh saint Brynach of Nevern – little is truly known about Brannoc, other than that he is believed to have eventually settled, and died, here. In addition to the well and church, the Anglican parish church of Braunton is also dedicated to him. According to folklore, he built his first church where he found a sow with seven piglets, an event foretold in a dream, and which is depicted in a roof boss in the church. He had originally tried to build on Chapel Hill where there is still a ruined chapel of St Michael, but the Devil nightly took the stones down the hill. St Brannoc's church was built in the late 1950s on the ruins of an earlier chapel, with a statue of the saint being erected over the porch. The well water was traditionally used for baptisms.

St Brannoc's Well at Braunton in 2004. An image of Our Lady of Lourdes has been placed in a shrine above the well.

Fitz's Well near Okehampton, covered by massive stone slabs, its location marked by a granite cross. Photo: Roy Fry.

Location: Braunton is five miles north-west of Barnstaple and the well is on the west side of the A36, in the grounds of St Brannoc's Roman Catholic Church. The entrance is opposite Frog Lane: take the lower lane down to the church. SS487374

Fice's Well, Princetown: The simple stone well-house in a stone-wall enclosure carries the letters I.F. and the date 1568: it was one of three wells built by Sir John Fitz (the other Fitz's Wells are at Okehampton and Tavistock). It was said that he and his wife had got lost – perhaps piskie-led – while riding on the moor. They came across the spring and took a drink, whereupon the mist cleared and they could see where they were. Sir John erected a stone shelter over the spring so that other travellers could also make use of it. The water was believed to be good for eye complaints. Public footpath to well signposted off the B3357. SX578759

Fitz's Well, Okehampton: This is another well said to be linked to Sir John Fitz, and the identical story about him being piskie-led, as is told at Fice's Well, is also told for this well. The water was said to be good for sore eyes; and the well was visited by youngsters on Easter Sunday to try and learn something of their future loves. Today's visitors tie rags to a nearby tree. The well can be found close to a lane south of the town and south of the A30, its location marked by a granite cross. SX591937

St Gudula's Well, Ashburton: This well has been restored in recent years, along with St Gudula's Cross close by. The water was once used to cure eye problems, and within living memory, people used to fill bottles with the water to keep in their medicine cabinets. Beside the Old Totnes Road ; steps lead down to the well. SX754694

Lady Well at Sticklepath.
Photo: Paula Veen-Voskuijl.

Ladywell, Pilton: A plaque with the well name is above an arched recess protected by a grille. The well was restored in the 1980s and was blessed by Metropolitan Anthony of Sourozh, a senior member of the Orthodox Church. The water has been used for baptisms and healing. It is in a lane behind Pilton parish church (north-west corner of churchyard). SS557341

Lady Well, Sticklepath: The well is beside the road through the village, a small stone trough into which the water flows from a pipe in the stone surround; above is a carved stone saying 'Lady Well – Drink and Be Thankful'. SX639941

Leechwell, Totnes

Terry Faull considers this 'one of the most ancient and important Holy Wells in Devon' – sadly I have not yet visited it myself. A stone-walled enclosure protects three spouts which direct water into three separate stone troughs, and each spring has a name and a different use. The water from Long Crippler cures the eyes, that from Toad cures skin problems, and the water from Snake helps snake bites. The name 'Leechwell' also tells us that the water had healing functions, since 'leech' meant 'doctor' and leechcraft was the art of healing. Traditionally the wells were also used in fortune-telling rituals, and possibly there was a connection with the leper hospital. The town also used the wells as a water supply. They were once so popular that wardens were appointed to oversee them. Today they are still much visited by holy well devotees, as the rags, flowers and other offerings attest.

Location: Reached from the upper end of High Street, Totnes, down the narrow Leechwell Lane next to the Kingsbridge Inn. SX800602

St Leonard's Well, Sheepstor in 2001.

St Leonard's Well, Sheepstor: The elaborate stone surround was from one of the old windows, reused when the church was restored in the 1850s. The spring originally rose in a field, but was piped to the roadside for ease of access. It is beside the road below the church: one field to the east of the church, on the north side of the road. SX560676

St Nectan's Well, Stoke

This is an important holy well, but unfortunately it did not have a good atmosphere when I visited. Perhaps its history still resonates: this was the place where St Nectan lived, and where he carried his head after he had been beheaded by thieves. It was said that bloody marks remained on a stone by the well where he placed his head, though these are no longer identifiable. St Nectan was a Welsh hermit who settled near Hartland in the sixth century; it was the theft of his two cows that brought about his murder, after he tried to convert the thieves to Christianity. In the centuries which followed, a flourishing cult preserved the memory of St Nectan in this area of North Devon, where five churches were dedicated to him. He was enshrined at Hartland, where an image beside the altar shows him with a spare head, commemorating the head-carrying exploit.

Left: *St Nectan's Well at Stoke is protected by a grille and a door in 2004.*
Right: *St Nectan with his well, as depicted on an icon which can be seen in Stoke church.*

There may once have been a sacred eel living in the well, because a twelfth-century story tells of two boys who dipped their cauldron in the well and then tried to heat the water over a fire. But it failed to boil, and they saw that St Nectan's sacred eel was swimming around in it. They hastily returned the eel to the well, whereupon the cold water began to bubble from the heat. Some holy wells did contain sacred eels or fishes, and more examples can be found in my book *Cures and Curses* in the entry for 'Fishes and frogs'.

St Nectan's memory is still strong in this area, and several depictions of him can be found in nearby Stoke church: in a window, standing beside his severed head on the reredos, and a copy of a modern icon. His image can also be found outside the church: on the church tower and the churchyard cross.

Location: Stoke is about twelve miles north of Bude and one-and-a-half miles west of Hartland. Close to the lych-gate entrance to the church, a path leads off the main street and down to the well. SS236247

St Nectan's Well, Welcombe: An archetypal holy well, very pleasing. The well-house is a Grade II listed building, fourteenth or fifteenth century, very much in keeping with the church dedicated to St Nectan a stone's throw away. There is a small icon of St Nectan in the niche. The water was once used for baptisms. Ten miles north of Bude. SS228184

St Nectan's Well, Welcombe in 2004.

St Urith's Well, Chittlehampton

There are three Devon saints around whom legends, and wells, have sprung up after their beheading: St Sidwell of Exeter, St Nectan of Stoke (see *St Nectan's Well* above) and St Urith of Chittlehampton. She was said to have been killed by haymakers with their scythes at the instigation of her stepmother. Since Urith is a Celtic name (from the Welsh version Iwerydd), she may have been a Christian victim of the pagan Saxons. A spring began to flow where she was killed, presumably the one at Chittlehampton that is more commonly known as Taddy Well or St Teara's Well ('Teara' is a dialect variant of Urith or its Latinisation Hieretha). Pilgrims came to visit her shrine and well, and the offerings were sufficient to build the fine church tower. Urith may still be buried somewhere in the church – her shrine is in an alcove to the north of the chancel – and she is depicted on the pulpit dating from around 1500. The annual pilgrimage to her shrine, which was stopped in 1539, has now been revived, and there is a procession to her well on her feast day.

Location: Chittlehampton is five miles west of South Molton, and the well is not far from the church, in a narrow lane near Rose Cottage. SS637255

ISLES OF SCILLY

St Warna's Well, St Agnes

Nothing is known of the origins or history of St Warna, and the name may originally have been Awana, though neither version appears before the seventeenth century. According to folklore, she was the patron saint of shipwrecks – and that is *not* protecting the sailors who found themselves shipwrecked, but luring the ships on to the rocky shore so that they could be plundered by the locals! It was said that the wreckers 'bowed daily before the altar of St. Warna, and daily threw pins into her well, and offered up their supplications for wrecks.' After one particularly gruesome event, when a priest and child were drowned with the wreckers looking on and making no effort to save them, the leader of the wreckers had a vision that same night in which the old man and St Warna came to him, prophesying that he and all five families living on the island would 'perish by a wreck'. Soon afterwards, all of them went by boat to St Mary's to attend a wedding, and on their way back they were shipwrecked in a storm and none of them survived. The boats drifted over to St Warna's Bay where they were later found – but the island was now uninhabited, 'nor was the worship of St Warna ever renewed.' But her well has survived. Stone steps lead down into a stone chamber where there is still water. It had become neglected and full of stones during the nineteenth century, but it is clearly now being cared for again.

Location: On the west side of the island, south of the village and above St Warna's Bay. Heading out of St Warna's Bay, walking south, the coast path climbs to a rocky outcrop. About thirty feet before reaching the fence at the outcrop, take a few paces to the right. The well can be found in a little hollow, its entrance facing out to sea. SV880078

St Warna's Well on St Agnes in 2007. Photo: Peter Griffin.

SOMERSET

Somerset is yet another south-western county that is overflowing with holy wells, and I have not visited all of them, so it has been possible to give details only of those that I believe can still be seen without too much difficulty. Phil Quinn's excellent book *The Holy Wells of Bath and Bristol Region* gives details of many more in that part of the county.

St Agnes' Well, Cothelstone

This well in a small stone building was judged by Dom Ethelbert Horne to be 'perhaps the most beautiful of the holy wells of Somerset.' To locate it you need to 'look for a small iron gate set in the side of the road to Cothelstone Hill. Cross a stream and turning right the well will be clearly seen... ' but it may be hidden under vegetation. St Agnes' Eve was a time when young people followed rituals to discover their lovers, and St Agnes' Well was said to be one place where such rituals were performed. ST184318

St Aldhelm's Well, Doulting

St Aldhelm lived from 639 to 709 and was abbot of Malmesbury in Wiltshire and bishop of Sherborne in Dorset. He died at Doulting, possibly while visiting the priory, and was buried at Malmesbury where a cult built up around his shrine. A local tradition linking Aldhelm with Doulting tells how he would do penance by sitting in the well while reciting the psalter. St Neot (see *St Neot's Well, St Neot, Cornwall*) was another holy man who used to do this. St Aldhelm's Well also developed a reputation as a healing well, and seems to have been much visited down the centuries.

The spring which forms St Aldhelm's Well flows from the hillside below the church and out through two pointed arches set against solid rock and into a stone trough. The water is also the source of the Doulting River. Many of the trees surrounding the well were felled in 1999, but new trees have since been planted and the well is still being cared for and maintained.

Location: Doulting is just to the east of Shepton Mallet and the well is beyond the garden of the former vicarage adjoining the church. There is parking in the lane behind the church and from here it is best to walk to the well. Where the road forks, take the right fork, past Old Bell House down a narrow walled lane and the well is at the bottom to the left, and in the woods above. ST645432

St Andrew's Well, Stogursey

The water gushes from three spouts into stone troughs. The right-hand well was considered to have the softest water and so was used for washing clothes. The wells provided drinking water, and the water was also believed to have healing properties. In a letter to me in 1984 the rector noted that he always used the well water for baptisms. The well is in the centre of the village: along High Street from the priory church, turn left at the stump of the market cross and it is a few yards further on. ST202428

St Andrew's Well, Wells

The city gets its name from the wells which spring up in the area of the cathedral, and St Andrew's is the one the authorities choose to show to visitors, albeit at the present time (2006) it is only viewable through a 'window' in a stone wall. Which well was originally St Andrew's is uncertain: Dom Ethelbert Horne suspects that the 'Bottomless Well' is a more probable contender. Confusingly, a pool in front of the cathedral is also known as the holy well of St Andrew. ST552458

St Anne's Well, Brislington

Dom Ethelbert Horne believes this to be 'one of the most interesting wells in Somerset.' When he visited it in 1922 it was in a sorry state with the stonework falling apart and the well hidden by weeds and rubbish. However Bristol Corporation soon took over the site and restored the well. The annual St Anne's Day pilgrimage, referred to by John Leland in his *Itinerary* following his visit to Bristol in 1542, was resumed in 1924 and has continued in succeeding years. In his book Phil Quinn described and illustrated the 1996 pilgrimage when forty people gathered and were sprinkled with well water by the priest. New stonework and a new statue of the saint were also erected in 1996.

A twelfth- or thirteenth-century chapel to St Anne once stood close to the well, and in the middle ages this was an important pilgrimage centre. Among the visitors were Henry VII who came in 1485 shortly after the Battle of Bosworth; and other royal visitors were also recorded. Bristol sailors would visit the well and chapel before setting sail, as too would sailors from Brittany before returning home. Up until the early years of the twentieth century, Breton onion-sellers would also visit the well before going back to France. (This interest by Breton people is probably explained by the fact that St Anne is the principal patron saint of Brittany.) Bristol cordwainers and weavers kept two enormous candles burning all year in front of the altar in the chapel, and others were burning perpetually in front of the statue of St Anne. Many votive offerings hung in the chapel, including silver ships left by the sailors. Everything changed at the Reformation when Keynsham Abbey and all its properties, including the chapel, became the property of King Henry VIII in 1539. In 1635 the ruined chapel was turned into a pottery, and was used for this purpose until 1800, after which the building became derelict.

Even though the chapel was lost, the well always seems to have continued in use. Local people visited in order to take advantage of the water's healing properties: it was believed to be good for scurvy, rheumatism, impure blood, infertility, and weak eyes. Coins were traditionally thrown into the well; abbey tokens and old Portuguese coins are among those found. Today the well is a small circular stone structure, enclosed by railings.

Location: Brislington is in south-east Bristol, and the well is in St Anne's Park north of Brislington, in a loop of the river. It is in a quiet valley, and an old pilgrims' path passes close to the well, which is at the foot of a wooded slope. ST621725

Chalice Well, Glastonbury

Dom Ethelbert Horne comments that there is no evidence of this having been considered a holy well at the time before the destruction of the abbey at Glastonbury, nor does the story of St Joseph of Arimathea having hidden here the Holy Grail (the cup that held Christ's blood) feature in the historical record, and it is more than probable that this well's reputation is of relatively recent origin. Nevertheless, it is now part of the modern legend that sees Glastonbury as a sacred site, and therefore merits a place in this guidebook. Along with the magical Tor which looms over the well, the impressive abbey ruins and the legend of the iconic King Arthur who was supposedly buried there, and the terrestrial zodiac which Katharine Maltwood claimed overlaid the ancient landscape around Glastonbury, the Chalice Well features significantly in the out-of-this-world experience which is Glastonbury in the Isle of Avalon.

The Chalice Well is also known as the Red Spring or Blood Spring, from its striking red (chalybeate) water which was seen as the blood of Christ from the Holy Grail. It is located in a peaceful garden, the actual well being covered by a lid, though water from it flows through the garden. It has been in the care of the Chalice Well Trust

*Chalice Well below
Glastonbury Tor.*

since 1958, and can be visited. It is located to the south of the town, at the foot of the Tor, at ST507385.

St Decuman's Well, Watchet

St Decuman was another of the head-carrying saints (see *St Nectan's Well, Stoke, Devon*). He is believed to have been a sixth-century Welsh monk who crossed the River Severn on a raft made of reeds, landing at the place still called St Decumans outside Watchet. He lived in north Somerset as a hermit, and one day while at prayer he was murdered. Despite being beheaded, he took up his head and carried it to the well which now bears his name. Or alternatively, the well sprang up on the spot where he was beheaded. According to a local version of his legend, he was in the process of building a church on a hill overlooking Watchet at the time, but the local people were unfriendly and it was one of them who decided to kill him. Undeterred, St Decuman went to the well and washed the blood off his head, before popping it back on again and resuming work on the half-built church. The people of the town were so surprised, and also ashamed of what they had done, that he received their full support in building Watchet's first church. The eagle-eyed visitor to the church will spot a small carving of St Decuman set into the wall of the church tower.

Location: St Decuman's Well is close to the church at St Decumans to the west of Watchet, which is along the coast 6 miles south-east of Minehead. From the church

St Decuman's Well near Watchet in 2004. From the stone well at the right the water flows downhill through stone basins.

follow the lane downhill (to the west) and the well is through a gate on the right. ST064427

Holy Well, Edington

The earliest written mention of the actual well is in 1791, though adjacent place-names suggest it was there many centuries before: 'Pipwell' in the form of 'Pypwyll' goes back at least to the mid thirteenth century. In 1791 John Collinson described it as smelling 'like the foul barrel of a gun' because of the sulphur content of the water. He commented that it 'has been found efficacious in scorbutick [scurvy] cases'. People would travel long distances to obtain cures for skin diseases both by washing in and drinking from the well. (The smell is said to be worse than the taste.) The well is a stone structure beside Holy Well Road, on a bend at the north end of the village. ST388399

St Joseph's Well, Glastonbury

This well, also called St Mary's in the Crypt and St Dunstan's, is in the crypt of the Lady Chapel, also called St Joseph's Chapel, at Glastonbury Abbey. The St Joseph referred to is of course Joseph of Arimathea, one of Christ's disciples who, so legend has it, brought the Holy Grail to Glastonbury. This precious vessel held the blood of Christ which flowed from his body at the Crucifixion, and it was said to be concealed in the Chalice Well (see above) and the cause of the red water there. The Holy Thorn

The holy well at Edington in 2007. Photo: Rosemary and Edwin Wilson.

is said to have sprung from St Joseph's staff, and he and his twelve disciples were said to be responsible for bringing Christianity to the area.

Archaeological investigation in the early 1990s supported the idea that the well is pre-Norman, and indeed it 'may well be a primary feature of the abbey site, perhaps even pre-dating the *vetusta ecclesia*! [the Old Church, now totally destroyed]' This wattle and daub structure may have been constructed in the seventh century, hence the exclamation mark in Philip Rahtz's statement, because if this well really did date back to the earliest religious development in Glastonbury it would be of major significance to the study of the link between water sources and early Christianity in Britain. The well would have been outside the Old Church, at the south-east corner, and if the well was Roman its location could have determined the position of the original church. The fine Lady Chapel was constructed in the late twelfth century, encompassing the remains of, or on the site of, the Old Church, and also incorporating the well in its structure.

Whatever the history of the Old Church may have been, it is unlikely to have any connection with St Joseph of Arimathea. William of Malmesbury's *Antiquity of Glastonbury* dating from around 1125 made no mention in its original version of either St Joseph or King Arthur, and it is probable that both of them became linked to Glastonbury in the late twelfth century during a period of crisis. (The alleged body of King Arthur was 'discovered' buried in the Abbey grounds in 1191.) The legends grew apace thereafter, and continue to be embellished even now.

Location: The well is below the crypt of the Lady Chapel in Glastonbury Abbey. Direct access is blocked by a locked gate, but the well can still be seen through the grille. The Abbey is subject to specific opening times and an entry charge; see their website for details. The entrance is in the centre of the town. ST501388

King Arthur's Well and Queen Anne's Well, South Cadbury

Both these wells can be found on the slopes of the Iron Age hillfort known as Cadbury Castle, and famous as King Arthur's Camelot, following John Leland's reference to this in 1542, an idea some believe to be supported by archaeological excavations in 1966–70 when traces of a large timber hall dating from Arthur's supposed time were discovered. The village of South Cadbury is five miles north of Sherborne and there is parking outside the church, from which point follow the footpath up into the fort. On entering the ramparts, keep straight ahead for King Arthur's Well which is about fifty yards ahead, up on the bank to your left, and looks like a small hole with a stone surround set into the bank. To find Queen Anne's Well, backtrack to the point where you entered the ramparts and, with the fort behind you, turn left and follow the footpath through the trees around the ramparts. You will reach the overgrown well, a brick tank, after five to ten minutes' walking. According to Dom Ethelbert Horne it was popularly known as Queen Anne's Wishing Well, and was probably originally a St Anne's Well. King Arthur's Well: ST630253. Queen Anne's Well: ST628254.

King Arthur's Well (left) and Queen Anne's Well (right), both in the ramparts of Cadbury Castle hillfort at South Cadbury, Somerset. Photographed in 2006.

St Mary's Well, Charlcombe

The water was originally piped from the spring to a well in the rectory garden, but in 1989 that outlet was closed and the well relocated to a public garden close to the church. The water is piped from the original spring to an old stone basin over which has been erected a modern stone carving of Christ being baptised in the River Jordan. Charlcombe is on the northern outskirts of Bath and the well is opposite the church. ST748673

Sacred Spring, Bath

Although strictly speaking not a holy well, the history of the sacred spring at Bath is traceable further back than any British holy well, and the uses to which it was put closely parallel the earliest uses of holy wells. There are significant remains from Roman times when the spring was of major importance, but its sacred history may go back even further – a pre-Roman causeway, and Celtic coins, have been found. Coins and curse tablets were thrown into the well during its Roman period, and good examples of these, together with other objects found during excavation, can be seen at the Roman Baths Museum. (There is more information on the Bath spring, and the curse tablets, together with photographs of the finds, in my book *Cures and Curses*.) Thousands of pilgrims would visit the spring to avail themselves of the water's healing powers in medieval times, and in later centuries it was turned into a spa. An impressive (and expensive) redevelopment has recently taken place as a millennium project, and the spa attracts over a million visitors a year. It is located in the heart of the modern city of Bath, which grew up around it. ST750647

England: South

Berkshire, Dorset, Hampshire, Isle of Wight, Wiltshire

BERKSHIRE

St Anne's Well, Caversham

This now largely forgotten well is claimed to have been once famed for its healing waters, and a plaque placed on the well in 1908 stated that it was: 'The holy well of St Anne, the healing waters of which brought many pilgrims to Caversham in the Middle Ages.' However this may not be strictly true, because the original attraction for the pilgrims was the shrine of Our Lady of Caversham, which was one of the most popular and prosperous in late-medieval England. There was also a medieval chapel of St Anne, which was built in the thirteenth century on the bridge over the Thames, but both shrine and chapel were destroyed at the Reformation. When a new bridge was built in the 1920s, pieces of stonework from the chapel foundations were saved and have been incorporated into a new shrine to Our Lady of Caversham in the Roman Catholic church of Our Lady and St Anne in South View Avenue.

The well probably acquired its name of St Anne's Well through its close proximity to the chapel and may not have been a holy well at all: these are, almost without exception, surface springs rather than deep wells. There is scant information about the well in its heyday. The Caversham antiquary John Loveday wrote that 'the religious went (in procession) at various times to a Well now in the hedge between the field called the Mount and the lane called Priest's Lane... This was formerly St Anne's Well. There was, in the memory of man, a large ancient oak, just by the well, which was held also in great veneration.' The well was lost in the mid-eighteenth century, only being rediscovered by workmen in 1906 who came across 'an ancient well, circular in shape.' When the well was excavated some bones, shells, pieces of earthenware and iron implements were discovered, but no coins. Two years after the well's rediscovery, a memorial drinking fountain was erected at the site.

According to tradition, the pilgrims who were cured would throw 'gold and gems' into the well until it was at risk of being 'choked by the accumulated treasures'. Not only that, it was said that local people, wishing to secure their wealth from the depredations of the Roundheads and other enemies, buried their valuables beside

St Anne's Well, Caversham, in an early twentieth century photograph.

the well – but nothing seems to have been found when the well was excavated early in the twentieth century.

Location: Caversham is just to the north of Reading, and St Anne's Well is at the top of Priest Hill, next to the junction with St Anne's Road, across from Caversham Bridge over the River Thames. The well is surrounded by a five-foot brick wall and topped by a grille, and is now dry. SU712750

Ladywell, Speen

The holy well is protected by a small stone structure surmounted by a semicircular carved stone, and its water was believed to have healing properties, especially for eye diseases – a quack doctor by the name of Parzianus Fisher once tried

The Ladywell at Speen in 2004. Photo: Paula Veen-Voskuijl.

unsuccessfully to promote it. Local children still visit the well, and throw a coin into the water while making a wish. A resident of Speen claimed to have seen a ghost standing beside the well, some time during the twentieth century.

Location: The ancient settlement of Speen is to the north-west of Newbury, by the A4. The Ladywell is about fifty yards from the graveyard of the church of St Mary the Virgin, to which a grassy track leads from the Bath road. A short distance down the track, a turning to the right leads to the Ladywell. SU455680

DORSET

St Augustine's Well, Cerne Abbas

The village of Cerne Abbas is best known for its hillside giant, but it also has an historic holy well. St Augustine's Well is located between the church and the ruined abbey, by the duck pond into which the well water flows. It is surrounded by a ring of trees known as the Twelve Apostles. A large (and visually obtrusive) stone marking the Millennium was placed at the well in 2000, between the water culvert and the back wall, and it bears an inscription quoting some words of Jesus on the subject of water.

The history of the well is confused and what follows is a simplified account of the probable truth. According to a Life of St Augustine written by Goscelin about 1100, he created the well by striking the ground with his staff when he and his monks were thirsty. St Augustine had been sent from Italy by Pope Gregory at the very end of the sixth century to convert the Anglo-Saxons, and he built the first cathedral at Canterbury. He only spent seven years in England before his death in about 604, and it is unlikely that he ever visited Cerne Abbas or created a well there in reality. The well that took his name is close to the ruined abbey, which was first founded in the ninth century, and it is possible that the well originally occupied the angle between the nave and the south transept of the now-vanished twelfth-century abbey church which is believed to have stood in the present graveyard. Indeed the church or a chapel dedicated to St Augustine may have actually been built around the pre-existing well.

In another version of its history, St Augustine's Well was the same as the Silver Well, and was the traditional site of the hermitage of St Edwold. He was a ninth-century brother of Edmund, king of East Anglia, and he had a vision that he must travel to a Silver Well, so he left home to begin his travels. In Dorset, it was said, he gave a shepherd silver pennies for bread and water, and the man showed him the well, which Edwold recognised as fulfilling his vision. He lived there as a hermit and performed many miracles before his death in 871. St Edwold's body was translated to the abbey at Cerne Abbas in the late tenth century ('translation' refers to the removal of a saint's body from its first burial place to a church or monastery where it was enshrined, and which often then became a pilgrimage site) and his shrine at Cerne was mentioned in a twelfth-century list of saints' resting places.

However, almost certainly the Silver Well and St Augustine's Well are not the same, and the Silver Well may have been St Edwold's Well at Stockwood, the confusion having arisen when St Edwold's remains were translated to the abbey at Cerne Abbas. Two centuries later, after the well at Cerne Abbas had become incorporated in the abbey that had been built after Edwold's death, it seems that the monks wanted a more illustrious patron, and so they hired Goscelin to rewrite its history, and it was he who wrote the legend telling of the well's miraculous formation by St Augustine. He told how St Augustine met some shepherds and asked them whether they would prefer beer or water to drink. When they requested water, he struck the ground with his staff and water began to flow. Another legend about St Augustine's link with Cerne Abbas tells that while overcome by a vision he struck the ground and cried out 'Cerno El!' ('I see God!' in Latin and Hebrew, and a pun on Cernel, the old name of the village); and in another bizarre tale he destroyed an idol, Heil, and thus annoyed its devotees who revenged themselves on the saint and his companions by fastening cows' tails to their garments and sending them away. But the joke rebounded on the heretics as they all grew tails themselves.

Numerous snippets of folklore have become attached to this well over the years. If you looked into the well first thing on Easter morning, you would see the faces of all those who would die during the year. It was also said to be a fertility well where maidens would drink some of the water, put their hands on the wishing stone, and pray to St Catherine for a husband. But this may be a twentieth-century 'tradition' deriving from a similar custom once practised at the site of St Catherine's lost chapel on a hill south of the village. There is a carved stone at the well which may be the wishing stone because it has been interpreted as depicting what is now known as a Catherine wheel. (According to her legend, St Catherine was to be tortured by being broken on a wheel, but it shattered and injured bystanders; Catherine was beheaded instead.) However, the 'wishing stone' with St Catherine's emblem is clearly part of an eighteenth-century chest tomb, placed by the well as an ornamental feature at some time.

In addition, women wishing to become pregnant were also advised to drink the well water; and it was believed to be efficacious in healing sore eyes and other ailments. It was once believed to be health-giving to new-born babies if they were dipped in the well as the sun first began to shine on the water. Echoing the well's fertility theme, it is interesting that the Cerne Abbas Giant, with its fertility connections, is located on a hill less than a quarter-mile to the north – although recent research strongly suggests that the giant hill figure was not created before the seventeenth century. A more modern tradition, dating only from the 1950s, tells that St Augustine's Well was also a wishing well: you had to make a cup from laurel leaves, fill it with water and drink while facing the south and making your wish.

Location: The village of Cerne Abbas is six miles north of Dorchester, and the well is to the north of the church and not far from the ruined abbey. Walk along the street towards the abbey with the church on your right, and at the abbey entrance go through the gate on the right: the path to the well is signposted. ST666014

St Augustine's Well at Cerne Abbas in 2006.

(Although the location of the Silver Well at Stockwood is not known, St Edwold's church, dating from the fifteenth century and one of the smallest in England, can still be visited. It is now in the care of the Churches Conservation Trust and can be found in the hamlet of Stockwood north-west of the equally small settlement of Melbury Bubb but accessed from the road linking the A37 with Chetnole.)

Holy Well, Hazelbury Bryan

This well had been lost, but a village resident remembered its location (in a field called Halliwell on a 1607 map) and it was excavated in 1999 by The East Dorset Antiquarian Society as a millennium project. It is a spring enclosed by a stone wall and with a rough paved area, situated at Hazel Wood which is a new Woodland Trust wood. The water had a reputation for being good for sore eyes. To find the well, starting from the war memorial at Pidney, head towards Sturminster Newton for a few hundred yards, then turn left at the bottom of a small hill on a public footpath into Hazel Wood. The holy well is on the left a few yards above the stream. ST747092

Holy Well, Holwell

The well's history is uncertain; also whether 'Holwell' was derived from the well, or vice versa. But the rector, writing in 1979, said the water was believed to be helpful in curing eye conditions, and a local resident had told him that she had obtained benefit from bathing her eyes at the well. Into living memory the water was used for baptisms and as a domestic water supply for The Borough. The well was excavated in 1968 and seven stone steps and a 'covered dip well' were found, the well fed by a pipe on the north side and drained by another pipe on the south side, 'thus maintaining a constant and convenient water level.' The area floods easily and so the well quickly gets silted up. It can be found not far from St Laurence's church, which is at The Borough north of Holwell. Follow the narrow track north of the church, cross Caundle Brook, and about fifty yards on, where the track crosses concrete culverts, the well is to the left. ST699121

Lady's Well, Hermitage

Park by St Mary's church and follow the footpath signposted to Lyons Hill – over bridge, through wood; halfway across field turn right to bottom corner of wood. The well will be found just inside. Hermitage was, unsurprisingly, once home to a succession of hermits in the fourteenth to fifteenth centuries. ST651068

St Wite's Well, Morcombelake

St Wite (pronounced Witta locally) is a saint shrouded in mystery, since no one knows who she was, or indeed what is her correct name. Some of the variants are White, Whyte, Wite, Witta, Vita, Candida (all of which approximately mean the same – 'white' or 'pure' or 'holy'), but the original form of the name was probably Hwita, making her an Anglo-Saxon saint. Other suggestions have been that she may have been a Breton brought over to England by Saxons and subsequently murdered by Vikings, but all this is conjectural. Whoever she was, she was revered as a martyr, and was buried at Whitchurch Canonicorum a short distance to the north. Her remains are still in her shrine in the church there, and the only other known instance of such a survival is that of St Edward in Westminster Abbey. Her thirteenth-century lead reliquary inside the stone shrine bears the inscription *Hic req[ui]esc[un]t reliq[ui]e s[an]c[t]e Wite* (Here rest the relics of St Wite) and when it was opened in 1900, the damaged bones of a woman aged around forty were found. A single thigh-bone lay on top of the relics, which confirmed the local belief that one of the thigh-bones was missing. Around 1910 a bone labelled 'the thigh bone of Saint Candida' was found at Lambeth Palace, presumably removed when the saint's tomb was opened in the sixteenth century.

The shrine has three holes in front so that sick pilgrims could touch the coffin and be healed by their physical proximity to the saint's relics – and twenty-first century pilgrims still leave cards and letters in the shrine's openings. Pilgrims used to offer cakes or cheese to the saint on her feast day, 1st June, and probably a pilgrimage to the saint's shrine would also include a visit to her well a mile to the south. The water still flows into a small stone basin, but there is no other structure. The well was restored in 1985. The Reverend Mr Coker mentioned it in his early eighteenth-century *Survey of Dorsetshire*: '... St. Wite a Virgin Martyr, whose Well the Inhabitants will shewe you not farre off in the Side of an Hill, where she lived in Prayer and Contemplation, unto whose Honour a Church being built was from her

St Wite's Well, Morcombelake in 2006.

named Whitechurch'. (It is uncertain whether this is the case, or whether the name, like that of many other Whitchurches, meant nothing more than a church built of white stone, or plastered and whitewashed.)

Water from the well was once used to cure sore eyes, and in order for it to be effective, they had to be bathed at first light. Bent pins were thrown into the well as a votive offering, and the supplicant would also say: 'Holy well, holy well, take my gift and cast a spell.' Periwinkles growing on the hill above were called Saint Candida's Eyes.

Location: Halfway between Bridport and Lyme Regis, the well is a short distance south of Morcombelake, across the A35. The lane to take off the main road is Ship Knapp Lane and it has two entrances. Drive a short distance up the lane and the well is signposted to the left. There is a small parking space by the lane. Follow the track across the field on foot and you will shortly find the well in a small enclosure beside the track on your right-hand side. SY399938

Wishing Well, Upwey

The spring that feeds the well is said to be the most powerful in the south of England, and is the source of the River Wey. It has been a tourist attraction since tourists started visiting Weymouth in the late eighteenth century, and although there appears to be no recorded evidence for this being a holy well, in recent times it was known as the Healing Well, with a reputation for helping eye problems. In its tourist heyday the well was probably on the itinerary of most visitors to Weymouth – indeed Joseph Pennell wrote in 1914 that the Weymouth holiday-makers 'come here in hundreds, mostly in coaches and wagonettes' – and as an indicator of its popularity the former railway station in Upwey was called Wishing Well Halt.

Upwey wishing well in 2006.

As befitted its status as a wishing well, a ritual had to be invented, and it involved making a wish while drinking some well water from a cup or glass (or laurel leaves, a detail copied from the well at Cerne Abbas, and believed to have been taken from a twentieth-century novel) while standing with one's back to the well and, having wished, it was necessary to throw the remaining water over one's left shoulder into the pool. I do not know whether anyone follows this procedure, but when I visited in 2006 the well was full of coins, showing that many visitors still make a wish there while throwing in a coin. The well is situated in a very pleasant water garden close to the church in Upwey (four miles north of Weymouth); reached through the tea-room. Heavily signposted in the area. Open daily except at Christmas. SY661852

HAMPSHIRE

Holy or Wishing Well, Binsted

The well is covered by a neat beehive-shaped stone house, and was dry when visited in the summer of 2006 but probably sometimes contains shallow water. Although probably ancient, judging by its location beside an old road and near to an ancient river crossing, nothing seems to be known about its history. It can be found three miles north-east of Alton, and half a mile south of Upper Froyle: below Mill Court

The well near Binstead in 2006. Photo: Rosemary and Edwin Wilson.

Lodge a mile north-west of Binsted village, beside an old road which may once have led to a ford across the River Wey. SU755417

Holy Well, Sopley

Red-brick steps lead down to a basin into which water trickles from an animal's head. A plaque above has a figure of Christ and the Alpha and Omega signs. This well has mistakenly been given the name of St Michael's Well, based solely on the church dedication. Across the river from the church, the well is beside the gateway to the Bible College on the B3347. SZ157969

Holybourne Springs

There are a number of springs around the church which feed the pond by the side of the church which is the source of the stream running into the village, the Holybourne, from which the village takes its name. Some of the springs rise under the sanctuary of the church, specifically under the altar and at the west end of the nave, and the water from the stream was reputed to have healing properties for eye troubles. Being close to the Pilgrim's Way, the church, which dates back to Norman times, was probably a marker on the pilgrims' route to the shrine of St Swithun at Winchester, and to the shrine of St Thomas Becket at Canterbury. SU732412

Iron's Well (or Lepers' Well), Fritham

The chalybeate water was once used to treat leprosy, and later to cure mangy dogs. The well is north-east of Eyeworth Pond which is north-west of Fritham; there is a car park at the pond. SU229147

ISLE OF WIGHT

St Lawrence Well, St Lawrence

The water flows from a dolphin's mouth into a scallop shell, inside an early nineteenth-century sandstone well-house. The poet Henry Brinsley Sheridan's poem *St Lawrence's Well – A Fragmentary Legend*, published in 1845, was inspired by this well. It is linked with the White Well via the Pilgrim Path (see next entry). SZ541767

White Well, Whitwell

This simple well situated at the base of a stone wall, with stones and ferns around it, may have been visited in the Middle Ages by pilgrims who may have been visiting the nearby church which is dedicated jointly to the Virgin Mary and St Rhadegund. The well was uncovered in recent years and is now linked to St Lawrence Well by a two-and-a-half mile Pilgrim Path. The path is waymarked and there are eight information panels along the route. To find White Well from Whitwell church (two miles west of Ventnor), cross the main road, walk a few yards up the hill, then turn into a grassy lane between two bungalows and the well will be found a few yards further along. The Pilgrim Path also follows this lane: more information is given in a leaflet, *Holy Wells and Pilgrim Paths,* available locally. SZ523777

White Well at Whitwell (2007). Photo: Susan and Peris Sinnett-Jones.

WILTSHIRE

Cat's Well, Bratton

Cat probably derives from St Catherine, one of the saints to whom nearby Edington Priory Church is dedicated, and perhaps the well was once a marker on the boundaries of the church's land. A phantom black dog is said to run along Stradbrook Lane past Cat's Well. The parish boundary, Stradbrook Lane and the stream the Stradbrook all follow the same line, and it is likely that the dog is patrolling the boundary, as black dogs have been noted on ancient boundaries elsewhere in Britain. The well has been quite recently restored. Two steps lead down to the rectangular stone well, where water still flows.

Location: In the village of Bratton seven miles south of Melksham. The well is beside Stradbrook Lane, a narrow lane which leads south from the B3098 at the Edington end of the village. The lane forks, and the left fork continues up on to the downs; there is a notice concerning restricted access. The well is on the right under the hedge, and has a name-plate (St Catherine's Well). ST917522

Daniel's Well, Malmesbury

Daniel's Well is named for an early abbot of Malmesbury's magnificent abbey who, according to the twelfth-century historian William of Malmesbury, would regularly immerse himself in the water as an act of penitence. 'That he might reduce the force of his rebellious body, he used to immerse himself up to his shoulders in a spring near the monastery. There, caring neither for the frosty rigour of winter nor for the mists rising from the marshy ground in summer, he used to pass the night unharmed.' (For more information on the practice of ascetic immersion, see 'Immersion' in my *Cures and Curses*.) In later centuries, the pool was regularly used by the women of the town to do their household washing. Nowadays the spring which flowed into the pool is not traceable, but the pool's location can be pinpointed as it was beside the simple bridge of stone slabs crossing the stream.

Location: Beside the River Avon, on the west side of Malmesbury, and reached by footpath from the town centre – a walk down alleys and steps taking only a few

Cat's Well on the outskirts of Bratton in 2006.

The site of Daniel's Well close to Malmesbury in 2006.

minutes. The route can be most easily found by obtaining a walks leaflet from the information centre. ST931872

Ladywell, Bradford on Avon

This is a strong spring which flows from a pipe in the wall. There is a good atmosphere here, with all the ivy and a plaque to Our Lady. The well probably took its name from the dedication of the old chapel of St Mary Tory which is higher up the hill. Below the chapel and above the well, beside the road opposite the house named Ladywell, is a dry water source which has Christian symbolism in the form of a Chi-Rho (first two letters of the Greek *Khristos* = Christ) on the well surround.

Location: Above the river in Bradford on Avon (five miles south-east of Bath). The well is beside a footpath which runs below Newtown, below the house named Ladywell, and below St Mary Tory Chapel. From the Saxon church of St Lawrence (also well worth visiting), walk uphill with the town church on your left. Climb the steps and part of the way up follow a narrow alley behind the houses to your left, and you will find the well on your right. Alternatively climb to the top of the steps to the road, turn left, and at the house named Ladywell some steps lead down to the well. ST823608

Left: *The Ladywell at Bradford on Avon in 2006.*

Right: *Now-dry water source at Bradford-on-Avon with Chi-Rho inscription.*

Monkswell, Edington

Not easy to find, but worth the effort, even though it probably is not a true holy well. Park on the priory church car park, walk back to the main road and towards Bratton. Pass Monkswell Cottage and Conduit Springs, and immediately before the railings an indistinct path leads through the hedge and downhill. There are tall nettles in the summer, and the path is probably boggy in winter. Keep walking away from the road, and on the right, below the high bank, is a fifteenth-century stone well-house, now a Grade I listed building. It was probably built by the monks of Edington Priory to channel the water from the spring rising in the hillside; even in the dry summer of 2006 there was a plentiful flow of water. The water flows out of the rock in the back corner of the building, through a stone trough, and is piped out of the doorway and into a stream. ST924530

England: South-East

Greater London, Kent, Surrey, East and West Sussex

GREATER LONDON

Caesar's Well, Keston

The well is a circular brick construction with steps down into the water. It is the source of the River Ravensbourne, and the water flows into Keston Pond. The early history of this well is unknown, but in the late eighteenth century it was known as Caesar's Spring and was a public cold bath with a changing room. Presumably the people who visited the well and immersed themselves in its water did so in hopes of a cure, but it is not known when it acquired a reputation as a healing well. The tradition that has grown up links this well with the nearby earthwork, an Iron Age hillfort that has acquired the name Caesar's Camp. It was said that Caesar and his men camped here when marching towards London. However they had no water supply, and while they were pondering what to do about it, they indulged in a spot of bird-watching. They noticed that a raven often came to a spot near the camp and appeared to be drinking. On investigating they found a spring, which they were able to use for their water supply, and which was afterwards known as the Raven's Bourne or the Raven's Brook. In the early nineteenth century the well was known by the local people as the Old Bath and the Cold Bath, and it was still being visited by people with weak or sprained limbs, as it was believed that a cure could be obtained by dipping the affected limb in the water. It can be found south of Bromley, on Keston Common, next to Keston Pond, downhill from the car park. To the north-west of the earthwork known as Caesar's Camp. TQ419640

Caesar's Well, Wimbledon Common

Not to be confused with the Caesar's Well at Keston (see above), despite the fact that this one too is located close to an Iron Age hillfort called Caesar's Camp! TQ224715

St Eloy's (or Loy's) Well, Tottenham

The saint is St Eligius: his legendary repute as a blacksmith led to him being a patron of horses and horse-handling in the later middle ages. Eloy and Loy come from Eloi, the French form of his Latin name. Beside Holy Trinity Church, near High Cross. TQ338895

St Mary's Well, Willesden

The name 'Willesden' is thought to mean 'well by the hill' and 'Willesdune' was recorded in a royal charter in 939, when the land was given to the Canons of St Paul's by the Saxon king Athelstan. The earliest church on the site may date from the tenth century; another church was built around 1170 and dedicated to Our Lady of Wellesdone. The first spring was said to have started to flow in the churchyard when St Mary appeared in a vision to a pilgrim, but no date for this event is recorded. Possibly pilgrimages to the shrine of St Mary were made from very early times, but their heyday was from the late fifteenth century until 1538, when the Reformation caused the destruction of many shrines and images, including a statue of Our Lady from Willesden. The shrine at Willesden was not revived until the late nineteenth century, when a new statue was carved from an oak tree that had grown in St Mary's graveyard. The restored shrine was relocated in the Catholic church, a new building opened in 1931 and dedicated to Our Lady of Willesden. Also in the twentieth century, the shrine at St Mary's church (now Church of England) was revived, a statue of Our Lady being erected in 1911. A new lime-wood statue was blessed by the Bishop of Willesden in 1972; and in 1980 an ecumenical procession was organised involving the two churches of St Mary's and Our Lady of Willesden.

The holy well seems to have moved its location more than once over the centuries. As mentioned above, it is believed that there was once a holy well in the churchyard at the place where St Mary appeared in a vision, where miraculous cures were obtained, but this disappeared at some point. From late Victorian times a pond in the vicarage garden was regarded as a holy well and its water was used for healing purposes. However a spring was recently discovered in the old boiler-house (a former family vault) below ground level, and the water is now pumped up into the church, where it can be obtained from a free-standing dispenser which has a tap and also a large bowl. People come to the church to obtain supplies of the water for healing purposes, and at least five miraculous cures have been claimed in recent times.

Location: Inside St Mary's Church, Neasden Lane, Willesden (London NW10 2TS), which is just off the Neasden Lane/High Road roundabout. The nearest underground station is Neasden Station on the Jubilee Line; local buses are 260, 266 and 297; there is car parking beside the Parish Centre. The church is open daily.

KENT

The Black Prince's Well, Harbledown

A few steps lead down to this well-maintained well, which still contains water. It is protected by a small stone structure surmounted by a stone arch, the keystone bearing three feathers, a feature of the arms of the Prince of Wales. However this carving was probably brought here from elsewhere and placed on the well in the nineteenth century; and the topmost stone was added in the last fifty years.

The Black Prince's Well in 2007. Photo: Bob Trubshaw.

The Hospital of St Nicholas at Harbledown was founded by Archbishop Lanfranc in 1084 for the relief of lepers, and one of the reasons for its siting here may have been the proximity of healing waters. The hospital was later converted to almshouses, and over 900 years a succession of buildings has been built. Among the hospital's treasures (no longer on display) were eight mazers (maplewood bowls), one from the fourteenth century containing a large oval crystal said to be the buckle from St Thomas Becket's shoe, the leather long since having perished. This relic may have attracted pilgrims to Harbledown; Erasmus (Dutch humanist, 1466–1536) described in his *Peregrinatio religionis ergo* (part of his *Colloquia Familiaria*) how when he visited Harbledown in 1519 the buckle was offered to him to kiss, and one of the brothers sprinkled him with holy water. In addition pilgrims on their way to Canterbury may have called here; and many pilgrims probably sought healing at the well.

The Black Prince's Well got its name from the tradition that Edward, Prince of Wales, eldest son of Edward III, known as the Black Prince, sent for water from the well during his last illness in 1376. There is also a tradition that he visited the well in 1357 and drank the water. Another version tells that he visited it often when passing by en route to Sandwich to board ship for the Continent. He was said to have suffered from a mild form of leprosy, and the well water was believed to help that condition, as well as being good for eye complaints.

Location: Harbledown is on the western side of Canterbury, and the well is to be found at the west end of the grounds behind the old leper hospital. Travelling west through Harbledown, turn left up Summer Hill, then go down Church Hill, and St Nicholas Hospital and Church are on the left. The well is on the left-hand side of the path just inside the gate. TR129581

St Edith's Well, Kemsing

The well is keyhole-shaped and steps lead down to the water. It was dry during 1988–92, but usually still contains water. The notice at the well states that it was originally within the precincts of the convent where St Edith lived when first born, and 'hallowed by her presence its waters became a source of healing'. Edith was born at Kemsing in 961, the daughter of King Edgar. Her mother was a nun, Wulfthryth, whom Edgar had removed from her nunnery in Wiltshire, and when Edith was still a baby they back went to Wilton near Salisbury where Wulfthryth had been a novice, and Edith was brought up there. She preferred to live her short life (she died aged 23 in 984) in obscurity in the nunnery and refused all opportunities to raise her status to abbess, or even to queen. Her death was followed by miracles at her tomb at Wilton and her cult was thus established.

An image of St Edith was erected during the twelfth or thirteenth century in the churchyard at Kemsing and people would bring corn to be blessed: the priest would take some, sprinkle the rest with holy water, and then add it to the main corn store. Probably people coming to Kemsing to evoke St Edith's aid in preserving their grain, would also at the same time visit her holy well close by, as too would pilgrims walking along the nearby Pilgrim Way to Canterbury also detour to visit Kemsing.

St Edith's Well at Kemsing in 2007. Photo: Bob Trubshaw.

St Leonard's Well at West Malling in 2007. Photo: Bob Trubshaw.

The well water was believed to be good for healing eye ailments, and the well was visited for that purpose as late as the twentieth century, when a correspondent living in Kemsing noted that 'I have personally witnessed a blind boy descending the steps to bathe his eyes in the water in the hope of a cure.' The water was also used as a village water supply until the early twentieth century. In 1926 the annual procession from the church to the well was revived, being held on or near to St Edith's Day (16 September); and this custom was again revived in 1961 after a war-time lapse. The saint and her well are depicted on the village sign.

Location: The well is in its own garden near The Bell Inn in the centre of the village of Kemsing, three miles north-east of Sevenoaks. TQ555587

St Ethelburga's Well, Lyminge

Once the village water supply, the well is now covered by a wooden shelter, beside the road not far from the church. TR162409

St Leonard's Well, West Malling

Very close to the eleventh-century St Leonard's Tower: the spring flows from below a stone arch by the Mereworth road. TQ675570

St Margaret's Well, Broomfield

Located near the church, indicated by a wooden cross. Well-dressing now takes place here on the Sunday nearest to St Margaret's Day (20 July). TQ839525

SURREY

St Anne's Well (Nun's Well), St Anne's Hill, Chertsey

There was once a chapel dedicated to St Anne close by the well, and both were probably once much visited by pilgrims. Locally the well water had a reputation for healing diseases of the eye. There is still water in the well, which is housed in a structure resembling 'a ruined dark brick igloo'. In 1719 John Aubrey described it as 'a fine clear spring'.

Location: On the north side of St Anne's Hill which is a mile to the north-west of Chertsey. Can be found by following the Nature Trail. TQ028676

St Anne's Well, Stanwell

The village took its name from the well, being in the Domesday Book recorded as Stanewelle, the stony spring, and presumably the name 'St Anne's Well' is a back-formation from the later village name. The water was believed to have healing powers. The well can be found on the edge of a playing field, on Town Lane, opposite Stanwell Hall Hotel, south-west of the church. It has a concrete cover and is surrounded by a low wall. TQ056742

Anne Boleyn's Well (or Queen Anne's Well), Carshalton

Legend tells how the spring burst from the ground where Anne Boleyn's horse struck its hoof while she was riding with King Henry VIII, but the well was probably originally named for St Anne. It is outside Carshalton churchyard wall, where Church Hill joins the High Street, and is fenced in with railings. TQ279645

St Anne's Well on St Anne's Hill near Chertsey, Surrey. Photo: Lionel Beer.

St Catherine's Spring close to the River Wey. Photo: Lionel Beer.

St Catherine's Spring, St Catherine's Hill, Artington

There is a ruined chapel on top of the hill, which would have been visited by pilgrims walking along the Pilgrim's Way. St Catherine's Chapel dates back to 1317, and may have replaced an even earlier chapel on the site. It had five doors, and is thought to have housed a relic which would have been venerated by the pilgrims. They would then have paused at the saint's spring as they walked down to the river crossing, once known as Pilgrims' Ferry. In the late nineteenth century it was still customary for children to bring bottles containing some sugar or treacle to the spring, mix in some water and then drink the concoction. The water was also reputedly a cure for sore eyes. A good flow of water runs from the spring in a stream down to the river, passing under a Victorian stone bridge.

Location: At the foot of St Catherine's Hill, a mile south of Guildford, where the Pilgrim's Way crosses the River Wey. The spring can be seen beside the path leading to the ford. SU994482

St Edward's Well, Sutton Park, Guildford

This well is in the churchyard of St Edward's Roman Catholic church, reached from the west through the gates of Sutton Place. It was said that the well was on the site of King Edward the Confessor's hunting lodge, but there is no historical evidence for a direct link with the eleventh-century king, who was a popular saint in the Middle Ages, being considered one of England's patron saints, along with St Edmund of East Anglia and, in the later middle ages, St George. The well may originally have simply been a water supply – there is no evidence for it ever having been a genuine holy well – and the wellhead and ironwork probably date from the middle of the twentieth century. TQ005538

St John the Baptist's Well, Bisley

The square stone structure is a Grade II listed building, and was restored by volunteers in 2002. Water flows from a pipe in the side of the well, and the chalybeate spring is said to have never run dry nor frozen. There is evidence that this is a historic well, as it is mentioned in the Pyrford Charter Bounds of 956, and Bisley church may have been built away from the village because of the well. It was said that the monks from the Abbey of Chertsey built a shrine near the well as thanksgiving for its refreshing water, and that the present church developed on the same site. For many centuries the well was famed for the medicinal value of its water. The local people believed that the well water was holy and insisted that it was used for their children's baptisms. Rowland G.M. Baker's wife's grandmother, born at Bisley in 1876, told how her mother used to send her down to the well with a bottle to get water 'to wash the babies in', and it was used for baptisms until around 1900.

Location: Near Bisley church, three miles north-west of Woking. A footpath opposite Clews Farm in Clews Lane leads to the well, and continues to the church. Steps lead down from the footpath to the well. SU956595

Mag's Well (or Meg's Well), Mugswell

Handily located in the garden of the Well House pub in Chipstead Lane, it now looks like a traditional wishing well, but was once famed for healing many complaints. The name may originally have been St Margaret's Well. TQ258553

St Mary the Virgin's Well,
Dunsfold. Photo: Clive Fewins.

St Mary the Virgin's Well, Dunsfold

The well, in a peaceful location surrounded by large trees, has been protected since 1933 by a sizeable structure made of oak with a shingled roof. There is also a carving of the Blessed Virgin Mary. The well may be an ancient one, with the church having been built close to it, since the church is nearly a mile from the village. Dedicated to St Mary and All Saints, it was built in the late thirteenth century, and is a rare period survival with benches that are contemporary with its construction, and among the oldest in England. The canopy over the holy well was designed by W.D. Caroe, funded by the Dunsfold Amateur Dramatic Society, and dedicated by the Bishop of Guildford in October 1933. Tradition tells of numerous visions of the Blessed Virgin Mary occurring to pilgrims at the well, whose water was believed to be good for eye ailments. The water is used for baptisms in the church.

Location: Close to Dunsfold church, 8 miles south of Guildford; a signposted footpath leads downhill from the church to the well. SU997363

EAST AND WEST SUSSEX

Bone Well, Willingdon, East Sussex

This well beside the road through the village is notable for being decorated with cows' knuckle bones set in flint. TQ588021

Ludwell Spring, Horsted Keynes, West Sussex

The spring, which is still flowing after five hundred years or more, and is said never to dry up, feeds a small pond and horse drinking trough. The area is now maintained by a team of villagers.The spring used to be the village's main water supply. The water is chalybeate – rich in iron – and is said to have curative effects, especially for animals. The 'lud' part of its name probably means 'loud', referring to the sound of the water, rather than having any connection with Lud, who was a mythical king of Britain. Horstead Keynes is six miles south of East Grinstead, and the Ludwell is on the western side of the village, beside the road to the Bluebell railway station. TQ379282

St Peter's Well, Lodsworth, West Sussex

This is beside a track by the church, two hundred yards downhill (north) from the church, but hidden behind a hedge, so easily missed. The water was said to cure eye problems. SU931229

Spring at Fulking, West Sussex

The Victorian well-house beside the village street carries a text from Psalm 104: 'He sendeth springs into the valleys which run among the hills. Oh that men would

The spring at Fulking, photographed in the early 1970s.

praise the Lord for his goodness.' Shepherds used to wash their sheep in the stone basin. On the opposite side of the street is a Victorian fountain, known as Ruskin's Fountain as it was the author John Ruskin who helped organise a water supply for the village. TQ247113

England: South Midlands

Bedfordshire, Buckinghamshire, Gloucestershire, Herefordshire, Hertfordshire, Northamptonshire, Oxfordshire, Warwickshire, Worcestershire

BEDFORDSHIRE

Holy Well, Stevington

The well, which is said to have never frozen or run dry, is under an arch in the churchyard wall surrounding the ancient church of St Mary which has Saxon stonework in the lower part of the tower. The water issues from the limestone rock

The holy well below Stevington church in 1984.

on which the church was built, and the well was much frequented by invalids and pilgrims in the middle ages. An ancient manor-house south of the church (now replaced by a farmhouse) used to serve as a hospice for them. It was said that Ann, the wife of the Black Prince, died at the well around 1386. However its reputation had sunk so low by the late nineteenth century that it was being used as a sheep wash.

Location: The village of Stevington is four miles north-west of Bedford; the well is in the churchyard wall: turn left on coming out of the church gate and follow the wall for a few yards. SP 991536

BUCKINGHAMSHIRE

St Osyth's Well, Bierton

St Osyth of Aylesbury may be a different saint from the more familiar St Osyth of Essex; there was until 1502 a shrine to the former at Aylesbury only a mile away – or was it in fact at Bierton? Also known as Uptown Well, this well is close to the church and may be the reason why the village developed here. Its circular brick structure was restored in 2001 as a community project. To find the well, walk about thirty

The recently restored but now vandalised well of St Rumbold on the outskirts of Buckingham in 2006.

yards from the church towards Aylesbury and then turn left along a footpath. SP836152

St Rumbold's/Rumbald's/Rumwold's/Rumwald's Well, Buckingham

The strange story of St Rumbold can be found in the entry for his well at King's Sutton in Northamptonshire, where he was born. He died there aged three days and was buried at Buckingham, where there was a shrine before the Norman Conquest. Today his well survives on the outskirts of the town, though it is now dry. It was restored in 2002, but was sadly uncared for when I visited in 2006. Yet the site still has atmosphere, despite the vandalism. Approaching the town from the south along Tingewick road (signed to Tingewick Industrial Park), after some houses on the left but before the industrial park there is a wooded area and a footpath (with a discreet sign to Riverside Walk) following the course of the old railway line. Follow this path in an easterly direction for several hundred yards, then go up some steps to the right (but not the first set of steps), still among the trees. At the top you emerge from the trees at a stile and the well is just outside the wood, in a fenced enclosure. SP690335

Schorne Well, North Marston

The well's name commemorates Sir John Schorne, rector from 1290 to 1314, and it was used as a healing well, especially for ague and gout. In addition, 'A glass of the water drunk at night was said to cure any cold ere daybreak.' The relics of Sir John were placed in a shrine in the village church and in the fourteenth century the village flourished as a result of all the people coming on pilgrimage to the shrine. The church chancel was rebuilt using the money offered at the shrine, and even after the relics were translated to St George's Chapel, Windsor, in the fifteenth century, pilgrims still came to North Marston. It is likely that the well rose to prominence at this period, in replacement of the lost relics. The Windsor shrine was destroyed in 1585, but there are some remains of a fourteenth-century shrine in North Marston church.

Traditionally the well was said to have been created by Sir John Schorne during a drought. He struck the ground with his staff and a spring burst forth. (This is one of several ways in which a holy well might come into being; more details can be found under 'Creation of Wells' in *Cures and Curses.*) Because of the cures that were claimed at his tomb and well, Sir John became venerated as a saint. His other main claim to fame was his defeat of the Devil, whom he managed to capture in a boot, and thus bring about a cure for gout – being primarily a disease of the foot, gout may have been described as the 'Devil in the boot' – an event depicted on numerous rood-screen paintings as well as on pewter tokens which were made for sale to pilgrims.

The well originally had four steps down into the water, but by the 1990s it was in a bad state of repair and there was only a pump and a structure like a coal-bunker. The villagers have since restored the well, erecting a triangular oak building with a tiled roof, a brick floor, and a new pump and trough. There was a service of blessing in May 2005.

Left: *North Marston residents at the newly restored Sir John Schorne's Well early in 2005. Photo:* The Buckingham and Winslow Advertiser.
Right: *Sir John Schorne has conjured the Devil into a boot. Artwork by Anthony Wallis.*

Location: The village of North Marston is five miles north of Aylesbury: the well is in Schorne Lane off Church Street, about one hundred and fifty yards from St Mary's church; signposted. SP777225

GLOUCESTERSHIRE

St Anthony's Well, Forest of Dean

This is an impressive well in an unusual location. It is not in a village, beside a lane, or close to a church – instead it is hidden away in a fine beech wood, seemingly far from human habitation, and is well worth seeking out. There are three springs about fifty yards apart near the foot of a steep hill, and it was said that the yield of water in 1922 was 200,000 gallons a day. The spring which feeds the holy well flows first into a small chamber and then into a large stone bathing pool, with steps leading

St Anthony's Well in the Forest of Dean in 2007. Photo: Bob Trubshaw.

down into it on the south side. The present bathing pool was created two hundred years ago, but the well was being used for cures long before that. The water was believed to be helpful in curing skin diseases, and not only for humans: dogs were thrown into the water to cure mange. Samuel Rudder writing in the eighteenth century said that:

> I have been told by people of merit and judgement in the neighbourhood, that bathing in this water is an infallible cure for the itch, and other cutaneous disorders; and a gentleman of Little Dean assured me that his dogs were cured of the mange by being thrown into it two or three times.

T.A. Ryder remembered St Anthony's Well from his boyhood in the first half of the twentieth century:

> ... a stone-lined hollow fed by a stream whose water is always icy cold, even on the hottest day. It was a favourite picnic place for myself and other children years ago, and we always brought back home a bottle of the water, for we believed it would cure any eye troubles such as soreness or styes. In the eighteenth century, people used to take their dogs there to wash them if the animals had mange or distemper. Earlier still, the monks of Flaxley sent sufferers from skin diseases to St Anthony's Well with instructions to bathe in its waters on the first nine mornings in May.

The bathing pool at St Anthony's Well. Photo: Bob Trubshaw.

The well is believed to date from the founding of nearby Flaxley Abbey in the twelfth century, and it has even been sceptically suggested that the monks invented the cures in order to attract pilgrims. However the well retained its popularity after the dissolution of the monasteries, and people continued to visit in order to cure skin diseases and rheumatism. It was still believed that for the former it had to be visited on nine successive days in May, while to cure rheumatism twelve visits were required. The St Anthony for whom the well was named was probably St Antony Abbot (St Antony of Egypt), who was invoked throughout the latter half of the middle ages for the cure of skin diseases, erysipelas being known as St Antony's Fire (St Antony was often depicted standing in fire).

Location: The well is hidden in the woods north of Cinderford, and I will describe the approach from the north (although it can also be reached by lanes and paths from Cinderford and Flaxley). On the A4136 travelling towards Monmouth: after Mitcheldean, on reaching the Plump Hill sign, take the lane to the left (Jubilee Road) and drive for about two miles until a Forestry Commission sign is reached. You can park here and walk the rest of the way. Keeping right past the industrial area, the track then continues straight ahead towards the trees. Here there is a large pool, and the well is uphill to the right: the water flows down into the pool, so investigate the streams flowing into the pool until you find the well. SO670158

The water can be seen issuing from the wall beneath the base of the cross at Calmsden in 2004.

St Bride's Well, St Briavels

This well is to be found in the village centre, below the Tump at the point where Lower Road begins. SO557045

Calmsden Cross Well

It is unusual to find a large cross erected above a spring, but there is one in the hamlet of Calmsden (and there was also a spring beneath the cross on Condicote village green). There appears to be no record of these springs having ever been considered as holy wells, however, but some religious intention must have been behind the act of planting sizeable stone crosses on top of them. Crosses were regularly used as markers on boundaries or paths, and perhaps they were also used to mark a source of good water. The Calmsden example can be found by the junction of the roads to North Cerney and Cirencester. SP045086

St Kenelm's Well, Winchcombe

The story of St Kenelm is a dramatic one, and two of the places which feature in it are still marked by holy wells. Kenelm was a son of Coenwulf, king of Mercia in the ninth century, but he died before his father, possibly in 812 or 821, and was buried at Winchcombe Abbey. His father was also buried there, and the location has been identified in recent years as the crypt of St Pancras church in Winchcombe. From the tenth century, Kenelm came to be regarded as a martyr and a saint, and legends grew

Top: *The well-house built over St Kenelm's Well, Winchcombe; photographed in 2006.*

Right: *The carving of St Kenelm above the door.*

up around him. His shrine at Winchcombe was a focus for pilgrimage before the Reformation, and many miracles were said to have been performed there.

According to the legendary Life of St Kenelm, he was only seven years old and had reigned as his father's successor for a few months when he was killed by his tutor at the request of his jealous sister, Princess Quendreda. The evil deed was said to have been done in the Clent Hills in Worcestershire, the site now being marked by a holy well close to the church of St Kenelm at Romsley, and how the murder came to be discovered will be revealed in the separate entry for this well (see Worcestershire below). Kenelm's body was carried across country to Winchcombe for burial beside his father. On the way, the party rested on Sudeley Hill, and where they laid the body, a healing spring arose. As they entered Winchcombe, Queen Quendreda, realising her part in the murder would be revealed, was reciting a psalm backwards, perhaps using black magic in order to protect herself. But it rebounded against her, for her eyes were suddenly and magically torn from her head, landing on the page of her psalter and spattering it with blood. There is a carving on the west front of Wells Cathedral which shows the crowned St Kenelm and Quendreda who is falling on an open book.

St Kenelm's Well outside Winchcombe can still be seen, now protected by a neat Cotswold limestone well-house apparently erected in the sixteenth century, but which certainly appears to have been substantially reconstructed in the nineteenth century. Inside, the well, four feet six inches square and two feet deep, almost fills the building. A carving of St Kenelm, based on a depiction in a fourteenth-century manuscript, was erected over the doorway in 1887. There was at one time a chapel close by for the many pilgrims, but it was demolished in 1830. Gerry Stewart has devised a sixty-mile route for modern pilgrims that links the two St Kenelm wells using mainly footpaths and bridleways.

Location: Winchcombe is five miles north-east of Cheltenham, and the well is a mile east of the town. Approaching from Winchcombe along the lane that leads to Guiting Power, a mile out of town there is a farm on the left, with space to park by the roadside. A footpath sign points across a field uphill to the left, but there is no mention of the well. Having crossed the field, a stile will be reached, and having walked straight across the next field there is another stile. From here the well building can be seen to your left. The door was unlocked at the time of my visit in 2006. SP043278

Our Lady's Well, Hempsted

The history of this well with its sizeable stone well-house appears to be unknown, though a Canon Bazeley believed that it was probably built in the late fourteenth century by the Canons of Llanthony Priory at Gloucester not far away. The building is certainly medieval, and there is a worn relief of the Virgin and Child on the exterior rear wall. Fantasy has filled the gap in its history, with the local belief that the Virgin Mary was going to visit Joseph of Arimathea at Glastonbury when her boat was swept up the River Severn (which is at the bottom of the hill) by the Severn Bore and subsequently she made her way uphill and discovered the spring which then

The well-house for Our Lady's Well near Hempsted church now stands alone in a field above the River Severn; photographed in 2006.

took her name. Another local belief was recorded at the well by R.C. Skyring Walters early in the twentieth century, that it was known locally as the Lady's Wash-house because it was the place where ancient ladies washed. Possibly they did their washing there, a practice which still continues at some holy wells in Brittany. Or the 'washing' may have been medicinal bathing, for the water was reputed to have healing qualities.

Sadly it is no longer possible to bathe or drink at the well. Laurence Hunt noted in 1994 that cattle were undermining the sides of the well when going to drink from the trough below it. When I visited in the autumn of 2006 the water appeared to have been diverted to a cattle trough at the bottom of the hill, leaving the well standing dry, and the trough shown on old photographs and drawings is no longer present.

Location: Hempsted is on the western edge of Gloucester, above the east bank of the River Severn, and the well is found by entering the churchyard gate and immediately turning right. Follow the path across the churchyard, then cross the next field slightly to the left, and enter a narrow footpath that passes to the right of a cottage. Enter the field straight ahead and the well-house will be seen a short distance further on. SO814173

Our Lady's Well, Lower Swell

Nothing seems to be known about this tiny stone-covered well sunk into the ground, though its name suggests it was once of great local importance. A fragment of folklore survives, which tells us that 'When the Wittelstone or Wissel Stone heard Stow clock strike, it went down to Our Lady's Well to drink.' This was a standing stone once sited above Lower Swell church, and the saying is probably a joke, because of course the events could never take place. The well can be found beside the drive to Abbotswood (public right of way on foot only), a short walk from the A4068 through Lower Swell. SP176258

(photograph overleaf)

The neat little spring at Lower Swell known as Our Lady's Well; photographed in 2004.

Seven Wells, Bisley

This unusual collection of seven springs is best seen after wet weather when water is pouring from all the spouts. The water comes from the hill on which the church was built, and is channelled through five outlets in a semicircular stone structure, with one more outlet on either side, these two being added when the wells were restored in 1863 by the Reverend Thomas Keble at the same time as the church was restored. The wells appear to have been used as a village water supply and there is no record of them ever having been thought of as holy or of having healing properties, but their 'adoption' by Keble took them into the church fold, and he gave them a kind of religious status when he had this inscription carved into the wall: 'O Ye Wells, Bless Ye The Lord: Praise Him and Magnify Him For Ever. Restored A.D. 1863.' He also initiated a well-dressing ceremony at the Seven Wells, annually on Ascension Day, which starts with a church service, followed by a procession down the hill to the wells. The children carry floral tributes: two stars of David, the letters of the word 'Ascension', the numerals of the current year, and the letters A and D, together with smaller tributes. These are all laid on the wells, which are then blessed by the vicar.

Location: Bisley is three miles east of Stroud, and it is an interesting village. Parking is difficult because of the narrow streets: we parked north of the church, found our way into the churchyard and then went downhill. The wells are on the south side of the church beside one of the narrow lanes leading off the main street. SO903058

On a wet autumn day (October 2004), the springs at the Seven Wells in Bisley were flowing freely.

HEREFORDSHIRE

St Ann's Well and Lady Well, Aconbury

Both wells are to be found on the north-east slope of Aconbury hillfort, and both are close to, but not on, footpaths. St Ann's is covered by a stone structure, and the first water taken after midnight on Twelfth Night was medically potent, especially for the eyes. It was said that the water bubbled up after midnight and a blue smoke arose from it; villagers would compete to get the first bucketful, and the water was bottled and kept by the winner. Lady Well, in woodland at the top of the field, is haunted by the spirits of two lovers, one of whom murdered the other, then died of a broken heart. The footpaths link the hillfort to the lane heading west from Aconbury church. St Ann's Well: SO511333; Lady Well: SO511332.

St Clodock's Well, Clodock

Clodock is the same as Clydog or Clydawg: he was a king, being a member of the local ruling family of Brychan, and he lived probably in the sixth century. He was killed while out hunting by a comrade who was jealous of a nobleman's daughter's love for Clydawg. His body was placed on a cart and taken to a place where the River Monnow could be forded, but the yoke broke and the oxen would go no further, so the body was buried there and a church was built at the spot, which is today St Clydawg's church at Clodock. The well is a few minutes' walk away from

St Clodock's Well: A simple holy well which yet somehow sanctifies this spot. Photographed in 2004.

the church on the other side of the river, and there is a tradition that the original site of the church was on the same side as the well and closer to it.

Location: Clodock is in the remote west of the county, fifteen miles south-west of Hereford and almost on the Welsh border. To reach the well from the church, pass the pub (Cornewall Arms) on the left, cross the river, and take a footpath to the right beside the river. The well is on the left before the house is reached. It is close to the river and is submerged when the river floods. SO326273

St Edith's Well, Stoke Edith

St Edith's connection with this place appears to be only legendary, for her main link is with Wilton in Wiltshire. She was only twenty-three when she died in 984, after which a cult developed at her tomb in Wilton church. The Herefordshire legend has her building a church, and carrying water from a brook to mix the mortar. This being an exhausting task, she prayed for water, and the well sprang up. The water comes from a bank under the church and flows into a bathing pool with an archway over it. It was so popular with the local people who wished to bathe here and benefit from its healing powers that Lady Emily Foley had a grille installed to keep them away!

The covered bathing pool at St Edith's Well, Stoke Edith, just below the church, photographed in 2004.

Location: The hamlet of Stoke Edith is 5 miles east of Hereford, just south of the A438. The short lane from the main road leads to the entrance to Stoke Edith House, and the well can be seen just inside the gates. SO604406

St Ethelbert's Well, Hereford

Ethelbert was a king of the East Angles in the eighth century who was murdered at the behest of King Offa when Ethelbert was visiting the king's daughter whom he wished to marry. He was buried at Marden and a well sprang up when his body was removed from its grave. St Ethelbert's Well at Marden still exists and is inside the church, but is not included here as a well to visit because although I have seen it, the last time I tried to visit in 2004 the church was firmly locked.

After being exhumed Ethelbert's body was translated to Hereford, a shrine being erected there in 795, followed by the earliest cathedral, and the saint's relics were visited by many pilgrims right up until the Reformation. The body was presumably carried by boat from Marden to Hereford because the River Lugg which flows past Marden links with the River Wye which flows through Hereford. On arrival at Hereford the body was rested on the ground close to the river and a miraculous spring appeared on the spot. Its water was famed for curing ulcers and sores, and pins were used as votive offerings, a number being found when the well was cleared out over a hundred years ago. At some point the water was pumped to a fountain but sadly it is now dry; however the structure still survives, surmounted by a stone head of St Ethelbert wearing a crown.

The site of St Ethelbert's Well near to the cathedral in Hereford in 1983.

Location: The site of the well is at Castle Hill near Castle Green in Hereford (between the Cathedral and the river). SO511396

Holy Well, Garway

The original church at Garway was a round one built by the Knights Templar; the Knights Hospitallers built the present church, where interesting carvings can still be seen, including a swastika. The holy well is a spring located just outside the churchyard at the south-east corner: the water flows from a spout into a small pool in the churchyard, though it is sometimes dry. SO455224

Holy Well, Luston

This well provided water for the village until late in the last century, but it also had a reputation for healing eye infections. The water was obtained from a pump, which still exists, though the water supply is no longer reliable. The village's Millennium project was to restore the site, and it has been surrounded by old paving stones and a low wall. A plaque of Welsh slate has the inscription 'Peace be to all who pass by here', and a gold fish to show the Christian connections. The pump was decorated with greenery for Christmas 2006, and the well is clearly still an important feature in the village. It can be found beside the main road through Luston, at the bottom of the hill, by the crossroads signposted to Eye and Moreton. SO486634

St Peter's Wells, Peterchurch

There were once three wells or springs here, but sadly they have almost not survived. I have not visited the location myself, but Jonathan Sant gives directions on how to find them: 'St Peter's Wells are half a mile from the church, on the hill above the

The sacred fish which was said to have been caught in the Golden Well at Dorstone, with a gold chain already round its neck. It was then placed in the well at Peterchurch by St Peter, and this image of it is in Peterchurch church.

village. They are off the Madley road just beyond Wellbrook, beside the footpath and track to The Wells Cottage.' The surviving spring flows from a stone head, now almost buried in concrete; 'he is just visible from the footpath below the wells'. The water used to flow into a bathing pool where pilgrims would bathe in order to cure their rheumatism. The head was said to represent St Peter, and he put a sacred fish into the well, a representation of which can be seen in Peterchurch church. (More information on magical fish can be found in the entry on 'Fishes and frogs' in my book *Cures and Curses*.) Two springs used to flow from holes in the stone wall beyond the head, and their water was used to cure eye problems. SO353388

HERTFORDSHIRE

Amwell, Great Amwell

One source of the New River (see *Chadwell Spring* below) constructed in 1613 by Sir Hugh Myddelton to carry drinking water to London. Amwell was commonly believed to derive from Emma's Well, with Emma being the wife of King Canute; the eleventh-century Domesday book has the name as Emmewelle. The well can be found by the New River just below Great Amwell church, two miles south-east of Ware. TL372125

Chadwell Spring, Ware

Although sometimes known as St Chad's Well, the name does not derive from St Chad but means 'cold spring'. It is the other source (with *Amwell*, see above) of the New River and produces up to four million gallons of water daily. According to sixteenth-century folklore, this spring and Amwell were linked by an underground passage. A 'haunted duck' which dived into the well-head swam along the passage and emerged at Amwell Spring 'featherless and bare'! The spring (a circular basin twenty yards across) can be seen from the A1170 linking Ware and Hertford. Permission is needed from the Thames Water linesman's house if closer access is desired. TL349136

*The monument marking
Chadwell Spring near Ware.*

Holy Well, St Albans

Alban was an early (third century) Christian martyr: according to legend he was a citizen of the Roman city of Verulamium who was killed because of his conversion to the Christian religion. He had been converted by a priest he was sheltering, and when the soldiers came for the priest, Alban dressed in his clothes so that the priest could escape, and was arrested and condemned to death. It was said that on the way to the execution, there were so many people on the bridge that there was no room to cross, but when Alban lifted his eyes to Heaven, the stream miraculously diverted. At this one executioner was converted, and another had to be fetched. As Alban walked up the hill to his death, he prayed for water to quench his thirst and a spring flowed at his feet. This may be a different well from the holy well still to be seen today: it may have supplied water to the abbey which grew up on the site of Alban's martyrdom. His shrine soon became a place of healing and was visited by pilgrims for hundreds of years up until the Reformation. The elaborate fourteenth-century shrine which can still be seen in St Albans Abbey (now cathedral) has many carvings depicting scenes from the saint's life.

When St Alban was beheaded, the executioner suffered the misfortune of his eyes immediately dropping from his head. St Alban's head rolled down the hill and where it finally rested, another spring began to flow, this being the present-day holy well. The name 'Holywell strete' appeared in ancient documents, as this was the main road taken by pilgrims visiting the saint's shrine, and it later became known as Holywell Hill. The site of the well was apparently lost in the mid twentieth century, but the persistence of local residents ensured it was rediscovered and saved from being built over.

Location: In the centre of St Albans, on Holywell Hill turn left down Belmont Hill and then turn right down De Tany Court. Shortly you will see a garden containing a fenced enclosure, in the centre of which is a low wall forming a square, which is the site of the well. TL146067

NORTHAMPTONSHIRE

Becket's Well, Northampton

The original name of this well may have been Swinewell, which does not sound much like a holy well! Its elevation to holy well status may have come after the murder of archbishop Thomas Becket in Canterbury Cathedral in 1170, when a Canterbury pilgrim assigned the well to the special protection of St Thomas. He may have done this by pouring in some water from St Thomas's Well in Canterbury Cathedral, which was said to have had Becket's blood mixed with it, and which pilgrims took away from Canterbury in ampullae. (See entries for 'Ampullae' and 'Blood' in my *Cures and Curses*.) More fancifully, Becket is said to have had a confrontation with King Henry II in Northampton Castle in 1164 before he took refuge in France. While in the town, he paused at a spring on Bedford Road, which

St John's Spring in the bank below the east wall of the ruined church at Boughton Green in 1972.

thereafter took his name. The well has been restored and murals by local schoolchildren depicting the life of St Thomas Becket have been installed there. It can be found on Bedford Road fifty yards from the Bedford Road/Victoria Promenade/Derngate/Cheyne Walk crossroads. SP761602

St John's Spring, Boughton Green

To see Boughton Green now, on the edge of industrial Northampton, with the old church in ruins, and a slightly sinister air about the place, one can hardly begin to imagine what it must have been like 'in the good old days' when the church was thriving, and a fair was held annually on 24th to 26th June on the 'beautiful green of 17 acres'. Traders would set up their booths, there would be football and wrestling and horse-racing, and horses and cattle were sold. The people must also have trod the maze, as there was until the early twentieth century a Shepherd's Race miz-maze cut into the green. Before the fair started, John the Baptist's birthday, 24 June, was celebrated with a service in which the clergy from six miles around prayed and preached for an hour. All this has now gone and the church is derelict – but the ruins and the churchyard are maintained, and the spring still survives. It is down the slope below the east wall, only about four yards from the church, and its opening is about a yard square. The water was used for baptism at the church.

St Rumbold's Well: The replica well-head and water source (dry since the late 1960s) near King's Sutton in 2006.

Location: The village of Boughton is on the northern outskirts of Northampton, just east of the A508, and Boughton Green is half a mile away on the lane to Moulton. The ruined church is set back from the lane and not easy to see as you drive along, so you should watch out for a large parking area on your left with churchyard gates just visible at the far end. Inside the gates there is an English Heritage information board. You can see the ruined church down to your left, and the spring is further down the slope, below the east end. My original visit was in the early spring and I then found the spring without difficulty. My latest visit was in August when the slope was thickly overgrown with nettles, so the summer is not a good time to visit! SP765656

St Rumbold's Well, King's Sutton

St Rumbold (or Rumbald/Rumwold/Rumwald) has already been mentioned in the entry for his well at Buckingham (see above), and more evidence of his presence can be found at King's Sutton where he was born in the mid seventh century, a grandson of Penda, king of Mercia. He died aged only three days, but during his short life he several times professed 'I am a Christian', asked for baptism and holy communion, and preached a sermon. He said he would die soon, and asked to be buried first at King's Sutton, then at Brackley, and finally at Buckingham.

The original and ancient St Rumbold's Well is in the grounds of Astrop House. The medicinal qualities of the water were discovered around 1657, and the spring was

When a font was needed to baptise St Rumbold, a shaped boulder was found by supernatural intervention, and the font inside King's Sutton church is believed to be the same one.

developed as a spa, being known as Astrop Spa. Many patients visited the spa, where there was a tea room, a dancing room, a kitchen, a music room, an assembly room, and other buildings in addition to the spring enclosure. Patients would take the waters, and then indulge themselves in eating and drinking, dancing and card playing, and the spa was popular for around 100 years, having gone out of fashion by 1771.

When Astrop House had a new owner around 1866, he diverted the road which passed the spa and erected a facsimile of the ornamental well-head, together with a replica statue of the saint, beside the new road. This became known as Astrop Well, and a supply of the chalybeate water from the original well was piped to it. This is the well which can be visited today, and although it is being maintained, the statue has gone and so has the water. It is a dispiriting place and a far cry from either the original holy well or the spa in its heyday.

Location: King's Sutton is on the Northamptonshire/Oxfordshire border four miles south-east of Banbury. The church is in the centre of the village and well worth visiting, for it contains the very font in which St Rumbold is said to have been baptised. Astrop Well is at the eastern end of the village on the road to Newbottle. If approaching King's Sutton from the south, when you reach the centre the church is visible to your left. Turn right and follow the road through the village towards Astrop, past the village green. After the houses end, the well will be seen on your left, but is easily passed as it is partly hidden behind a bank. SP507362

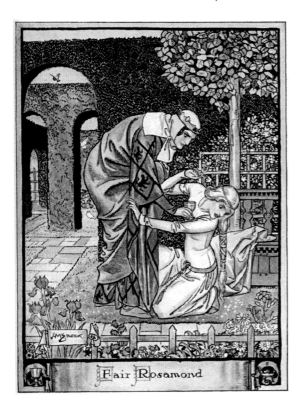

The poisoning of Fair Rosamond, as depicted by H.M. Brock in A Book of Old Ballads *(1934).*

OXFORDSHIRE

Fair Rosamond's Well, Woodstock

This well, once known as Everswell, is the oldest element of the complex that is now Blenheim Palace and its grounds, and it is said to have never dried up. Its present name refers to Rosamond Clifford, who was the lover of King Henry II in the twelfth century. At that time the well was in the grounds of the old royal palace at Woodstock, and its surroundings were more elaborate with three pools, a cloister, and a group of buildings which were used as a royal retreat. Popular tales told how Fair Rosamond was killed by Eleanor, King Henry's Queen, who was understandably jealous: she managed to penetrate the labyrinth woven around the bower by Henry to protect his lover, and once inside, she offered Rosamond the choice of death by sword or poison, and Rosamond chose the latter. But this was only a legend: in reality Rosamond was not poisoned, but retired to Godstow nunnery where she died some time around 1176. She was popularly venerated as a saint for a time after her death, and her tomb was visited as a shrine, so it is not impossible that this well functioned as a holy well at that time.

Location: Blenheim Park is at Woodstock north-west of Oxford, and the grounds are open daily. The well is on the north shore of the lake, so having crossed the bridge with the Palace behind you, turn left and follow the lake shore until you reach the well enclosure. SP436165

Fair Rosamond's Well in Blenheim Park, with the lake visible beyond. The water issues from the base of the long stone wall just visible at the right. Photographed in 2004.

Lady Well, Wilcote

I am reliably informed that although this is sometimes given as Lady's Well, locally it is known as Lady Well. It is very close to Bridewell Farm, so was it at some stage dedicated to St Bridget? The one-time vicar of Wilcote, J.C.S. Nias, informed me that when he first went there around 1956, 'numerous members of country families used to go to that well on Palm Sunday with jam jars containing crushed peppermint and (I think) liquorice and they would pour water from the well on to this mixture which, they believed, would then be a specific for certain ailments during the following year.' Local historian Margaret Rogers noted in a letter to me in 1984 that 'local people do not any longer visit it on Palm Sunday'. She added, 'Occasionally one elderly lady visits it, but way back in 1934 there used to be a substantial number of people going down on Palm Sunday to make liquorice water. Quite a few elderly members of the village remember with indignation that they did not get Sunday School stamps for going down there.'

Sadly neglected as it now is, the well is still very much worth visiting. Its rural location, seemingly miles from anywhere, and the approach by a country walk from Wilcote church along an avenue of old ash trees, give a strong feeling of history and tradition. Mrs Rogers noted that the shallow and clear water flowed into a stone sink

Lady Well, with the trackway from Wilcote passing close by, through the avenue of old ash trees on the skyline. Photographed in 2004.

St Margaret's Well close to Binsey church in 2004.

and thence into a series of medieval fishponds. The water was during the nineteenth century taken up to Wilcote Grange and Wilcote Manor for drinking water.

Location: Wilcote is between Finstock and North Leigh, north-east of Witney. From Wilcote church, take the footpath heading south-east towards North Leigh, and the well will be seen on the left-hand side at the end of the avenue of ancient trees. SP374147

St Margaret's Well, Binsey

It was St Frideswide, the patron saint of Oxford, who brought this well into being, through her prayers to St Margaret. She lived *circa* 680–727, but her legendary life was first told by William of Malmesbury in the twelfth century. He told how Frideswide hid herself in a forest retreat at Binsey to escape from the unwanted attentions of a suitor: he was blinded following her prayers to Saints Cecilia and Catharine, but later his sight was restored by Frideswide. At Binsey she founded a church and created the holy well. There is little factual information about her life, but it is thought that she founded a monastery at Oxford. In 1180 her relics were taken to a new shrine in the church dedicated to her which eventually became Oxford Cathedral. She also still has a strong association with the little church at Binsey which she founded; although dedicated to St Margaret, it is in the parish of 'St Frideswide with Binsey'.

Evidence inside Binsey church that pilgrims still visit this ancient place, with offerings arranged around a statue of St Frideswide.

It seems that this well has been visited by pilgrims for more than 1,200 years. The early church was totally rebuilt around 1181, and a statue of St Frideswide was placed in a niche in the south wall of the chancel which was venerated by all the pilgrims who came to drink the water or bathe in the well. The water was said to be especially good for the eyes, and for curing infertility. Votive offerings attesting to successful cures were hung up in the church; and the well became so popular that a locked stone house was erected over it, and the water sold at a guinea a quart. Pilgrims in the Middle Ages would first visit the saint's shrine in the cathedral, and then go to the well at Binsey; among royal pilgrims were King Henry VIII and Catherine of Aragon. So many pilgrims came in the well's heyday that the nearby village of Seckworth, now disappeared, had twenty-four inns to house them.

The stone well-house was pulled down in 1639, after which the well became disused and overgrown until the Reverend Prout took it in hand. He restored it in 1874, creating the present stone structure with several steps leading down into the well which is in a round basin under an archway. A contemporary of Revd Prout was the Revd Dodgson, better known as Lewis Carroll. There is a story that when Prout was requesting ideas for an inscription to go above the well, Dodgson suggested 'Leave Well Alone'. It is also said that the treacle well referred to in *Alice in Wonderland* is in fact the holy well at Binsey, an old meaning of 'treacle' being a remedy or something with medicinal properties.

Although so close to Oxford, Binsey church and well are in a rural setting in meadowland, although sadly now close to the busy A34. There is evidence that both well and church still receive many pilgrims, and Binsey is an oasis of calm.

Location: Best approached from the west, along the A420 into Oxford from Botley. In New Botley/Osney follow the lane heading north to Binsey, and keep on this lane until you reach its end, where you will find the church, with the well outside its west end. SU485080

WARWICKSHIRE

Berks Well, Berkswell

'Berk' is thought to derive from the personal name Beorcol, and the place-name was given as Berchewelle in the eleventh-century Domesday Book. The 'well' is a stone tank sixteen feet square and five feet deep, possibly used for baptism by immersion. It was restored in the nineteenth century. Berkswell is five miles west of Coventry, and the well is to the south of the church, outside the main gate and beside a footpath. SP244790

Holy Well, Burton Dassett

Visitors to this quiet rural scene today would never imagine that there was once a prosperous market town called Chipping Dassett ('Chipping' meant 'market') here. The Black Death, and the land-owner's desire to create vast sheep pastures, eventually resulted in the disappearance of the town. However the fine unrestored thirteenth-century church has survived, and just outside is a holy well with a stone well-house dating from around 1840, described by Pevsner as 'latish Grecian with a few medievalizing touches'. The water used to be used for baptisms.

Location: The countryside hereabouts is now a Country Park, where pursuits such as mountain biking and kite flying take place. There are fine views from the hilly open countryside, and plenty of places to park, but there is a parking fee if you wish to

Berks Well in 1984.

This photograph of the holy well at Burton Dassett in 2006 does not do justice to the golden stone from which the well-house is made.

linger there. I approached the Country Park via the M40, leaving at Junction 12 to Gaydon: travel south-east along the B4100, then left over the motorway towards Burton Dassett, following signs for the Country Park. Follow the tarmac road across the hills, past the parking machine on the left, and shortly on the right is a dead-end road leading downhill to Burton Dassett church. Follow this, and on the left, in a large open parking area in front of the church, stands the holy well. SP398515

Holy Well, Southam

This mineral spring was first mentioned as 'Hallewell' in a document of 1206 but is probably much older. The present stonework is late eighteenth or early nineteenth century and the well is now a Grade II listed building and a scheduled ancient monument. Possibly this is the well mentioned in the legend of St Fremund, a local saint who was beheaded at nearby Radford Semele following a battle in 869, according to the legend. He then carried his head to a point between Harbury and Long Itchington, and with his sword he pierced the soil and said a prayer, whereupon water began to flow, in which he washed his head and body before dying. The well's water was believed to help cure eye ailments, and was said to be especially cold; this and other springs were the town's water supply until the 1920s. A recent grant of over £100,000 from the Heritage Lottery Fund has enabled the well

The newly restored holy well at Southam, with plenty of water flowing through it in the wet summer of 2007.

An old postcard of Druid's Well in Sutton Park.

to be restored, this work being completed in 2007. This interesting well consists of a semicircular pool with two lots of steps leading into a separate trough fed with water from the main pool through the mouths of three carved heads, traditionally said to represent Mary, Joseph and Jesus. The pool is inside a walled enclosure surrounded by green oak palisade fencing and with matching gates and bench, and a new outflow for the well water has been constructed on the nearby river bank.

Location: The holy well is located to the west of Southam (which is five miles south-east of Royal Leamington Spa), on the route of a new Holy Well Walk (leaflet available), and is accessed along a wheelchair-friendly footpath from Wattons Lane (reached by taking the lane alongside the church). There are information boards on the Wood Street car park, at Wattons Lane, and by the well. SP410618

Rowton's Well, Sutton Park

Sutton Park is one of the largest urban parks in Europe covering more than 2,200 acres; it is a National Nature Reserve with free access. There are seven lakes, ancient woodlands, and three named wells. The water of Rowton's Well was said to have

St Ann's Well, Great Malvern in 1983.

medicinal properties. The other named wells are Keeper's Well and Druid's Well (or St Mary's Well). Sutton Park is to the north-west of Sutton Coldfield; there are many points of access, with car parks and footpaths. Rowton's Well is a mile north-east of the car park at Banners Gate (SP093965). Keeper's Well is on the feeder stream to Keeper's Pool; Druid's Well is at the south-west end of Bracebridge Pool.

WORCESTERSHIRE

St Ann's Well, and Holy Well, Malvern Hills

There are at least sixty wells, springs, spouts and fountains in the Malvern Hills, and so it is hardly surprising that Malvern water should have become so famous, and Great Malvern itself famed as a spa town. All the visitable water sources can be explored with the aid of Cora Weaver and Bruce Osborne's guide *Aquae Malvernensis,* or the Malvern Hills website – I have room to describe only two of the best-known wells. Anyone planning to visit the wells may be interested to know that a well-dressing competition is held annually (details on Malvern Hills website) when a large number of the surviving wells are decorated with flowers and foliage.

St Ann's Well: The well-house and its octagonal extension, both built in the nineteenth century, are listed buildings. However, the earliest use of the name 'St Ann's Well' is on an estate map of 1744 and Weaver and Osborne wonder if it was originally St Werstan's Well, with 'Ann' deriving from 'Werstan'. St Werstan's hermitage was below the present-day St Ann's Well building, and their detailed investigation of his legend can be read in their most recent book. The water can be sampled from a spout from which the water flows into a basin of Sicilian marble, dating from 1892.

Location: Half a mile west of Great Malvern town centre, and reached via a steep path which is signposted from the top of Church Street. SO772458.

The Holy Well at Malvern Wells in 1983.

Holy Well: The building dates from 1843 but the earliest written reference to the holy well is from 1558. As at St Ann's Well, the water can be sampled here.

Location: At a hairpin bend on Holy Well Road, Malvern Wells, to the south of Great Malvern. SO770423.

St Katherine's Well, Bredon Hill

There was once a medieval chapel close to this well, and excavation has revealed foundations. The spring water flows into a stone trough. It can be found on the steep north flank of the hill, directly below Parsons' Folly, on the corner of a wood. After parking near Woollas Hall Farm, a path leads past Woollas Hall and uphill to the right of the well. The stream seen on your left has the well as its source. SO953403

St Kenelm's Well, Romsley

Kenelm was a prince, and son of a Mercian king, who died early in the ninth century and was buried at Winchcombe in Gloucestershire. The Kenelm Legend began to develop in the eleventh century and a Latin Life of the saint was written by a monk named Wulfwine in the twelfth century, followed by a thirteenth-century Life written in Old English. According to his legend, Kenelm reigned as king at the age of seven, until he was murdered at the instigation of his jealous sister Quendreda. The holy well at Romsley – 'Seint Kenelmes Welle' – marks the site of the murder, an event which was miraculously revealed to the world when a white dove carried a scroll to the pope in Rome which bore the message: 'In Clent cow-pasture under a thorn, of head bereft lies Kenelm, king born.' A search party was sent out to look for the body, led by the bishop of Mercia, and they were shown the grave by either a ray of light, or a miraculous cow which never ate yet remained fat, lying under a thorn tree which had grown from Kenelm's staff. As the body was exhumed the church bells rang of their own accord and a spring began to flow in the grave, as was recounted in the Old English Life (here translated):

> Anon as this holy body they took up, a well sprang up there
> In the place that he lay on that still is clear and good.

St Kenelm's Well in the Clent Hills, in its present-day location, photographed in 1983.

> For there is a well fair enough, and ever since hath been
> In the place where he lay, as you may there see,
> And they call it St Kenelm's Well, that many a man hath sought,
> That many out of sickness through that water have been brought.

The body of Kenelm was carried to Winchcombe in Gloucestershire, where another well came into being (see *St Kenelm's Well, Winchcombe, Gloucestershire*) at the spot where the body was rested on the ground. Gerry Stewart has devised a long-distance walk linking the two main Kenelm sites – see his *St Kenelm's Way*.

The site of Kenelm's murder in the Clent Hills became a place of pilgrimage – though the location of the well has been moved three times. Some people think that the original well may have been located in a field to the north of the church, where the medieval village of Kenelmstow once stood. However it seems sensible to assume that the church was built at the original well-site: there was once a stairway at the bricked-up archway at the east end leading to a spring sited under the altar, which was visited by lepers seeking to bathe in the water. This well was destroyed at the Reformation, when the Bishop of Worcester campaigned against the superstitious pilgrimage to wells. The well was later reopened some yards away, and the present-day well is visually insignificant, being nothing more than a small stone-lined cavity under a bush, but its location can easily be seen as pilgrims place rags on the branches all round. In 1985 a brick well-head was erected close by, for reasons unknown as it does not mark the site of the well.

The whole site was sensitively landscaped in 1995, and modern carvings by Michael Fairfax of scenes from the life of St Kenelm have been placed there. There are also ancient depictions of the saint to be found at the church: there is a wooden statue of him above the lychgate; the stone figure on the exterior south wall may be Kenelm; the stained-glass window in the north wall depicts the legend; and there was once a series of fourteenth-century wall paintings which told St Kenelm's story. These paintings were lost at the time of restoration (desecration?) in 1846, but tracings of some had luckily been made.

Location: The rural oasis of the Clent Hills is located west of the M5 motorway, south of Dudley. The church of St Kenelm is north-east of the village of Clent, and north-west of Romsley. There is car parking beside the lane, and a footpath leads from the east end of the church into a wooded valley where the well will easily be found. SO944807

England: East

Cambridgeshire, Essex, Lincolnshire, Norfolk, Suffolk

CAMBRIDGESHIRE

Holy Well, Holywell

Holywell, two miles south-east of St Ives, is mentioned in the Domesday Book, as Haliewelle, so this well was important at least as far back as the eleventh century. During the 1980s well-dressing was introduced, a service of Blessing the Well and the Church Flower Festival being held late in June to coincide with the patronal festival of St John the Baptist. The well is easily found behind the church. TL336707

The holy well close to Holywell church, photographed in 1974.

Holy Well, Longstanton

Longstanton is six miles north-west of Cambridge city centre. Two parishes were amalgamated and St Michael's church, dating back to the thirteenth century, was made redundant in 1953; it is now in the care of the Churches Conservation Trust. The age and history of the holy well in the churchyard are unknown, but it has been restored on more than one occasion, with the present round-arched structure over the well probably being Victorian, and incorporating four-hundred-year-old brick floor tiles. In the mid-1980s well-dressing festivals were held here, but this custom appears to have been discontinued. The well can be found in the churchyard of the redundant St Michael's church (take the road to the Barracks and turn right down St Michael's Lane), beneath a big chestnut tree and protected by railings. TL403658

Holy Well (St Cloud's Well), Longthorpe

This holy well is said to comprise a natural spring bubbling up through oolitic limestone, around which have been built three stone chambers enclosed in an artificial mound now overgrown. The well's history is uncertain, but it may have been a medieval holy well that was incorporated into a grotto in the eighteenth century. R.B. Parish wonders if the structure was built as a 'folly-hermitage' as part of the story that a hermit called St Cloud once lived at the site. There was also said to be an underground tunnel linking the well to Peterborough Cathedral, built by monks so that they could come and bathe in the water, but this is surely part of the legend and never was a reality. Despite the well's ambiguous nature, it seems worthy of inclusion: the water was said to be good for rheumatism, gout, skin diseases and the eyes; and Parish, writing in 2002, also noted that 'It is one of my favourite holy wells, despite being much neglected.'

Close by is a series of ponds which may once have been fishponds linked to a medieval manor (no longer standing); they are now known as Holywell Ponds. Longthorpe is two to three miles west of Peterborough city centre and the well is south-east of the village. There is limited car parking, and restricted access by car via Thorpe Road at the junction with Longthorpe Green. From there, walk through to Larklands and follow an unmade footpath to the well and ponds. There is also a public footpath south of Thorpe Hall running parallel to and north of the Longthorpe Parkway. TL168981

Red Well, Knapwell

As its name suggests, Red Well is a chalybeate spring and was believed to have medicinal properties. It is probably an ancient well: in the late eleventh-century Domesday Book the village is called Chenepewelle, but it is unclear whether the well in the village name is the Red Well, since 'Chenepe' (Cnap and Cnapen in references earlier in the eleventh century) may be the name of a person.

Knapwell is seven miles north-west of Cambridge, and the well can be found in Boxworth Wood which is now the Overhall Grove Nature Reserve. At the north end of the village a track leads to the church, from where a footpath can be followed into

The Red Well at Knapwell in 1977.

the wood. Pass the information box and then take the path right into the woods. The well is due east of the church, at TL337630.

ESSEX

St Cedd's Well, North Ockendon

Close to and south-west of the church is this well, with a pointed-roofed structure over it. St Cedd has strong connections with south Essex, having built several churches including (possibly) the one still surviving at Bradwell-on-Sea which is a contender for the title of oldest church in England. He is said to have blessed a spring at North Ockendon and carried out baptisms here. Follow the tree-lined path past the church and cut across the grass, keeping left until you find a gap in the hedge: this leads down to the well. TQ587848

St Peter's Well, West Mersea

This well was once attached to the lost priory of St Peter and St Paul, and was restored in 2000. Accessible by path from Coast Road. TM006124

The Running Well, Runwell

The first element of the place-name, *run*, may mean 'secret' or 'council' and may indicate that the well was a meeting-place. It is clearly an old site as the name was Runewella in the eleventh-century Domesday Book, and there are even earlier references to it. Archaeological investigation has unearthed a wide variety of remains, and it is believed by some that there was an ancient chapel, based on a reference in the parish register of 1602 to a 'Shrine of the Bl. Virgin of the Runnynge Well'. A colourful early twentieth-century vicar of Runwell, the Revd John Edward Bazille-Corbin, created several 'legends' for Runwell, including the 'Priory of Our Lady of the Running Well'. In truth, apart from early references to the well, nothing is known of its history. The well is two miles north of Wickford, reached along a footpath to the east of the Running Well Equestrian Centre. TQ750965

LINCOLNSHIRE

There are many interesting springs and wells in Lincolnshire – see Ian Thompson's guide – but most of them are not holy wells, and those that are, are mostly derelict or inaccessible.

Holy Well, Sempringham

A circular stone basin in the south-east corner of the churchyard is now known as a

The holy well in Sempringham churchyard in 2006.

holy well, but although mentioned in a twelfth-century document, it has no history as a holy well and may have simply been a spring supplying water to the now-lost St Mary's Priory which stood to the south of the church. Although the church is situated among fields some way from civilisation, there is a driveable track all the way from the B1177 (church signposted) at Sempringham north of Bourne. Just south of the church, where the track turns right, note the moving Gwenllian memorial. This has nothing to do with holy wells but is worth noting nonetheless. It commemorates a Welsh princess who was removed from Wales to Sempringham by order of Edward I in 1283 while still a baby and was imprisoned at the abbey which then stood here, until her death in 1337. TF107328

St John's Well, Bottesford

This is protected by a Victorian stone well-house; the water is in a sunken stone trough. It is located in a southern suburb of Scunthorpe, at the junction of Manor Road and Church Lane. SE898070

Kell Well, Alkborough

Neolithic flint arrowheads and a stone axe-head have been found at Kell Well. In his 1697 diary Abraham de la Pryme referred to 'pretty stones' called 'kestles and postles' (actually fossil crinoids) which used to be found there too. The well's former petrifying qualities appear to have been lost, but the water still flows, from a pipe in

Two of the Spring Wells at Billingborough, on opposite sides of the pool, in 2006.

a stone wall, down to the River Trent through a series of tiny waterfalls. Kell Well is close to the cliff path a mile south of Alkborough (where the ancient turf maze known as Julian's Bower can still be visited). SE873207

Lud's Well, Stainton-le-Vale

'Lud' probably means 'loud' and is not the name of some pagan god. The spring rises in a tiny cave 'guarded by a strange rock shaped like an animal's head', and the water falls into a pool. Downstream a rag bush has come into being. The well and bush are in a steep wooded dell beside a public footpath linking Stainton to Kirmond le Mire. TF176937

Spring Wells, Billingborough

Five springs feed an ornamental pool west of the church, with two of them (one on either side of the pool) visible within enclosures. An elderly resident claimed that water from the Spring Wells used to be used for baptism, so one of them may once have been a holy well. TF117342

NORFOLK

Walsingham Wells

Hidden away in the north Norfolk countryside can be found the most surprising, and inspirational, holy site in the whole of England: the Anglican Shrine of Our Lady of Walsingham. It was an important shrine before the Reformation, and has become a great shrine again since its restoration in the early twentieth century. There is also a Catholic shrine close by, and three separate holy wells can be visited, each with its own fascinating history.

The first location actually has two wells side by side, which may have been in existence as early as 1061 (according to tradition – in reality they may date from the twelfth century) when Richeldis de Faverches, the widow of a local lord of the manor, had three visions of the Blessed Virgin Mary and was taken in spirit to Nazareth. Richeldis was asked to build at Walsingham a replica of the Holy House of Nazareth (the home of Joseph, Mary and Jesus), and this she did, the building being set up not far from the wells. A priory was built beside the Holy House, and in the next four hundred years the shrine flourished, with the pilgrims including many kings and queens. In 1538 the shrine was forcibly closed at the time of the Reformation, and the shrine and priory church were destroyed. The wells survived, and in subsequent centuries their water was considered to have healing powers, especially for headaches and stomach ailments, but they later degenerated into wishing wells. A special ritual had to be followed for the wish to succeed. The wisher must kneel on a stone between the two wells and dip a hand into each while silently making a wish, and finally drinking a little water from both wells.

The two ancient wells in the priory grounds at Walsingham, close to the site of the original shrine, photographed in 1999.

Location: The wells are in the priory grounds, close to an archway. The grounds are open to the public at certain times of the day, with access from the village centre.

In 1897 Pope Leo XIII blessed the re-founding of the Shrine of Our Lady of Walsingham in Kings Lynn, and the first post-Reformation pilgrimage took place to the Slipper Chapel (see below) and to Walsingham. A little later, the then Anglican Vicar of Walsingham, the Revd Alfred Hope Patten, was responsible for the restoration of the shrine in Walsingham village, beginning in 1922, and ten years later a site was found where a chapel could be built to accommodate a new Holy House, as close to the site of the original shrine as possible. Before building started, Patten instructed that the site should be investigated, and the finds included a cobbled courtyard, a cross base – and a well. The men who were digging had only gone down a few feet before water gushed forth, and they found a disused ancient well built upon a base of four tree trunks, which had been deliberately sealed with clay and debris, including sixteenth-century shoe soles. It was found to link directly with the two wells in the priory grounds, and was incorporated into the design of the new chapel, where it now plays an important role in pilgrimages to Walsingham. Many people have claimed to have been healed by the water, and there are many ex-voto plaques attesting to these cures in the shrine church. A Sprinkling service

The rediscovered holy well inside the Anglican Shrine at Walsingham, guarded by a statue known as Our Lady at the Well, photographed in 2006.

takes place daily at 2.30 p.m., and plastic bottles stamped with the image of Our Lady of Walsingham may be purchased in which to take away the water.

Location: Inside the Anglican Shrine in the centre of the village of Little Walsingham. Access is open to all. Just inside the main entrance, steps lead down to the holy well under the reconstructed Holy House.

There is also a Roman Catholic Shrine at Walsingham, centred on a fourteenth-century chapel known as the Slipper Chapel which was built as the last pilgrim chapel on the way to Walsingham from London and the South. After the Reformation it became a farm building, but was rescued in 1896 and later restored. In recent years the Catholic Shrine has acquired its own 'holy well' in the form of a fountain, known as the Holy Water Font, where pilgrims can collect holy water.

Location: The Catholic Shrine is at Houghton St Giles half a mile from Little Walsingham: there is a large car park. The fountain will be found outdoors among the complex of buildings, close to the shop, where bottles for the water can be purchased. The direction sign points to 'Holy Water'.

General Information and Location Details: The Anglican and Catholic shrines at Walsingham welcome pilgrims of all faiths and none, and there is open access to both shrines. Many pilgrims stay in the village, where there is a pilgrimage guesthouse and also other accommodation. Walsingham is four miles north of Fakenham, and well signposted off the main roads. There is a large car park in the village from where it is a short walk to the Anglican Shrine, and the Catholic Shrine at nearby Houghton St Giles has its own large car park. Both shrines have their own websites, where full information will be found. There are always plenty of pilgrims at Walsingham, but especially during the pilgrimage season from Easter to October.

The Catholic 'holy well' or Holy Water Font: water flows constantly into the basin where bottles can be filled for personal use. All around the base are plaques illustrating the theme of water in religion – one shows the baptism of Christ, another has the legend 'I will give you living water.' Photographed in 2006.

St Walstan's Well, Bawburgh

Walstan was a local Norfolk saint, said to have been born at Bawburgh between 960 and 970, and possibly a prince. When he reached the age of twelve he decided to leave his home and become an agricultural labourer, which career he followed for more than thirty years. He was known for his charity, and he lived in poverty, giving his food and belongings to the poor. He became the owner of two white oxen and a small cart, since he had had a vision from an angel telling him to look after them as they would take him to his burial place. He also had other visions, and one foretold his death, which took place in the fields, possibly in 1016. A spring began to flow beside Walstan's body at the time of his death. He was placed on his cart as he had requested, and the two oxen pulled it where they chose, for Walstan had instructed that this should be allowed to happen. They carried him to Costessey Woods, and where they rested, another spring began to flow. The marks of the cartwheels and the oxen hooves were permanently imprinted on the water of a ford they went through near Costessey, which could still be seen centuries afterwards, or so it was said.

A third spring flowed just below Bawburgh church when they reached that place, and this is the well that can still be seen today. St Walstan was buried at the church

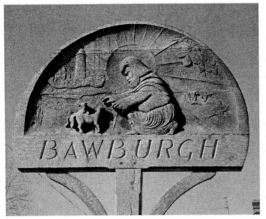 

Left: *Bawburgh village sign depicts St Walstan in his traditional role caring for farm animals.*
Right: *St Walstan's Well, Bawburgh in 2006.*

and over time his shrine received so many pilgrims that enough money was given to rebuild the chancel in 1309. Farmers would come on the anniversary of St Walstan's death, 30 May, to obtain his blessing for themselves and their livestock. The well water was sought as a remedy for sick animals, even being sold on the streets of Norwich. Sadly the chapel and the shrine were demolished at the Reformation. But Walstan is still remembered at Bawburgh, being depicted on the village sign, and his well is being looked after. St Walstan's death is commemorated each year with a service held in the church, and a procession to the well where prayers and singing take place.

Location: Bawburgh is about five miles to the west of Norwich city centre. There is parking by the church gates: to reach the well, do not enter the churchyard but continue along the lane and follow it round to the right, and the well can be seen in an area of grass and trees to the right beyond the house. TG153087

St Withburga's Well, Dereham

The church in Dereham (formerly known as East Dereham) was founded by St Withburga in 654 and she is still strongly present there. Today inside the church it is possible to see a statue of her, a fresco in the reredos of the high altar, a window depicting her legend, and a banner carrying her image. And of course just outside the church is her holy well. She was the youngest daughter of Anna, king of East Anglia, and went to live in solitude for religious reasons. She is usually depicted with two tame does, which are said to have daily provided milk for her nunnery. She died before the buildings of her community at Dereham were completed, and was buried in the churchyard, but when she was exhumed fifty years later her body was found to be incorrupt and so was placed in a shrine in the church. However it was stolen in 974 by the abbot of Ely, who took her to be buried near her sisters. He had gained

Left: *A nineteenth-century depiction of St Withburga inside Dereham church, accompanied as always by the two does which provided her with milk.*

Right: *St Withburga's Well in the churchyard at Dereham in 2006. The plaque above the arch gives a brief history of St Withburga.*

the king's approval before taking possession of the coffin by subterfuge: the people of Dereham did not want to lose her, but were unable to stop the theft. Indeed it has never been forgotten, and in 1985 there was an attempt by the town to get her remains back from Ely Cathedral. The water was said to be running stronger and fresher than ever, and a ghostly lady had been seen in the churchyard, both considered possible signs that Withburga herself was in favour of the move.

The present holy well is the site of her first burial at Dereham: the water began to flow in the grave when she was first exhumed. The water became famed for its healing virtues, and the well must have been visited by many pilgrims down the centuries. Some remains of a chapel survive there, but not the 'hideous' bath-house built in 1793 in an effort to emulate popular spas like Buxton or Bath. It was never popular, and was torn down in 1880.

Location: Dereham is fifteen miles west of Norwich, and the well is easy to find in the churchyard of St Nicholas's church on the west side of town. TF986133

SUFFOLK

The Lady's Well, Blythburgh

Alternative names for this well were the Wishing Well, the Lady's Fountain, and Queen Anne's Well. Its history is uncertain: legend had it as the place where King Anna was killed in the Battle of Blythburgh in AD 654, the spring flowing miraculously where his body fell. (He died at Bulcamp only half a mile to the west.) The present structure is an arched shelter, a pillar on either side, and two stone seats inside. There used to be brass cups chained to the shelter so that travellers could drink the water. The well is set into an earth bank beside the Blythburgh to Beccles road just before the turning to Blyford. TM450762

England: North Midlands

Cheshire, Derbyshire, Leicestershire, Nottinghamshire, Rutland, Shropshire, Staffordshire

CHESHIRE

Three wells on Alderley Edge

The three wells are the Holy Well, the Wishing Well and the Wizard's Well. Their antiquity is debatable, but nevertheless being in such an atmospheric location they are well worth visiting. Alderley Edge is a wooded escarpment with fine views out over the Cheshire Plain; the nearby village has the same name. The woods are in the care of the National Trust and are accessible to the public. All three wells are stone basins under the rock face. The water from the Holy Well was believed to be a cure for barrenness, and bent pins were once the traditional offering. The Wishing Well is just along the same path, and it is probably best to leave the rhododendron leaf in place, which guides the water dripping into the well, or else seven years' bad luck is said to follow its removal. These two wells often get mixed up, but I understand that the Wishing Well is the circular well and the Holy Well is the rectangular one.

The Wizard's Well is in a different location, and gets its name from the wizard Merlin of the Arthurian legends. One day Merlin met a local farmer who was taking a white horse to market. He offered to buy the horse, but the farmer refused to sell, and Merlin told him he would not sell it that day. Sure enough, in the evening the farmer led the horse back unsold – and again was met by Merlin, who led him to a rock in which were iron gates. They opened, and the farmer saw that inside the rock were caverns full of sleeping men and white horses. Merlin told him they were King Arthur and his knights, asleep until such time as their country needed them, and he said that they needed another horse to make up the numbers. The farmer grabbed the purse of gold which Merlin offered him, and ran from the cave as the gates closed behind him. That cave has never been found again – though there are plenty of caves to be seen on the Edge, the result of industrial working in past centuries. The Wizard's Well has a face carved on the rock above it, said to represent Merlin. This carving, and the inscription 'Drink of this and take thy fill for the water falls by the Wizard's will', are said to have been added by Robert Garner, the great-great-grandfather of author Alan Garner who wrote several magical children's books set in Cheshire, such as *The Weirdstone of Brisingamen* and *Elidor*.

Left: *The Wishing Well on Alderley Edge. Note the barely-visible rhododendron leaf which directs the flow of water into the stone basin. Photographed in 2006.*

Right: *The carving of the wizard's face and inscription above the Wizard's Well. This photograph was taken quite a few years ago, and the carvings are less clear today.*

Location: Alderley Edge village is six miles north-west of Macclesfield, with access to the Edge and wells from the B5087. Ignore the National Trust car park: the lay-bys are closer to the wells. *Holy Well* and *Wishing Well:* Park in the second lay-by along the Macclesfield road from Alderley Edge village (by the house), enter the wood and veer left to the Beacon (with monument on top). Beyond is a steep hillside. Follow the path to the left until steps down are reached. Follow this path downhill, and the holy well, then the wishing well, will be found on the right under the rockface. *Wizard's Well:* This well is closer to the village along the same ridge, so park in the first layby on the Macclesfield road (by 30 mph signs), enter the wood and go down steps by two stone posts. Follow the path to the left, with rock outcrops on your left, and you will soon reach the Wizard's Well. *Holy Well and Wishing Well:* SJ858779. *Wizard's Well:* SJ855781.

St Chad's Well, Chadkirk, Romiley

The well is close to Chadkirk Chapel, both being in the grounds of Chadkirk Country Estate. It is one of several surviving wells dedicated to St Chad, who was a seventh-century bishop of Mercia. According to local tradition he founded a monastic cell here, and carvings inside the chapel depict scenes from his life. There was a church on the site in the early fourteenth century; the present building has some Tudor black and white walls and other interesting features and is well maintained, being open to the public on Saturday and Sunday afternoons. The well is accessible at all times.

The simple well of St Chad close to Chadkirk Chapel at Romiley. Photographed in 2006.

Since the late twentieth century well-dressing has taken place here annually to coincide with Chadkirk's Summer Festival at the end of July.

Location: The Chadkirk Country Estate is south of Romiley (east of Stockport), to the east of the A627. If travelling from the south, turn right shortly after the two sharp bends. There is a car park to the left, and the well is then reached on foot. You can either walk straight up the lane, past the chapel, and past the farm: the well is on the left as you go uphill. Or you can follow the waymarked circular walk round the estate grounds which also passes the chapel and well. SJ939904

St Patrick's Well, Bromborough

According to legend, this well was blessed by St Patrick when he visited the area in 432. However it is probably of no great age. The water was said to be good for the eyes. There was also a Boiling Well with warm water at Bromborough, and a Shod's Well (for St Chad's Well) at nearby Spital. St Patrick's Well is in Dibbinsdale Local Nature Reserve, which is signposted off B5137 Spital Road. From car park, take footpath nearest the road, going downhill, and walk through woods with the road high up on your right. Where the path divides and the right branch goes over a stream, the well (with its name beside) is on the right. SJ345829

There is no structure at St Patrick's Well, and without the notice you would be unlikely to recognise it as a holy well. Photographed in 2007.

St Plegmund's Well, Plemstall

St Plegmund, who was an archbishop of Canterbury, was born some time in the ninth century and died in 914. For part of his life he lived as a hermit on an island near Chester, and the place-name of Plemstall derives from his name. The well is clearly ancient, as there is a reference to it as Seynt Pleymondes Well from 1302. I have no information as to its supposed virtues or how popular it was, but the mere fact of its survival indicates that it was once a significant well. Today it is a stone-lined pit with two steps down into it, surmounted since 2002 by a large wrought-iron structure bearing the well's name. As is becoming customary elsewhere, modern-day visitors are starting to leave 'rags' in the trees.

St Plegmund's Well at Plemstall in 2005.

Location: Plemstall is a hamlet in the parish of Mickle Trafford two miles north-east of Chester and the well is beside Plemstall Lane which leads from the A56 to Plemstall church. It is on the north side of the lane about two hundred yards west of the church, by a bridge, and is easy to miss among the foliage despite the large superstructure. SJ455701

Whistlebitch Well, Utkinton

Although visually this well does not rank highly, it is worth including because it was once so important and is now almost lost. Four hundred years ago, two thousand people came daily to this well, a fact difficult to comprehend now. A pamphlet written in 1600 gives details of the cures that were being reported; but the well's popularity was its downfall, since the deer in the Queen's forest were seen to be under threat, and so the forest was closed, the area once again sinking into obscurity. The pamphlet notes that the well was formerly St Stephen's Well, which must date it to the medieval period; it was the New Found Well in 1600; and the Whistlebitch is its current name, though no one knows how far back that name goes. The 'rediscovery' of the well four hunded years ago was actually the survival of a medieval well cult.

The sad remains of this once-famous well can be found on the edge of Primrose Wood a mile north of Utkinton (Quarrybank), itself two miles north of Tarporley.

The title page of an account of the medicinal powers of the Whistlebitch Well, written in 1600 by a Cheshire man to his friend in Northamptonshire.

From the War Memorial in Utkinton, go up Chapel Hill, and turn left at the school into Tirley Lane. Follow this road to its end, at the T-junction. Opposite, a track leads into a wood. Where this track turns sharp right, go straight ahead along an overgrown green lane, a fragment of the ancient road to the well. At its end, cross the intervening few yards of field, and the Whistlebitch will be below you, almost lost in the luxuriant undergrowth (especially in summer). The water rises in a sunken wrought-iron lidded tank, and flows into a large oblong cattle trough, before flowing off down the valley. SJ549669

DERBYSHIRE

St Alkmund's Well, Derby

The body of St Alkmund, a Northumbrian martyr who was killed about 800, was translated from Shropshire to Derby, and a church built over his shrine. An elaborate ninth-century stone sarcophagus, found in the church of St Alkmund when it was demolished in 1968, was believed to be his shrine (now held in Derby Museum). This city-centre well, close to the former church of St Alkmund, is said to be one place where the saint's remains were laid when being carried to the town, and the water had healing properties from that time. The earliest reference to the well is in a fourteenth-century charter. It is now to be found four hundred yards north-north-west of St Mary's Bridge, at the junction of Bath Street and Well Street. SK351370

St Anne's Well, Buxton

This must be the only holy well in Britain where people still queue up to collect the water! However they are not doing it for religious or therapeutic purposes, but because it is a free source of the famous Buxton mineral water. Like Bath, Buxton was also the site of a Roman bath and was known as Aquae Arnemetiae – 'the waters of the goddess of the grove.' This became St Anne's Well, and late in the twelfth century a chapel was built and dedicated to the saint, where pilgrims who had been healed left their crutches and other votive offerings. Reputedly a miraculous image of St Anne had been found in the well, which is why it and the chapel were given her name. It has been suggested that a statue of Arnemetia, the Roman nymph of the spring, was mistaken for St Anne – but it seems unlikely that any Roman cultic artefacts from the shrine of Arnemetia would have survived several hundred years of Christianity.

The chapel was closed in the sixteenth century on the orders of Thomas Cromwell, an agent of Henry VIII, with the saint's image and the votive offerings removed from the chapel, and the baths and wells sealed. But in the time of Queen Elizabeth I the baths and St Anne's Well were open again, and many patients came to bathe in the warm water and to drink it. The seventeenth-century traveller Celia Fiennes came to Buxton and bathed in the spa. She also described St Anne's Well: 'about 10 or 12 yards distant [from the bath] is a spring called St. Anns Well which is for drinking, they have arch'd it up that its much hotter, it heates the cup you take it up in, but not

St Anne's Well, Buxton in 2006.

a near so hot as the Somersetshire Baths and Springs are, [the Buxton water is 82 degrees F/28 degrees C] the taste is not unpleasant but rather like milk, they say its Diaretick I dranke a part of a cup full.'

The water from the well, around 200,000 gallons a day, supplied the successive Pump Rooms; but because of the Enclosure Act there also had to be free access to St Anne's Well, and so a pump was placed outside the Pump Room. This was replaced by another in the 1940s, which is where visitors can obtain the water from St Anne's Well today. It is a stone structure with a constant flow of water from a pipe, and it has a niche containing a statue of St Anne.

Location: Outside The Micrarium (the former Pump Room), at the bottom of The Slopes, a sloping public garden, in the centre of Buxton.

Holy Well, King's Newton

This well is clearly ancient, the earliest documentary reference to 'Halywalsiche' being dated 1366, and an arch built over the well bore an inscription dating from the late seventeenth century, but there is no folklore linked to the well, or any memory

The holy well at King's Newton before the first arch collapsed.

that it was supposed to have healing virtues. The arch collapsed in the 1950s, but thankfully in 1984–5 the well was restored by the Melbourne Civic Society who had a new stone arch erected, together with a plaque giving the old inscription: FONS SACER HIC STRVITVR ROBERTO NOMINIS HARDINGE 16XX [1660]. King's Newton is north of Melbourne, and the well is signposted down Ward's Lane, which runs from the Packhorse roundabout to Swarkestone Bridge. SK386262

Mompesson's Well at Eyam in 2006.

Mompesson's Well, Eyam

This is not a holy well as such, but commemorates a tragic event in local history. William Mompesson was rector of Eyam in the 1660s when the plague was brought in from London. He isolated the village, to stop the disease spreading to other villages, and his wife became one of the victims. The well is a mile from the village, and on the boundary line beyond which the villagers could not go, so it was used as a place where outsiders left supplies. The rector left money in the well to pay for the goods, and he also left a note informing the outside world of the number of deaths. When the plague ended, only 83 villagers survived from the original 350. Every year on the last Sunday in August a commemoration service is held at Cucklet Delph where Mompesson had held open-air services. Well-dressing also takes place in Eyam at this time. Eyam is five miles north of Bakewell, and the well is to the north-east of the village, beside the lane to Grindleford. SK223773

Roman Baths, Stoney Middleton

There was a St Martin's Well here, and it might have been at the place where the so-called Roman Baths are today – or perhaps nearer to the church at the place where the medieval unroofed bathing pool was situated. The water was said to be 'beneficial for any unnatural sharpness and saltness of blood, heartburn, too great heat, contraction of stomach, shortness of breath and stuffiness of the lungs.' Another account added rheumatism, scrofula and bad eyes. This bath was replaced in 1815 by the present bathhouse in Blind Lane, a stone's-throw north of the church, as it was hoped that the waters could be developed as a spa, but this never happened. The building is now listed, and was restored during 1985–92. The bathhouse was fed by the most substantial of a number of adjacent springs, the water from one of which flows through a pool beside the building, and well-dressing takes place here annually. SK232756

Tissington wells

Probably none of the six wells in and around the village was ever a true holy well, though Hall Well (opposite the Hall), which is the most elaborate well, was once

The double bathhouse known as Roman Baths at Stoney Middleton in 2006. It contains two separate chambers, one for women and one for men, and was still in use into the mid-twentieth century.

Hall Well, Tissington, photographed in 2006.

called St Helen's Well. The Tissington wells are famous for the annual well-dressing, which takes place here on Ascension Day, and Crichton Porteous refers to Tissington as the 'mother-place of well-dressing' for the custom there is the longest-established. One tradition cites 1350, when the pure water saved the village from the Black Death; another claims the custom began in 1615 after the wells kept flowing through a drought. Whenever it started, the tradition is as popular as it ever was, and has now spread into neighbouring Staffordshire, and even further afield to many other locations throughout the UK. The ornate pictures set up around the wells are made from flower petals, seeds, leaves, bark, moss, pebbles and any other natural materials that can be found, all pressed individually into a base of wet clay. Well-dressing can

Well-dressing at Hands Well, Tissington, in the 1940s.

be seen in many Derbyshire villages throughout the summer. The six Tissington wells are the Hall Well, Children's Well, Yew Tree Well, Hands Well, Town Well, and Coffin Well; a walk which passes them all is publicised in the village. Tissington is three miles north of Ashbourne, and there is a large car park to the south, on the old railway line which is now the Tissington Trail. SK177522

LEICESTERSHIRE

Holy Well, Ab Kettleby

Holy wells are scarce in the county, and this is the best of what survives. Look for the strange truncated pyramid topped by a stone basin, close to the village pond. Bob Trubshaw surmises, probably correctly, that the basin was once what the water flowed into; now it disappears under a grating. The water was believed to be good for rheumatism. To find the well, turn left off the main road into the village (from the south), then left into Church Lane. The pond is on your right, the well to your left by a footpath. SK724229

The holy well at Ab Kettleby in 1989 before the grating was added. Photo: Bob Trubshaw.

Holy Well, Beeby

Another strange truncated stone pyramid marks this well, dating from 1855 (restored in 1953), though in 1804 it was depicted with a normal well-house with a pitched roof. It was then known as the Stockwell, with 'excellent mineral waters' which were good for stomach disorders. It can be found on the roadside just below (north of) the church. SK664084

King Richard's Well, Bosworth Battlefield

Although not a holy well, this is famous for being the place where King Richard III (allegedly) drank during the fateful Battle of Bosworth in 1485, the last battle of the Wars of the Roses, in which he was killed. The stone cover was erected in 1813 and restored in 1985. There is public access to the battlefield (between Shenton and Sutton Cheney) and the well will be found a short walk away from the car park. SK402000

NOTTINGHAMSHIRE

St Catherine's Well, Newark

This well came into existence when two knights, Sir Everard Bevercotes and Sir Guy Saucimer, fought over their love for the same woman, and Sir Guy killed Sir Everard, on St Catherine's Eve. A spring burst forth where the dead man fell; Sir Guy left for the Holy Land full of remorse; and their beloved Isabell died of grief. Sir Guy caught leprosy while away from home, and on his way back he had a vision of St Catherine who told him that the water from the spring could cure his leprosy. He built a hermit's cell beside the spring, but the river flooded the site and he moved to another spring close by where he built a house with chapel attached, where he placed a statue of St Catherine. He enclosed the spring with a stone wall, and lived there for the rest of his life. He was venerated locally, and known as St Guthred. The spring now known as St Catherine's Well is close to the Civil War fortification known as the Queen's Sconce, by the River Devon, but it is in a cottage garden so please do not trespass. SK790530

St Catherine's Well, Westhorpe, Southwell

There were once four holy wells at Southwell, and two of them, the Holy Well and the Lady Well, were in the Minster. Now only St Catherine's Well survives – but it was always the most famous, the water being known for curing rheumatism. A chapel dedicated to the saint was built next to the well in 1482, but didn't survive the Reformation; nor did an attempt in 1720 to develop the spring as a spa fare any better. Bath Cottage was built on the site of the spa buildings, and today the well is by this cottage, on the left-hand side of the unadopted Bath Lane about two hundred yards from the crossroads in Westhorpe. The well has a square brick structure over it, and is situated in the grounds of Bath Cottage, where permission to view should be sought. SK684534

RUTLAND

Wishing Well, Ashwell

The well has also been referred to as the holy well, and the village name may have been taken from it. The village was Exewelle in the Domesday Book, Essewell in 1202, and Asshewell in 1291. The inscription over the well reads:

> All ye who hither come to drink,
> Rest not your thoughts below,
> Look at that sacred sign and think
> Whence living waters flow.

The cross ('that sacred sign' of the verse) on top of the well-house is a recent one dating from the late 1990s and replacing one which was lost ten or more years earlier. The well is easily found on the west of the village, in a clump of trees where the Langham road turns off the Oakham road. SK864137

The wishing well or holy well at Ashwell in 2004.

SHROPSHIRE

St Cuthbert's Well, Donington

This well had a reputation for curing sore eyes bathed with its water. It has a stone canopy, and can be found in a wooded dell below St Cuthbert's church. Donington is close to Albrighton, north-west of Wolverhampton, but not signposted, so if travelling along A41 look for Rectory Road. SJ808045

St Julian's Well, Ludlow

A small stone well-house which is Grade II listed covers this well, which was originally a water supply in an Augustinian friary. It can be found under a large tree in the middle of Livesey Road: SO518750

St Milburga's Well and St Owen's Well, Much Wenlock

Both wells are looked after but are now dry; they have plaques giving their names. Well dressing takes place annually at both wells in June. St Milburga's Well cured eye diseases, and girls who threw in a pin would acquire a sweetheart. It is near the Guildhall, off Barrow Street (SO625998). St Owen's Well is in the wall of St Owen's Well House, an old cruck-framed building on Back Lane (SO622999).

St Cuthbert's Well near Donington church in 1984.

St Milburga's Well, Stoke St Milborough

Milburga was the daughter of Merewald, king of Mercia, and she became the second abbess of the nunnery of Wenlock. According to the eleventh-century Life by Goscelin, she had miraculous healing powers and was a saintly woman. After her death in 715, her tomb was venerated, but its location was later lost. However a document found at Wenlock priory described the site of her grave and the monks excavated there in 1101. Some boys fell into a grave where there were bones and a coffin and altar. Cures started to occur at the grave, which was identified as that of St Milburga, and her cult then began to spread, with five churches being dedicated to her. One of them was at Stoke St Milborough, where a holy well was also miraculously created. The legend tells of Milburga being chased by her enemies and riding on a white horse for two days and nights before falling in a faint to the ground. Some men working in the fields ran to help her, but there was no water to bathe the wound caused when she struck her head on a stone. She told her horse to strike the rock, and a flow of water gushed forth. She commanded the barley the men had been sowing to grow quickly, and she told them that if anyone came asking for a lady on a white horse, they were to say that she had passed by when they were sowing the barley. That evening the barley was ready to harvest, and while the men were cutting it, St Milburga's pursuers came past and asked about her. The men were able to tell them the truth, that she had passed by when they were sowing their barley, and so her enemies went away baffled.

Down the years the well had a reputation for curing sore eyes, and the local women would also wash their clothes there. During the twentieth century the water was piped to a small reservoir and used to supply the scattered houses and farmsteads. At the end of the last century the well was restored.

Location: Stoke St Milborough is six miles north-east of Ludlow and the well is not far from the church. On entering the village from the south, head for the church but do not drive into the dead-end lane to the left that leads to the church entrance (with red postbox). Keep going up the hill and round a sharp left-hand bend, after which there is a wide entrance on your left, and immediately afterwards a rustic gate leading to the well. SO567823

St Oswald's Well, Oswestry

St Oswald was a king of Northumbria who died a martyr in 642. His link with Oswestry came about because he was killed only eight years into his reign by the pagan king Penda of Mercia at the Battle of Maserfield, which is generally identified with the present-day Oswestry. Penda ordered that his limbs and head be cut off and displayed on stakes, and according to legend, an eagle seized an arm and flew off with it. Where it dropped the arm, a spring gushed forth which became the saint's well. His body was buried firstly at Oswestry (Oswaldestre or 'Oswald's Tree', i.e. wooden stake), but later parts of him were taken to different places as relics (his head went to Lindisfarne, and then to Durham, where it is still in St Cuthbert's coffin) and so his cult spread. The ruins of a chapel built over the well could still be seen in the late eighteenth century but there are now no traces of it. The well still survives in good condition, and contains water, but iron railings keep all visitors away from it.

The water was once considered a cure for eye ailments, and was carried away in bottles for that purpose. In addition, pilgrims would bathe in the well, even as late as the mid-nineteenth century. But it degenerated into a wishing well with an elaborate ceremony required if the wish was to succeed. There were in fact several rituals, including going to the well at midnight, taking some water in one's hand and drinking some of it whilst wishing. The rest of the water should be thrown on to a stone at the back of the well: it was a carved head with a crown which was believed to depict St Oswald, but over the years was damaged beyond recognition, presumably because it featured in the wishing rituals. Another of the rituals was to bathe one's face in the water while wishing; yet another was to find a beechnut husk resembling a human face and to throw it into the water face up, then count twenty, and if the husk floated during the count, the wish would be fulfilled.

Location: On the west side of Oswestry. To find the well from the town centre, go to the crossroads with traffic lights near the parish church and take the Trefonen road westwards, then turn second right into Oswald Place and follow this road along Oswald's Well Lane. The well is on the left-hand side, close to the road but hidden from view in a hollow with trees around. There is a plaque at the entrance; and the new housing close by has adopted the name Maserfield. SJ284293

St Oswald's Well, Oswestry in 2005.

St Winifred's Well, Woolston

This well marks the place where St Winifred's body rested when being carried from Gwytherin in Denbighshire to Shrewsbury in 1138. (The full story of St Winifred can be found in the entry for *St Winefride's Well, Holywell, Flintshire, Wales.*) The spring began to flow at Woolston where the body lay, and on the stones could be seen red markings like bloodstains. The water was supposed to be good for healing wounds and curing broken bones. The folklorist Charlotte Burne saw it being used in this way during her visit in 1885: a man with a broken arm had been instructed by his doctor to bathe it every morning in the well. Another small spring further downstream was said to be good for the eyes.

The surviving structure at the well is elaborate, with three enclosures. The spring rises under the cottage which now stands over the well and the water flows through the enclosures which have stone-slab walls with holes in them. These can be blocked so that the baths fill with water; the main bath is two to three feet deep. A chapel originally stood over the well, and the use of dendrochronology (dating the ancient wood in the structure) shows that it was built around 1485. The chapel was converted after the Reformation into a courthouse for the manor, and the building used as such until around 1824. It was then converted into a small cottage, and has in recent years been renovated by the Landmark Trust and is available through them for holiday lets. (Hardy visitors only: the ablutions are in a building outside!)

A corner of the half-timbered cottage above St Winifred's Well, Woolston, with some of the bathing pools visible. Photographed in 2005.

Location: The hamlet of Woolston is four miles south-east of Oswestry, and the well is not easy to find, as it is not signposted. From Maesbury Marsh turn left into Woolston, then where the road turns right you should follow the track to the left. It shortly comes to an end, but a small wooden gate on the right leads to the well (no signpost). Through the gate a path through shrubbery soon reaches the cottage, and the well and pools can be found on the lower side. The footpath continues down past the cottage and well. An alternative approach in fine weather is to walk from Maesbury Marsh: follow the canal bank in an easterly direction as far as the bridge, then turn right across the fields to Woolston. SJ322244

STAFFORDSHIRE

St Bertram's Wells, Ilam

Very little is known about Bertram (Bettelin) who may have been a very local saint – a hermit living in the area in Anglo-Saxon times. Anyone visiting his wells (there are two) at Ilam should also look in the church, where the substantial remains of the saint's shrine can still be seen. In medieval times the shrine was a focus for pilgrimages, and the pilgrims would probably also have visited St Bertram's Well. One of the wells linked (though perhaps in name only) to St Bertram is located between the church and St Bertram's Bridge over the River Manifold, in the grounds of Ilam Hall. It is surrounded by a stone wall and fenced off for safety reasons, but a good view can still be had of the gushing water. This was probably never a true holy well but simply a local water supply. The real St Bertram's Well is an insignificant spring with tumbledown stonework located on Bunster Hill above the village. I have to confess that my attempt to reach it ended in failure, due to an excess of mud on the hill (but it was April 1st!). A venerated tree, St Bertram's Ash, used to overlook the well and it was considered unlucky to damage it.

Location: Ilam is four miles north-west of Ashbourne; the pseudo St Bertram's Well can be found south of the church. The real well is to the north, close to footpaths crossing Buntser Hill, and I am indebted to Tim Prevett for these directions: 'Walk north past the large cross near the bridge, and a footpath is signposted up the hill. Bear to the right keeping to the east of the field boundaries… The well will be on the right, in a low U-shaped structure.' *Warning:* This is a very popular tourist area, because of the breathtaking scenery, including Dove Dale, and Ilam Hall Country Park, so best visited out of season.

St Bertram's Well on Buntser Hill: SK137515; pseudo St Bertram's Well: SK133507.

St Chad's Well, Stowe, Lichfield

Chad was the first bishop of Mercia and Lindsey at Lichfield in the seventh century. He had earlier succeeded his brother Cedd as abbot of Lastingham in North Yorkshire, where wells dedicated to both saints can still be seen (see *Lastingham* entry). His move to Lichfield was at the end of his life: he arrived in 669 and died in

Although not a genuine holy well, the alternative St Bertram's Well close to the church at Ilam is still worth seeing. Photographed in 2006.

672. In this brief three years he established a monastery or hermitage north-east of the cathedral, close to a spring where he baptised converts, and where, according to Bede, he was accustomed to stand naked on a stone in the water to pray. After his death he was buried at Stowe, his bones being removed to Lichfield Cathedral around 700. Placed in an ornately decorated shrine, the relics were afterwards visited by many pilgrims. In 2003 during archaeological excavations in the cathedral some remains claimed as being from the shrine were discovered, three well-preserved fragments of painted limestone carving depicting the Archangel Gabriel.

The site of both the well and St Chad's church close by can be dated with certainty to the seventh century, though nothing of the original church now remains, it having been rebuilt in the twelfth century. The well too has changed: both its appearance and its location. Apparently since St Chad's time it has been relocated to several spots within a twenty-five-yard radius. In the 1920s it was located in the gardens of three cottages, and three women 'looked after' the well on alternate weeks,

Left: *This old photograph probably dates from the 1920s; it comes from R.C. Skyring Walters' book on Gloucestershire wells and shows St Chad's Well when it was in cottage gardens and still had its stone well-house.*
Right: *A modern photograph taken in 1984.*

presumably supervising the many pilgrims who still visited. It used to have an octagonal stone cover, which was demolished in 1949 and replaced by a pitched roof on four legs, one standing on each corner of the pool, a structure likened to a bandstand and which somehow lacks the atmosphere one expects from such an important and historic well. Up until the early nineteenth century the well was decked with flowers and greenery on Ascension Day, and a service in the church was followed by a procession to the well, another service, and then merrymaking and feasting in the churchyard. People bathed in the water to cure sore eyes, skin complaints and rheumatism, and it was also drunk. By the early twentieth century it had degenerated into a wishing well, with wishes being granted by placing one's hand against a granite stone built into the well-house, which was said to be the stone St Chad used to stand upon.

Location: Stowe church is to the north of Lichfield, on the northern edge of Stowe Pool, and the well is in the churchyard. SK122103

Egg Well, Bradnop

The detailed history of this well is not known to me, nor why it was called the Egg Well. Did the name have some obscure esoteric significance – or did the water perhaps smell of bad eggs? This intriguing well is housed in a simple building, unroofed until some time in the nineteenth century, inside which is a substantial bathing pool measuring about six by four feet, with a step in each corner leading down into the water. Around the rim is the inscription: 'Renibus et Spleni Cordi, Jecorique Medetur, Mille Maelis Prodest Ista Salubris Aqua' – 'The liver, kidneys, heart's disease these waters remedy, and by their healing powers assuage full many a malady.' There are also the initials of William Stanley, the owner of nearby Ashenhurst Hall between 1744 and 1752, suggesting that the present well structure was constructed at that time. The Egg Well was probably one of those wells which straddles the line between healing well and simple spa.

Left: *The Egg Well near Bradnop in 2006.*
Right: *A view of the interior showing the bathing pool and part of the inscription round its rim.*

Location: Bradnop is two miles south-east of Leek and the well is a mile away, reached along lanes to the south. Follow the lane across the main road from Bradnop village; you can drive as far as the entrance to Middle Cliff Farm, and then park on the verge. Walk down the lane, turn left at the entrance to Ashenhurst Hall Farm and follow the lane leading to Roost Hill Farm. The well building will be seen under trees on the grass verge at the next junction, opposite the bungalow Fernleigh. SK006541

St Helen's Well, Rushton Spencer

In earlier centuries this well would sometimes suddenly dry up early in May, even in a wet season, and this was taken to foretell some great calamity. It is said to have dried up before the outbreak of the Civil War and before the execution of Charles I. Well dressing used to take place until the 1920s. Rushton Spencer is four miles north-west of Leek and the well can be found beside a minor road off the A523 to the south-east of the village. However the road is used as a shortcut and therefore busy with fast traffic so care is required. The well is in a deep, walled chamber next to a telegraph pole, uphill from the Royal Oak. SJ941622

Holy Well, Sandwell Valley

This holy well is in Sandwell Valley Country Park next to the ruined Sandwell Priory: the name Sandwell presumably came from the well. The priory was founded in the twelfth century and closed in 1525, after which a succession of grand houses was built on the site, the last being demolished in 1928. The well is inside a concrete structure but the water flows out through a trough at the front. It is dressed annually by local pagans on the Sunday nearest to Imbolc (February 2nd). The Country Park is east of West Bromwich and bisected by the M5 motorway; the well is located south of Swan Pool and east of Park Farm, not far from the Heritage Centre. SK024914

Wulfruna's Well, Wolverhampton

Also known as Lady Wulfruna's Well, this is now marked by a memorial erected in 1901 but it is not on the exact site of the well, which was probably close to St Peter's church, Wolverhampton, as that was originally a monastery founded by the Lady Wulfruna in the tenth century. She was a Saxon noblewoman who was regarded as the founder of Wolverhampton. There is an account of the well in a sixteenth-century document where it is referred to as 'Ladie Wulfruna's Sprynge' 'where she used to come and wash. It is said that the lady prayed for it' (which suggests that the well was believed to have sprung up at her request). This early account also said that the water was believed to have healing powers, miraculously healing the lame, the weak and the infirm. The present small gabled structure was originally a drinking fountain, but the tap and drinking cup are long gone. It carries an inscription: In remembrance of the Lady Wulfruna – and is now protected by railings. Its location is in Gorsebrook Road. From Wolverhampton town centre, follow the A449 towards Stafford and after about one-and-a-half miles take Gorsebrook Road which leads to the racecourse. After two hundred yards the road goes under a railway bridge, and shortly afterwards the well memorial will be seen on the left, opposite the racecourse fence.

England: North

Cumbria, Durham, Isle of Man, Lancashire, Northumberland, Yorkshire: East, Yorkshire: North, Yorkshire: South and West

CUMBRIA

St Andrew's Well, Kirkandrews-on-Eden

Also known as Neddy Well, this baptismal well is in the old graveyard below the site of the ancient church (no trace of this to be seen). Take the left-hand path down the side of the graveyard (overgrown) downhill, and just beyond the house on your left, the location of the well is indicated by a flow of water under the bank. NY354585

St Cuthbert's Well, Colton

This well, set into a grassy bank below a remote hilltop church, was restored for the Millennium. It is approached through a small circular stone-built enclosure and is lined with sandstone; a large stone above it is inscribed 'St Cuthbert's Well'. The water used to be used for baptisms in the church. The well can be found beside an ancient path leading uphill to the church (opposite church gate) at Colton six miles north-east of Ulverston. SD318861

St Cuthbert's Well, Colton in 2007.

Even in dry weather, a steady stream of water flows from St Helen's Well at Great Asby into the beck. Photographed in 2007.

St Helen's Well, Great Asby

The water from a powerful spring flows into a large square stone basin walled on three sides – its size suggests it was constructed as a bathing pool. On the fourth side, the water overflows down the bank and into the stream which runs through the village. The water has never been known to fail, and when I visited, although the stream bed above the well was dry, downstream there was a good flow of water gushing from the well. It was once used for baptisms at the nearby church. The well can be found on the north bank of the stream on the green at the centre of the village, just east of the church. NY682133

St Kentigern's Well, Aspatria

In the churchyard to the north of the church can be found a small stone well-house built into a bank and approached by an open walled court, all now overgrown. The water was once used for baptisms. NY147420

St Kentigern's Well on the river bank at Caldbeck is in a beautiful location – even when it's raining. Photographed in 2007.

The door of St Mungo's Well near Bromfield church is normally kept secured for safety reasons: there is a deep well inside the small well-house. Photographed in 2007.

St Kentigern's Well or St Mungo's Well, Caldbeck

Kentigern's pet-name was Mungo, and this well appears under both names. Kentigern was a Scottish monk and bishop of Glasgow who died in 612; he was exiled for a time to Cumbria, hence his still being remembered there with several church dedications. At Caldbeck he is depicted in a church window, and his well is just outside the churchyard, to the west end of the church, below the stone bridge. There are steps down to the well – a simple stone trough on the river bank. NY325399

St Mungo's Well, Bromfield

Another well which sometimes went under the name of Kentigern; and it was also known as the Helly Well. It can be found in the field immediately to the north of the church – there is a path from the churchyard – but it may be lost in vegetation in the summer. The stone cover was added in 1890, and on its roof above the door is the inscription: '+ Therefore with joy shall ye draw water out of the wells of salvation. Isaiah XII'. The water can be seen in the circular stone shaft about two feet below ground level. Games were once held by the well, until suppressed by a zealous clergyman. NY176470

St Ninian's Well at Brisco in 2007: overgrown yet not completely lost.

St Ninian's Well, Brisco

Brisco is just south of Carlisle, and a grass track (signposted as footpath to Carleton Mill) leads off the main street to the well, which is now somewhat neglected and overgrown. The arch was erected in the nineteenth century by Sarah Losh and was inscribed in memory of her sister Katherine. When the field gate is reached, the path goes over a stile into some trees, and the well will be found at the far end of this small wooded area. NY423520

St Oswald's Well, Kirkoswald

This is a particularly interesting holy well in an atmospheric location. Although the spring which feeds the well is now below St Oswald's church, this was probably not the case in the early days of this church, perhaps a thousand years ago. The first church would have been much smaller, and may have been built beside the spring which supplied water for baptisms. When the church was extended westwards in the following centuries, the spring was built over, and a well supplied by the spring was therefore located outside the west end. The exact site of the spring is unknown, but in the early twentieth century Colonel Fetherstonhaugh stated his belief that it was under the nave, because the vault beneath the chancel was dry.

The well consists of a stone and brick superstructure in which is a circular hole protected by a metal cover. When this is lifted, you can see down into the well; this

Tristan Gray Hulse demonstrating the use of the cup on its chain at St Oswald's Well outside Kirkoswald church in 2007.

can also be accessed more directly down some steps to the side. A metal cup on a chain is provided so that you can lift water from the well.

Location: Kirkoswald is nine miles north-east of Penrith, and the church and its separate bell-tower are at the south end of the village. There is room to park one car by the entrance gate on the B6413. NY555409

St Patrick's Well, Patterdale

A substantial stone well-house covers this well, which is easily found beside the road. There used to be a chapel here too, now lost (1348: Capella de Patrickdale),

The archetypal well of St Patrick in Patterdale in 2007.

The roofless building that survives at Stanger Spa shows how lucrative businesses sometimes grew up around water supplies that were believed to have curative qualities. Sometimes these were formerly holy wells, but it is not always possible to be sure of this. Photographed in 2007.

and the name shows that St Patrick's name was also given to the dale. It is located just south of Glenridding, at the southern end of Ullswater: because of double yellow lines everywhere, it is best to park in Glenridding and walk to the well, or visit the café nearly opposite which has a car park. NY388166

Stanger Well, Embleton

Also known as Stanger Spa. Some people think that the name may originally have been St Anna, but this seems too contrived and it may simply derive from Susanna, as Fons Susannae (Susanna's Well) was mentioned in an early deed. Whether this was ever a holy well is uncertain. It may simply have been a private bath that was developed as a spa when its water was found to be curative. The water was said to be 'strongly impregnated with mineral salts' and 'very efficacious in the cure of skin diseases', and was sold at sixpence a gallon. A roofless building survives, restored by the Cockermouth and District Civic Trust: inside, a grating covers the water supply. It is in a field near the River Cocker, two miles south-east of Cockermouth and is accessible by bridleway from Stanger to the north-west (parking situation unknown) or from the B5292 to the south-east (parking in lay-by). NY141272

DURHAM

St Cuthbert's Well, Durham

Little is known about this well below Durham Cathedral. It has a large sandstone surround with the inscription FONS: CUTHBERT and a date (1600 or 1660). St Cuthbert of course is closely linked with Durham, and his grave is still to be seen in the cathedral, as too are his portable altar and late seventh-century coffin. Access to the well is difficult, down a steep path between the Cathedral and the River Wear. NZ272421

Holy Well, Wolsingham

There is a large building like a little house over this well, now a listed building, and the water is said to have been used 'for religious purposes' in a chapel which once stood close by, but nothing else seems to be known about its history. It is on the north side of the lane leading from the inn at the north of the village to the hospital. NZ077378

St Mary's Well, Gainford

Located close to the church, this well once supplied water for baptisms. To find it, go to the church on the village green, through the churchyard and down a steep path towards the river; the well is under the churchyard. The water flows into a stone trough and then away to the river. NZ169167 (Just to the north-east by the river can be found Gainford Spa, which grew up at a group of sulphur springs and led to the development of the village as a health resort in the nineteenth century.)

St Oswald's Well, Durham

When the monks of Lindisfarne were forced to flee from the Vikings carrying St Cuthbert's relics with them, they placed the relic of St Oswald's skull in Cuthbert's coffin. The cult of St Oswald presumably came to Durham with his relic, hence the dedication of a church and well to him. (See the entry for *St Oswald's Well, Oswestry, Shropshire*, for more details of Oswald's death.) Depictions of St Cuthbert regularly showed him as a bishop carrying the crowned and haloed head of St Oswald, and the skull is still with Cuthbert's relics in his grave in Durham cathedral. I rely on Laurence Hunt's description of St Oswald's Well close to New Elvet. 'Situated just below the footpath leading from St Oswald's churchyard to Prebend's Bridge. Reached down a narrow, steep footpath about 20 yards after entering the trees below the church tower. Today this well consists of a large cavern cut into the sandstone rock outcrop part way down the steep, well-wooded banks of the Wear overlooking the Cathedral. A small rock ledge at the front of the cavern dams up a pool of water, the overflow pouring over the ledge and down to the river below.' NZ275419

ISLE OF MAN

There was once a large number of holy wells in the Isle of Man, many of which probably still survive, though only as overgrown springs. W. Walter Gill listed over one hundred named wells in his *Manx Scrapbook* of 1929, but that was nearly eighty years ago. I have not come across any recent survey of the wells of the island, and an up-to-date study is long overdue. Here I give details of a few wells that I am reasonably certain still survive; however I have never visited any of them myself and therefore location details are sometimes sketchy. The Isle of Man awaits the attention of dedicated well-hunters, who will find plenty of places to explore in Gill's list and in the other publications named in my Sources.

Well of the Baptism (Chibbyr y Vashtee), Patrick

This must be the most remote of the Manx wells, near the equally remote keeill (a keeill is an ancient Christian chapel or church, the remains of many of which are scattered throughout the island) (Lag ny Keeilley, 'The hollow of the chapel'), and some determination is required to reach it. It is located at the southern end of the Manx National Trust property of Eary Cushlin, with access as follows. From Dalby take the main road towards Round Table and turn off on rough cart track to right, one-and-a-half miles from Dalby. After a further half-mile is the entrance to Eary Cushlin: follow rough path (old packhorse track) south for three-quarters of a mile to a point 250 yards (another source gives 100 yards) north of the keeill. The well is on the lefthand side of the track, but might be difficult to find, being described by Gill as 'a spring of unimpressive aspect', though it was credited with healing powers. The keeill site consists of the ruined chapel, a hermit's cell, and a burial ground.

St Catherine's Well (Chibbyr Catreeney), Port Erin

This is a spring 'at the top of the beach', the water of which was believed to have 'miraculous qualities' and healing powers. It was said that 'any woman who drank its waters would be as fascinating as a maiden of seventeen, however great her age'. The well was at one time covered by a pump, and acted as a local water supply, but the pump was removed when piped water was made available, and the water now wells up through the sand again. There was also a carved stone at the well, its inscription reading 'St Catherine's Well, Keep Me Clear', placed there by William Milner in the mid-nineteenth century. It is a few yards from the site of Keeill Catreeney, suggesting it is an ancient well. Its location is said to be 'in the shore wall' just below the present St Catherine's church.

St Mary's Well (Chibbyr y Woirrey), Ramsey

Certain herbs had to be dropped into the water of this well so that it could be used for love divination. Its location was noted in 1929 as 'about 300 yards west of the Parsonage'. A Ramsey Town Centre Walk found on the internet includes mention of this well: 'The "Bayr Chibbyragh" road sign refers to Chibbyr Y Woirrey, a well in Coronation Park said to have healing properties.' This appears to be in an area bordered by Tower Road, Albert Street and Parsonage Road.

St Maughold's Well, Maughold

This is the best-known and most atmospheric of the accessible Manx wells, its cliff-top site being especially noteworthy. However, it may not be the original St Maughold's Well. The Life of St Patrick written by Jocelin of Furness in the twelfth century described a spring at Kirk Maughold which flowed from a stone sarcophagus containing the saint's bones, the water of which 'healeth divers infirmities'. A hollow stone measuring around four by three feet and ten inches deep was found close to the church when a grave was being dug in 1830, but there was no spring. This was possibly the sarcophagus described by Jocelin, and the spring may have moved, for the churchyard was known to be 'full of water' until drained around 1860. Writing in the late nineteenth century, the Reverend S.N. Harrison described a stone trough or sarcophagus standing at the side of Chibbyr y Chrink, a stone-lined well, 'flagged on the bottom, with steps going down some ten or twenty feet'. Also in the churchyard are the foundations of three keeills, and two others have been recorded there. Close to the eastern keeill is a large circular stone well which has also been named as St Maughold's Well – and so it is possible that this well is the one described by Jocelin, or at least its successor in the churchyard.

The well on Maughold Head is the one that has been the focus of pilgrimage and ritual for some generations. It was described in 1874: 'A few stones form a square, open to the north, and within the inclosure is a small scooped stone into which the water flows from the rock, but so slowly that it is hardly perceptible.' According to folklore, it was created by the knee of St Maughold's horse when they landed after crossing from Ireland. Water gushed forth from the hollow, which was drunk by both the saint and his horse, and thereafter has been considered 'efficacious for the cure of all diseases'. It was said that there used to be a saint's chair close by, where barren women would sit and drink a glass of the well water in hopes of becoming fertile, but the chair is no longer to be seen. It was also customary to visit the well on the first Sunday of harvest, when the water had 'its full virtue' for the treatment of sore eyes, and pilgrims would leave strips of cotton, which they had used to wash their eyes, on the bushes by the well. They would also drop coins, or pins, or buttons, or beads into the well as offerings.

Location: Maughold is three miles south-east of Ramsey and the cliff-top well is 430 yards north-east of the parish church on the slope of Maughold Head; footpath signposted. SC495919

St Patrick's Well (Chibbyr Pherick), Lonan

This well was created, according to legend, by St Patrick's horse, which stumbled and dislodged a turf with its hoof, whereupon a spring began to flow. The water was said to be good for sore eyes, and it was also believed that anyone who drank from the well without leaving an offering would be unable to find their way home. Chibbyr Pherick Fair was held at the well every year on 12th May. The well may now not be easy to spot, if it has not been tidied up since it was described, 60–70 years ago, as 'half hidden by ferns and briars'. It is somewhere on the road to Glen Roy: 'on the hill-side above Lonan Church'; and 'on Lhergey Grawe, East side of Glen Roy, Lonan'.

St Patrick's Well (Chibbyr Pherick), Peel

This well on Corrin's Hill began to flow to mark the place where St Patrick first planted the sign of the cross on Manx soil. An alternative legend has it gushing forth from the hillside at the place where St Patrick's horse landed as it leapt on to the cliff from the sea. St Patrick crossed from Ireland to Man on horseback, and he was pursued by a sea monster which fell to its death as the horse leapt on to the land. Its petrified body is said to be still visible at the foot of the gully below. The well's alternative names were Chibbyr Noo Pherick (St Patrick's Well), Chibbyr Sheeant (Blessed Well) and Chibbyr yn Argid (Well of the Silver – from all the silver coins thrown into it as offerings), and its water was said to be efficacious against disease, as well as protecting against witches and fairies. Corrin's Hill is south of Peel, and Kermode gives a precise location: on the west slope by a footpath 217 yards west-north-west of Corrin's Tower.

LANCASHIRE

Holy Well, Hollinshead Hall, Tockholes

The substantial well-house is the main surviving building of Hollinshead Hall. The well's history is unclear, but it may be ancient as a now-demolished neighbouring farm was known as Halliwell Fold Farm, and an old bridge nearby was also named from the Halliwell. However these references could equally relate to another well, now lost. It has been suggested that the well-house may once have been used as a baptistery and chapel by local recusant Catholics – but the interior details make its use as either a chapel or a baptistery implausible and it looks more likely to have been nothing more than a bathhouse, or even just a grotto. The presence of a holy well led to its construction, but more research is needed before the well-house's history can be satisfactorily written. There is a collecting pool on the hillside behind and above the well-house, from where the water flows into the building through a lion's head (currently blocked) and into stone troughs on either side of the well spout. The water is said to have had a reputation for curing eye problems. The building is kept padlocked, but it is possible to look inside through the windows, and the well outside is accessible.

Location: The well is about two miles south of Tockholes, just to the south of Blackburn. It is accessible by footpath from the Slipper Lowe picnic and car park area, which is reached from the lane south of Tockholes, and is just under a mile north of the lane's junction with the A675 halfway between Abbey Village and

The well-house at Hollinshead Hall: the well is on the raised ground behind. Photographed in 2007.

Belmont. Hollinshead Hall is signposted from the car park: where the paths diverge (no sign at this point), go right downhill into the trees and you will soon see the low walls of the demolished hall, with the well-house off to the left. Back at the car park, the track through the gate also leads down to Hollinshead Hall (go left at the junction). SD663199

Ladyewell, Fernyhalgh Lane, Fulwood

The Catholic Marian Shrine centred on Ladyewell House has the holy well as its centrepiece: the site has been changing and developing since its distant (possibly Anglo-Saxon) origins. The romantic story told of its founding is said to date to around AD 1100 and tells of an Irish merchant, Fergus Maguire, who was crossing the Irish Sea when a storm blew up, and he vowed to God that if he reached dry land safely he would make payment for his safe deliverance. He came ashore on the Lancashire coast and while sleeping heard a voice telling him to find Fernyhalgh and to build a chapel by the crab tree with coreless fruit, overhanging a shrine. He searched in vain until, staying overnight in Preston, he overheard a girl saying she had been following a cow which had strayed to Fernyhalgh. So he was able to find the crab tree, and the spring, and a statue of the Blessed Virgin Mary, showing this place had already been a shrine in the past. He built a new chapel, and although it was later demolished, Fernyhalgh had become a pilgrimage centre which it remains today. The earliest safely documented reference to a chapel on this site is from the mid-fourteenth century.

The Ladyewell at Fernyhalgh in 2007: the water can be seen by lifting the small flap in the well-cover. The present statue of the Virgin and Child was erected in 1954.

Pilgrims are always welcome at Ladyewell House, where in addition to the well there are a chapel and library, a room holding saints' relics, a Padre Pio Memorial Garden, and many other features typical of a twenty-first century Catholic shrine. The well is the first feature to be seen (to the right) on entering the grounds, and it is set in a small hollow overlooked by a large statue of Our Lady where flowers, offerings and candles are left. At ground level a flap can be opened to gain access to the water, but the water is also available from two taps, and water bottles are on sale. Cures continue to be claimed by some of those who have used the water. It is possible to visit the well without visiting the rest of the shrine, but a wider exploration is recommended as Ladyewell has become one of the most visited places of pilgrimage in Britain over the last sixty years.

Location: Just north of Preston and very close to the motorway but tricky to get to. Leave the M6 motorway at Junction 32 (signed Preston, Garstang) and at the roundabout follow the Preston sign, immediately getting in the left-hand lane signposted Longridge and Ribbleton. At the next small roundabout turn right – there are numerous Ladyewell signs along this route. Continue to the large roundabout and follow the Ladyewell sign: the road goes over the motorway and shortly after this you need the right turn (again signposted Ladyewell). Along this lane on the left is a car and coach park for the shrine, just before the Catholic church (which was itself built, in the late eighteenth century, because of its proximity to the well). It is possible to drive all the way to the shrine but the lane becomes narrow and there are very few parking spaces at the shrine itself. If your visit coincides with a pilgrimage there will be a lot of people and vehicles in the lane and so parking in the first car park is recommended, but if all seems quiet you may safely drive all the way. SD 557334

St Oswald's Well, Winwick

St Oswald, King of Northumbria, died in battle in AD 642, either here or, more likely, at Oswestry in Shropshire (see *St Oswald's Well, Oswestry, Shropshire*). According to a local variant of the saint's legend, he clawed at the ground with his right hand as he lay dying, and at that spot a spring began to flow. Bede described how people carried away the earth at the site of Oswald's death, but his description does not mention a detail that has become part of the Winwick legend, that the well formed in the deep hole that was made. The beliefs that have grown up around the Winwick well appear to combine details from Bede, medieval legends of Oswald, and the local traditions of Oswestry. This well is probably old, though its legend is not.

The well survives in a field and is protected by a fence. Three stone steps lead down to the water, and a stone at the back bears the letters I.H.S. (an abbreviation of the first three letters of the name Jesus in Greek). The water used to be collected for its healing powers, especially for sore eyes. The name of the well's location, Hermitage Green, suggests that this was once a religious centre of some kind, perhaps focused on the holy well.

St Patrick's Well near Heysham church in 2007.

Location: Winwick is just to the north of Warrington, and the well is on Woodhead Farm at Hermitage Green, half a mile north of the village. Anyone wishing to visit the well is requested to knock at the door and ask permission first. SJ607941

St Patrick's Well, Heysham

This well, also known as Church Well, is set into the wall beside the entrance to the path to St Peter's churchyard. It has been restored in recent years and furnished with a pump. Almost certainly, the well was given its saintly dedication because of its proximity to St Patrick's chapel, whose remains, with unusual rock-cut graves, lie only a few minutes' walk away to the north-west of St Peter's church. The notice at the well states that its true dedication is 'long since lost'. St Patrick is said to have been shipwrecked at Heysham and while making his way northwards he needed water and thrust his staff into the ground and a spring burst forth. That St Patrick's Well is a short distance away at Slyne, but not accessible. SD411617

St Thomas's Well, Windle

St Helens Cemetery is now the location of this well, close to the stepped base and shaft of Windleshaw Cross, which itself is close to the ruins of the Gerard chantry chapel of St Thomas's, known locally as Windleshaw Abbey. There has been a Catholic burial ground here since the seventeenth century, and it is probable that the well is also at least that old. It is circular, six yards in diameter, twelve feet deep and lined with stone. A name plate with 'St Thomas's Well' and another with '1798' and 'H.W.E.' can be seen, the initials being those of William and Elizabeth Hill who owned the land when the well sides were raised. Windle is to the north-west of St Helens and the cemetery is south of the A580. SJ497969

NORTHUMBERLAND

St Cuthbert's Well, Bellingham

Also known as Cuddy's Well, this takes the form of a pant, a northern name for a public fountain or well. Its existence was recorded in the twelfth century by Reginald of Durham in his *Miracles of St Cuthbert*. The saint was said to have discovered the spring by dowsing, and consecrated it. The water was used for baptisms in the nearby church. The well is in a grassy lane just outside the churchyard wall. NY837833

St Cuthbert's Well, insignificant-looking but with a history going back at least 800 years. Photographed in 1993.

Lady Well, Holystone

This well is also known as St Ninian's Well; in the early eighteenth century it was St Paulinus's Well. It seems to have taken its name of Lady Well from the nearby house of Benedictine nuns dedicated to St Mary the Virgin. A description of three hundred years ago includes mention of the 'holy stone' which was at the west end of the well pool. It was three feet long and was said to be where St Paulinus (the first Bishop of York, died 644) knelt when baptising his flock. Today the well takes the form of a large pool with a Celtic cross standing in the middle, and there is a statue of St Paulinus at one end. The cross has an inscription claiming that Paulinus baptised three thousand Northumbrians there at Easter in 627 – however he was actually at York Minster at that time. This used to be a healing well, but degenerated into a wishing well, with bent pins or coins thrown into it. It is now in the care of the National Trust.

Location: Holystone is seven miles west of Rothbury, and the well is north of the village, reached by a short footpath from the village. NT952029

Lady Well in its dark copse can be a sombre place when the sun is not shining. Photographed in 1998.

Small pieces of metal can still be seen in the Pin Well today (2006), as people try to keep up the old tradition of throwing in a pin and making a wish. No bent pins are to be seen because no one nowadays carries pins.

Pin Well, Wooler

This is a rewarding well to seek out, as its location is quite magical and it is on an interesting circular walk starting at Wooler. It was once traditional to visit the well on May Day and drop in a bent pin and make a wish. The well was also known as the Maiden Well, and lovers would go there at midnight, throw in a bent pin and make a wish. On a rock overhanging the site was once a natural chair called the King's Seat, long since lost through quarrying.

Location: The well is to the south of Wooler and the circular walk starts (or ends) in Cheviot Street. Walk up past the youth hostel and after half a mile fork right, then shortly right again on to a track signposted Pin Well. Follow the track round the quarry, past the pool, and then the well is among boulders opposite where a ravine forks off to the left. To return, keep straight on to Waud House and along the bridleway, eventually coming out on to the road leading back down into Wooler. At this point the bridleway is signposted Wooler Common, and in town, at the bottom of Ramsey's Lane, there is a signpost to Wooler Common and St Cuthbert's Way. NT987271

St Mary's Well, Jesmond Dene, Newcastle

This was a healing well located close to St Mary's Chapel (the Chapel of Our Lady of Jesmond), built in the early twelfth century but now ruinous. At one time the area thronged with pilgrims, and a papal letter of 1428 referred to miracles wrought at the chapel, which may have been the cures obtained at the well. It was said that when a bathing place was created at the well, the water stopped flowing as if in revenge for the well being interfered with. However the flow later returned as strong as ever. The well has a stone arch over it carrying the word 'Gratia', said to be part of a once-larger inscription: Ave Maria Gratia Plena (Hail Mary Full of Grace). In the early 1980s an archaeological investigation was carried out which revealed that the present well structure does not date from earlier than the seventeenth century. There are known to have been at least two other springs near the chapel, and one of those may have been the original holy well. People still collect bottles of water from the well because of its healing reputation, and there is still an annual pilgrimage to the chapel with a service being held in the ruins.

Location: The well and chapel are in Jesmond Dene, a wooded area of Jesmond north of Newcastle city centre, and can be reached from Jesmond Dene Road: enter a small copse opposite the Banqueting Hall through a wooden gate. The well is two hundred yards west of the chapel.

St Mungo's Well, Holystone

This is not far from Lady Well; it is between the village and the Forestry Commission car park. The site is said to be where St Mungo preached and baptised converts. However, Binnall and Dodds say 'It is doubtful whether this is an old name. It may only have been applied to the well after the publication of Walter Scott's *Rob Roy*.' They also have its location as 'on the south side of Holystone burn', whereas it is now sited by the roadside. So this appears to be a holy well of dubious authenticity for more than one reason. NT954025

YORKSHIRE: EAST

Drummer's Well, Harpham

The name of this well comes from a story whose action dates back to the fourteenth century. Tom Hewson was a village boy who was part of the household of the St Quintin family, and one of his tasks was drummer to the village band of archers. During a parade in the field, the squire accidentally knocked Tom headfirst into the well and he died. His mother was fetched, and she, the village wise woman, announced that, although the death had not been intended, it had come from the squire's hand and therefore: 'Know, then, that through all future ages, whenever a St. Quintin, Lord of Harpham, is about to pass from life, my poor boy shall beat his drum at the bottom of this fatal well!' It was said that from that time, whenever a head of the house of St Quintin was about to die, Tom's drum could be heard in the

Although the Drummer's Well is protected by railings, it is also very overgrown with weeds, making examination difficult. Photographed in 2005.

well. In an alternative version, William the Conqueror, who was fighting a battle nearby, promised to give the village to whoever was first to set foot in it, and Tom was narrowly beaten by a St Quintin who knocked him out of the way, causing him to fall into the well. (There is more information on Drumming Wells in my book *Cures and Curses.*) The well is located in the field behind the church, and reached by footpath beside the church or opposite the pub in Main Street, Harpham (five miles south-west of Bridlington). TA091615

St Helen's Well, Goodmanham

The water from the spring under an ancient elder tree flows into a shallow triangular pool which may have been used as a bath. However there appears to be no surviving history. It can be found in a wooded valley south of Goodmanham and is reached from the lane leading from Market Weighton to South Dalton: a footpath to the left five hundred yards past the crossroads leads to the well which is close to the lane. SE891424 (There is also a spring known as Lady Well to the west of Goodmanham whose water was used for baptism; it is overgrown but still traceable in a rough pasture field: SE887429.)

St John's Well, Harpham

The well is dedicated to St John of Beverley, who was born in Harpham. He is said to have struck the ground with his staff, whereupon a spring began to flow. He was Bishop of Hexham in 687–705 and Bishop of York in 705–718, and he also founded Beverley Minster where he is buried, the location marked by a slab in the floor of the nave. He was a saintly man who healed the sick, and after his death in 721 miracles were reported and his relics were translated to Beverley. His feast day is 7th May and, since 1929, every year on the Thursday closest to that day, members of the choir and congregation of Beverley Minster go to Harpham church (dedicated to St John of Beverley) and then in procession to the well, which is decorated with flowers. An anthem is sung, and prayers are said, before the procession returns to the church for choral evensong. On the Sunday nearest 7th May there is a ceremony at the Minster in honour of St John, and children from Harpham take primroses gathered in the Harpham woods which are placed round the saint's tomb.

St John's Well, Harpham in 2005.

St John's Well was said to never run dry; and according to William of Malmesbury it had the power to subdue wild bulls and other savage beasts. The water was also said to be helpful in curing headaches and eye ailments. It is now scarcely visible inside the small stone well-house, though it can be heard if you throw in a coin. It is protected with railings like the Drummer's Well on the other side of the village.

Location: Harpham is five miles south-west of Bridlington, and the well is beside a lane just to the east of the village: from the church, go to the crossroads in the centre and turn right. The well is signposted. TA095617

YORKSHIRE: NORTH

This county is another one overflowing with interesting holy wells, though in various states of repair. It is impossible to list them all, so I am concentrating on those I have visited myself, which I know are worth visiting. Details of many others can be found quite easily (see *Sources*).

St Cedd's, St Chad's and St Ovin's Wells, Lastingham

Aside from the fact that this village has three holy wells, it is worth visiting anyway for the church and its unique eleventh-century crypt. St Cedd founded a monastery at Lastingham in 654, being succeeded as abbot by his brother St Chad. The monastery was rebuilt after the Norman Conquest, and the crypt dates from that

time. St Cedd died at Lastingham in 664 and was later re-buried in the crypt. According to Bede, St Ovin was a member of Queen Etheldreda's household who went to Lastingham carrying an axe which showed that he had come to work at the monastery. He later went to Lichfield with Chad, and died at Ely.

All three wells are on the roadside within walking distance of the church. Walking down into the village with the church behind you, St Cedd's Well is on your left. Turning right at the junction, St Ovin's Well is on the left in the front wall of Ovins Well House. Turning left at the same junction will take you up to St Chad's Well. St Cedd's Well has a well-house, and a lion's head from which the water used to flow; the other two are inset into walls and have stone arches: St Chad's has his name carved across the top. All three wells are now dry.

Location: Lastingham is five miles north-west of Pickering; there is roadside parking close to the church, which is open daily. SE728905 (church)

Dropping Well and Wishing Well, Knaresborough

Although the Dropping Well (often known as the Petrifying Well) is by far the best-known feature here, there is also a wishing well close by. The site is also linked to Mother Shipton who was a sixteenth-century prophet born in a cave close to the wells. So there is plenty for the visitor to Knaresborough to see on a scenic walk by the River Nidd. The water from the Petrifying Well Spring falls over a rock face from which have been hung many small objects such as teddy bears. The water deposits calcium carbonate onto them, and gradually a crust of new rock builds up, so that in time they appear to have been petrified or turned to stone. At the back of the rock over which the water pours can be found the wishing well in the form of a water-filled rock basin. To make a wish, place your right hand in the water, make your wish, then let your hand dry naturally.

Opposite: *The well-house marking St Cedd's Well in the centre of Lastingham in 2005. The church can be seen top left.*

Right: *A close-up view of the Dropping Well in 1993 with many small items hanging in the water flow and gradually petrifying.*

The Petrifying Well and the Mother Shipton story have been developed as a tourist attraction, so that there are also a museum, shop, café, toilets, picnic area, children's playground, and so on. There is also ample car parking space; but a sizeable entrance fee is payable before you can partake of any of this.

Location: Knaresborough is to the north-east of Harrogate, and the main entrance to the well is off the A59 Harrogate road, by the bridge over the River Nidd. SE348565 (Dropping Well)

Ebbing and Flowing Well (and Bank Well), Giggleswick

The name describes the rising and falling of the water level, seemingly independent of the amount of rainfall. Local legend has the ebbing and flowing as the breathing of a nymph who became one with the water after being chased by a spirit. Another Giggleswick well is Bank Well where a small lead figurine of a woman was found over one hundred years ago. Bank Well is in a stone trough by the gates of the old vicarage on Bankwell Lane; the Ebbing and Flowing Well is beside the road to the north-west of the village. Although easy to find, it is not easy to visit by car because the traffic is fast and there is nowhere close by to pull off the road. SD803654 (Ebbing and Flowing Well); SD812689 (Bank Well)

The roadside Ebbing and Flowing Well in 2005.

St Hilda's Well in Hinderwell churchyard, photographed on a frosty morning late in 2005.

St Helen's Well, Farnhill

Yorkshire has many wells dedicated to St Helen, several of which are still worth visiting. At this one, the water flows into a stone trough against a wall. Farnhill adjoins Kildwick four miles south-east of Skipton, and the well is near the junction to Low Bradley. SE005466

St Helen's Well, Kirkby Overblow

This well is next to St Helen's Cottage and the water flows out of the bank into a stone trough in a walled chamber. There was a chapel here in the eleventh century. Kirkby Overblow is a few miles south of Harrogate and the well is one hundred yards west of the church, to the north of the road. SE323492 (Further along the same road can be found Bird Well with water flowing into a large stone trough.)

St Hilda's Well, Hinderwell

St Hilda was abbess of Whitby in the seventh century; she was a proponent of education and highly respected by all manner of people from kings to the humblest citizens. After her death in 680 her cult grew, especially in the north, and Hinderwell church is one of several dedicated to her. It is possible that she had a retreat close by, perhaps even on the site where the church now is. Her well, a simple stone structure at the end of a flight of steps behind the church, is a strangely atmospheric site. It used to be the custom for children to mix the well water with liquorice on Ascension Day, which was here known as Spanish Water Day.

Location: Hinderwell is eight miles north-west of Whitby. NZ791170

Our Lady's Well, Threshfield

This is also known as Lady Well; the water was believed to have healing properties. It also was able to give protection against devils and demons, as one man found out, according to local legend. The area of the well was haunted by the ghost of a local dead schoolmaster known as Pam the Fiddler, and one night a man making his way home to Threshfield in a drunken state came upon the ghost playing his violin to a

Mary Magdalene Well, hidden away at the bottom of a grassy bank, in 2005.

crowd of dancing imps and fairies. He watched them, but suddenly sneezed, and the dancers, angry at being spied on, chased him. Knowing that the well was a refuge, he ran there and jumped into the water. So long as he stayed there, the angry fairies were unable to harm him, and he had to stay in the cold water until sunrise when the Little People were forced to retreat. The well is close to the River Wharfe, accessed from the road between Grassington Bridge and Linton, next to Bridge End Farm: a narrow opening in the wall reveals steps leading down to the well. SD998638

Mary Magdalene Well, Spaunton

A spring flows into a small stone trough at this unspoilt rural well, and the name is carved on a stone above. Fragments of Saxon and thirteenth-century pottery have been found, suggesting it is an ancient well. It is tucked into a steep bank just below the lane leading west from Lastingham, just north of Spaunton, close to cottages by a junction. SE722904

Old Wives' Well, Stape

The age of this woodland spring is not known, nor the origin of its name. A rough stone with the inscription 'Nattie Fonten' adds to the mystery. Not far away is the

Offerings of flowers and other natural decorations can be seen at the evocative Old Wives' Well. Photographed in 2005.

Roman road known as Wade's Causeway with associated legends about the giant Wade and his wife. Was she the 'Old Wife' after whom the well was named? Archaeologists are now wondering if the Roman road might overlie a Neolithic linear monument, which hints at other lost elements of this ancient landscape. The well can be found in Cropton Forest just north of Stape about six miles north of Pickering, beside the lane heading north to Wheeldale Moor. At the point half a mile north of Stape where there is a break in the trees and a 'forest drive' off to the right, park and walk back to the south. The well is just off the lane in the forest on your left (east of the lane). SE795941

YORKSHIRE: SOUTH and WEST

St James's Well, Midhopestones

This is South Yorkshire's best-preserved holy well: a small square stone chamber protected by railings. Along with the nearby Potter's Well, it is decorated annually and a blessing ceremony held. To the south-east is St James's Chapel, rebuilt in 1705 on the site of an earlier chapel. Midhopestones is two miles north-west of Stocksbridge, and the well is in a field to the north of a track leading to Midhope Hall: SK234995

Lady Well, Hartshead

Hartshead church dates back to Norman times or before; also dating back to the eleventh century is Walton Cross, carved with interlace, beasts and birds, which stands on the west side of the road a quarter-mile north-west of Hartshead church. The Lady Well is beside Lady Well Lane which leads to the church: its location is marked by a thorn tree in the hedge. The well has been neglected but the trough survives, sunk into the ground and divided into two halves by a large stone, one half being in the field, the other on the road side of the hedge. Hartshead is two miles east of Brighouse and the church is to the north of the village. SE179235

Peace Well, Dore

In 1959 this well was restored, and a temporary supply of water was provided from the mains when the first well-dressing took place in that year. The well is at the south-east corner of the village green in Dore (five miles south-west of Sheffield); also on the green is the King Egbert Stone which commemorates the proclamation of Egbert of Mercia as the first king of all England in AD 829. SK309811

Town's Well, Hampole

A Cistercian nunnery dedicated to St Mary was founded here in 1170, but there are no visible remains. Richard Rolle, a popular English mystical writer in the late Middle Ages, lived here as a hermit until his death in 1349. A local farmer had a dream in which he was requested to build a tomb for Rolle and by 1395 his body was located close to the high altar of the church, with miracles occurring and

The small stone head through which the water flows into the pool at White Wells. Photo: David Clarke.

pilgrims coming to the shrine. A plaque near to the well records that he lived 'close to this spot', on the south side of the village green at Hampole, six miles north-west of Doncaster. SE505103

White Wells, Ilkley

White Wells was developed as a spa from 1760 and was very popular for a hundred years or more, resulting in the growth of Ilkley. Rescued in 1974 after years of neglect, White Wells is now a tourist attraction and one of the baths is still in use. The water, which is noted for its purity, flows through a stone head into the small pool, and a sample can be obtained from a fountain behind the well house.

There is no suggestion that this was ever a holy well, but it merits an entry here because of a curious event which (allegedly) took place in 1815. William Butterfield was in charge, and one morning he was unable to unlock the door to the baths. He forcibly pushed it open, and discovered a host of unexpected visitors taking a bath. They were 'little creatures dressed in green from head to foot, none of them more than eighteen inches high, and making a chatter and a jabber thoroughly unintelligible.' He shouted 'Hallo there!' – whereupon 'away the whole tribe went, helter skelter, toppling and tumbling, heads over heels, heels over heads, and all the while making a noise not unlike that of a disturbed nest of young partridges.' When the fairies (for that is what they are presumed to have been) had left, he could find no trace that they had ever been there.

White Wells is open intermittently during May to December, such as Bank Holidays, afternoons during school holidays – and any time when the flags can be seen flying. No flags means White Wells is closed. Admission is free, and visitors' requirements are catered for (café, gift shop, parking, toilets). Located on the moor half a mile south of Ilkley Station and accessible by car, or by foot starting at Darwin Gardens Millennium Green. SE118468

Wales

Anglesey, Carmarthenshire, Ceredigion, Conwy, Denbighshire, Flintshire, Gwynedd, Monmouthshire, Pembrokeshire, Powys, South Wales

Wales is especially rich in holy wells, and the sacred landscapes of which the wells were often a part sometimes also still survive. Many traces of Welsh saints have been preserved, often well-hidden, with more exciting finds coming to light all the time. I have been and am still involved in research into the Welsh saints and their holy wells, and I hope eventually to publish a further guidebook to the holy wells of Wales. Meanwhile, the very best wells to be found in the principality (41 in total, all bar four visited by me) are described in this section.

ANGLESEY

Ffynnon Cerrigceinwen, Cerrigceinwen

This well is interesting in that it took its name from the village and not from the saint: 'Cerrigceinwen' means 'the stones of St Ceinwen'. The well may have been a central feature of the *llan* enclosure back in the sixth century, and an important factor in the choice of site. However nothing is known about this well other than that its water was believed to have healing qualities; but it is a pleasing example of a churchyard well, and very easy to find, being on the left of the path leading down to the church. There is no structure: the water trickles out of a small rock-face in the grassy bank. Cerrigceinwen is 3 miles south-west of Llangefni. SH423737

Ffynnon Seiriol (St Seiriol's Well), Penmon

The location of this well is particularly interesting, as it is close to the impressive priory church dating from the twelfth century: the first church was founded by St Seiriol in the sixth century. The other building you will notice is the fine stone dovecot dating from around 1600 which has a vaulted dome roof. The car park is opposite: turn left at the dovecot end of the car park and follow a short path leading to the well, above the former monastic fishpond. The well chamber is built up against a rock-face, and inside is a small pool and stone benches. The upper wall is of brick and dates from 1710 with the lower wall being earlier. Outside to the left of the chamber can be seen the circular wall of a hut or cell, and it has been surmised that St Seiriol himself lived here as a hermit. However this is unlikely as all the surviving remains post-date St Seiriol, and it may have simply been a changing room for the well, as it was clearly a bathing well. It was also used for divination. Penmon is four miles north-east of Beaumaris. SH631808

Ffynnon Seiriol at Penmon; photographed in 1983 but it still looks exactly the same today.

Ffynnon Wenfaen (St Gwenfaen's Well), Rhoscolyn

This well consists of a sunken square stone-built forecourt accessed by steps on the east side, and with four seats built across the corners. This gives access to an open oblong well chamber facing the steps, with the water flowing west under the

Ffynnon Wenfaen on a wind-swept cliff-top at Rhoscolyn in 2004.

142

enclosing wall into an uncovered oblong bathing tank accessed at either end by steps. From this pool, the water flows away to the west, falling over the cliffs into the sea. The water was once used to protect against mental problems, and it was noted in the eighteenth century that it was customary to throw in two white pebbles as an offering. Since the saint's name means 'white stone' this practice perhaps evolved from the name, though white quartz pebbles were also offered at other Welsh wells. The cliff-top location of this well is exhilarating, as too can be the walk to it in windy weather. Rhoscolyn is five miles south of Holyhead, and the walk starts near the church where there is room to park. Take the track heading south-west for about half a mile, and turn right at the coastguard lookout, following the path for another half-mile to the well. SH259755

CARMARTHENSHIRE

St Anthony's Well and Ffynnon Fair (St Mary's Well), Llansteffan (Llanstephan)

St Anthony's Well was once a healing well, and later a wishing well. It is in a walled enclosure, with the water inside a pointed stone arch, and a narrow stone ledge at the back was called 'the offerings shelf'. It's not known how long the well has been revered, but the stonework was in place by 1811. There is a walk of about a mile to get to the well from the village. Park near the church and walk down the road past the church which heads towards the castle. At the car turning circle, walk straight on through the wood and along the cliff-top path to St Anthony's Bay. Follow the garden wall of the one house on the bay, and the well is down some steps in the wall, about fifty yards along, at SN346099. There is a second well in the village, Ffynnon Fair (St Mary's Well), which was believed to have healing properties. From the church, walk uphill past The Castle and The Sticks Hotel and in thirty yards the well can be seen in the garden wall of Well House on the right.

Ffynnon Deilo (St Teilo's Well), Llandeilo

In the early medieval period, Llandeilo seems to have been a major centre of St Teilo's cult. His well is near the eastern end of the church, the water flowing into a twelve-feet-square alcove below the level of the raised churchyard. Although this

St Anthony's Well, Llansteffan in 1997.

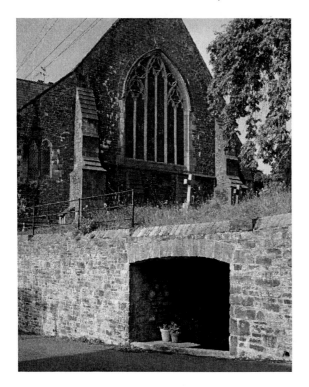

Below Llandeilo church can be found St Teilo's Well with a good flow of water. Photographed in 2007.

was a town water supply for centuries, its proximity to the church suggests it was once a holy well and perhaps used as a baptistery. Bishop Rudd's will dated 1614 mentions 'Tyrffynnondilo', which may be the same well. It can be found on the south side of the churchyard, in the wall along Church Street. SN629222

Ffynnon Gwyddfaen, Llandyfan

Although the Baptists created a baptistery here, there was a healing well long before they came on the scene. Edward Lhuyd refers to 'a medicinal spring' in the late seventeenth century, but it was in use even earlier, for in 1592 a large number of pilgrims were taken before the local magistrate, who refused to imprison them, saying they were 'poor, sickly persons who had gone to the well to bathe, hoping by the help of God thereby to have their health'. There was a medieval chapel here until the end of the eighteenth century, and this was clearly an important pilgrimage site. The water was said in 1813 to be 'efficacious in the cure of paralytic affections, numbness and scorbutic humours'. Today the well is a spring-fed pool within solid stone walls, with steps leading down into the baptism pool; the rusted mechanism which lowered a gate so that the water could be dammed still survives. Llandyfan is four miles south of Llandeilo, and the well can be found inside Llandyfan churchyard. SN642171

Top: *The impressive stone tank into which Ffynnon Gwyddfaen flows today.*

Bottom: *Ffynnon Gybi in Llangybi gives easy access to the living water.*

Both photographed in 2007.

CEREDIGION

Ffynnon Gybi (St Cybi's Well), Llangybi

An unpretentious spring with the water flowing from under a stone slab, in a fenced-off corner of a field. The antiquarian Edward Lhuyd called it Ffynnon Wen, and that is the name to be found on the OS map. People seeking a cure for scrofula, rheumatism or scurvy would go to the well on Ascension Eve, wash themselves in the water, and then go to a prehistoric stone with the name of Llech Gybi. They would try to sleep under it, as that would mean recovery. If they did not sleep, death was to be expected. This is an interesting example of incubation, a practice described more fully in my *Cures and Curses*. The stone appears to have gone, but the well can be found just off the A485 to the south-west of the village, opposite Maesyffynnon chapel; signposted. SN605528

Ffynnon Llawddog (St Llawddog's Well), Cenarth

A neat, well-maintained stone building with a slate roof covers this well, and on each end is a slate slab bearing the well's name. It was reputed to be a healing well. It sits on the south bank of the River Teifi in the centre of Cenarth, close to the B4332. SN268416

Ffynnon Llawddog beside the river in Cenarth, photographed in 2007.

Llangelynin Old Church and the well in the corner of the graveyard, photographed in 1988 after restoration. Today the well is surrounded by greenery.

CONWY

Ffynnon Gelynin (St Celynin's Well), Llangelynin

Remotely sited, yet well worth the effort to track down, this well is in a formerly roofed courtyard in the corner of the graveyard of Llangelynin Old Church. The water was used for baptisms in the church, but this was also a divination well, with the clothes of sick children being floated on the water. Recovery would be indicated

The solid stone building which now covers Ffynnon Drillo, photographed in 1988. The well is in the floor just behind the east wall facing the photographer.

if they remained floating, but death was to be the outcome if they sank. After being bathed in the water, the sick children would be carried to a nearby farm where beds were kept in readiness. The church is also worth exploring and is always open. On the south side outside, a demolished side chapel is still visible which probably housed St Celynin's tomb shrine, and which was probably the original place for the sacred incubation. The church is signposted at points along the lane from Henryd south of Conwy. Follow the lane in a south-westerly direction as far as it goes; there is plenty of parking by the house gateway, from where it is a short walk to the church. Go up the step-stile over the wall on the left, follow the path, and over another step-stile. Turn left and follow the track to the church. SH751738

Ffynnon Drillo (St Trillo's Well), Llandrillo-yn-Rhos (Rhos-on-Sea)

This coastal well is covered by a small chapel (Capel Ffynnon Drillo) whose date is unknown but it is probably a few hundred years old. There is some evidence that the 'chapel' was originally simply an unroofed enclosure surrounding the well. Inside, the well is under the modern altar table: a stone tank about three by two feet with steps leading down. The chapel has in recent years become a focus for written petitions and prayers left by visitors on the altar table, but it is not clear whether any pilgrims still come to take away water from the well. The chapel can be found at Rhos Point, a couple of miles north-west of Colwyn Bay (not far from the public toilets). There is plenty of parking along the coastal road; the chapel is below road level, by the shore. SH842812

Ffynnon Beuno after heavy rainfall in 2007, with water issuing from the mouth of the figure on the exterior wall of the bathing tank whose entrance gate can be seen at the right. The figure is illustrated in close-up in Cures and Curses.

DENBIGHSHIRE

Ffynnon Beuno (St Beuno's Well), Tremeirchion

The best-known feature of this well is the head through which water flows, but this is just the overflow from the actual well, which is on the other side of the wall and takes the form of a large rectangular tank bounded by tall walls. Nor is the head any kind of evidence for a pagan head cult, as closer examination will show that the figure also has part of a body and arms, and was a late addition to an earlier structure. The size and depth of the well indicate that this must once have been an important healing well where patients immersed themselves in hopes of a cure. The well is in the front garden of the house Ffynnon Beuno, formerly an inn, just south of Tremeirchion on the east side of the B5429 to Bodfari. There is a lay-by in front of the house (which has in recent years been a bed and breakfast venue, and a restaurant) and an information board to the side. SJ084724

Ffynnon Ddyfnog (St Dyfnog's Well), Llanrhaeadr-yng-Nghinmeirch

Today there survives only the large bathing pool, now deep in woodland, but once there were numerous buildings, for this well was visited by large numbers of people seeking cures for scabs and itch and other skin ailments, according to Edward Lhuyd in the seventeenth century. There were so many of them that their offerings were enough to enable the creation of the fine Jesse window in the nearby church in 1535. The water was said to have gained its potency from the influence of St Dyfnog, whose habit it was to do penance by standing for long periods under the flow of cold water from the spring. (See 'Immersion' in my book *Cures and Curses*.) Llanrhaeadr (as it is usually known) is between Denbigh and Ruthin; park by the church and walk to the right of the entrance door, through the graveyard, to the left of the almshouses, and into the wood. Follow the footpath over the stream and to the right and you will soon come to the bathing pool. It is difficult to imagine the well as it was in its heyday, but the site is still well worth visiting, as too is the church. SJ080633

The bathing pool at Ffynnon Ddyfnog seen from above, near the site of the original spring which fed it. Photographed after heavy rainfall in 2007.

Ffynnon Degla (St Tegla's Well), Llandegla

This atmospheric well has recently been sensitively restored and made more accessible. Details of the strange incubation ritual which was once practised here by patients seeking a cure for epilepsy can be found in *Cures and Curses*. Offerings of pieces of white quartz were once left in the well, many pieces being found during excavation in 1935. From the car park near the church in Llandegla (ten miles north of Llangollen), walk down the lane with the church on your right, over the bridge, and the well is signposted across the field to your left. SJ195523

Ffynnon Fair (St Mary's Well), Cefn Meiriadog

The sizeable chapel building here, Capel Ffynnon Fair, is a Grade I Listed Building, and a Scheduled Ancient Monument. Next to St Winefride's Well at Holywell, it is the most substantial and important Welsh well shrine. In brief it comprises the ruined chapel (mainly of two periods, the chancel being built in the fifteenth century), outside of which to the north is the well basin (completely rebuilt in the late fifteenth century). The design of the basin is reminiscent of that of St Winefride's Well, both being based on an eight-pointed star. Adjoining it is a nineteenth-century bathing pool, from which the water runs along a stone channel into the chapel. Despite the desolate appearance of the overgrown ruins today, this was once a very popular holy well even though it was remote, being hidden deep within the valley of the River Elwy. From Trefnant south of St Asaph, take the B5381 and after the hairpin bend

This aerial view of Ffynnon Fair, taken in 1997, clearly shows the unusual well basin beside the ruined chapel. Photo: Roger Brown.

you cross the River Elwy and then take the first lane to the left. Where the trees begin on your left, there is a steep track downhill which is the way to the well. Parking around here is difficult, so it is best to continue driving along the lane and park up the hill by the yellow bin where the lane widens on a bend. Walk back downhill and take the track to your right, past some houses. At the field gate the ruined buildings can be seen across a field to your right, under the trees; make your way across the field, which can be boggy in wet weather. This is private property, but access is tolerated so long as no damage is caused. SJ029711

Ffynnon Sara, Derwen

Who Sara was, no one seems to know, but in Lhuyd's time (seventeenth century) this was known as 'Ffynnon pyllie perl' after the nearby place-name Pyllau Perl. The

Ffynnon Sara in early 2007.

water was believed to cure rheumatism and cancers, and pins were left as offerings. There was once a cottage nearby where cured pilgrims left their crutches. Today the well has a gloomy feel, possibly from its location under dark trees, but the water still flows into the large stone bathing tank, on the edge of a rushing stream. Half a mile north of Derwen; beside the lane linking Clawdd Newydd and Melin-y-Wig. SJ064515

FLINTSHIRE

Ffynnon Wenfrewy (St Winefride's Well), Treffynnon (Holywell)

This is without doubt the most impressive holy well in Britain, not least because it is still in active use, and is visited by around 30,000 pilgrims and other visitors each year. Traditionally it came into being because of an attempted murder in the seventh century, when the virginal Gwenfrewy was trying to avoid the unwanted attentions of Caradog, a prince's son, who tried to rape her. He cut off her head with his sword and left her for dead, but he had not reckoned with the magical powers of her uncle, St Beuno, who quickly replaced her head and saved her life. The attack took place on the hill opposite the well, at another well called Ffynnon Beuno: the head rolled downhill to the site of what is now Ffynnon Wenfrewy and where it landed, the water began to flow. The well soon became a focus for healing, and has been a place of continuous pilgrimage until the present day. In the early sixteenth century an impressive two-storey shrine building, with a chapel above, was erected over the

The two-storey well chapel at St Winefride's Well, Holywell: the well is inside the building and the water flows into the large outdoor bathing pool. Photo: Roger Brown.

Pilgrims queueing to venerate the saint's relic at St Winefride's Well, Holywell, during a Catholic pilgrimage in June 1987. Some are taking the opportunity to gather well water from the bathing pool.

spring, which flows into a large swimming-pool-sized bathing pool. Countless cures have been recorded down the centuries, and they continue to occur today, with many sick people still coming to follow the traditional bathing ritual. (More information can be found in the entry for Holywell in my book *Cures and Curses,* and on www.saintwinefrideswell.com.) In addition to the well building, there are now also a museum, information centre, and shop; the well is open daily, and details of forthcoming pilgrimages can be found on the website. St Winefride's Well is signposted in Holywell – it is down the hill, beside the B5121 to Greenfield – and there is parking either opposite the entrance, or on a public car park at the top of the hill nearer the town centre. SJ185763

GWYNEDD

Ffynnon Beuno (St Beuno's Well), Clynnog Fawr

This well was closely linked to the nearby church, of historic interest in its own right, especially for the links with St Beuno. His shrine chapel incorporates the site of his first church, eighteen by ten feet, and it was here, after bathing in the well, that sick pilgrims would try to sleep on the saint's tombstone. This custom apparently ceased

Ffynnon Beuno at Clynnog Fawr is a square pool within solid stone walls. Photographed in 2007.

Ffynnon Beris is now agreeably overgrown with ferns and other greenery – but these make it difficult to see the structure. Photographed in 2006.

following the destruction of the tomb at the end of the eighteenth century. There is more information on the widespread custom of sacred incubation in my book *Cures and Curses.* The pilgrims also scraped powder from the stone columns and mixed it with the well water, believing this mixture to have curative powers. The well is not far from the church: it is a stone-walled structure containing a 6 foot square pool surrounded by stone seats. Clynnog Fawr is nine miles south-west of Caernarfon, and the well is two hundred yards down the road from the church, to the south-west, and on the opposite side: past the garage, and past the last house, Maes Glas. SH414495

Ffynnon Beris (St Peris's Well), Nant Peris

Some wells contained sacred fish or eels, with the future being foretold by their movements, or a cure may result from contact with them when bathing in the well. Ffynnon Beris had two trout – as late as 1896 a newspaper report said that two new ones had been placed in the well – and it was believed that if the patient did not see the fish when bathing in the well, it was a bad omen. The water was believed to be good for rickets, rheumatism, scrofula, warts and other ailments. Nant Peris is south-east of Llanberis, and the well is north-east of the church. Look for the group of houses called Nant Ffynnon and park there (or in the large car park across the road). Walk along the tarmac track and through the gate just to the right of the houses, up the track for a short distance to a cottage on the right (Tyn y Ffynnon). The well is in the front garden, opposite the front door, so please knock and request permission to view it. It is also requested that you do not interfere with or damage the well in any way, and leave it just as you found it. SH609584

Ffynnon Fair (St Mary's Well), Bryncroes

The structure of this well has been well maintained and it is worth looking at, though nothing is known about its history. A record of 'an ancient chapel, called Ty Fair' (St Mary's House) hints that this may once have been a local pilgrimage site. The well pool is walled around but not roofed; steps lead down to the water. It can be found beside the road not far from the church at Bryncroes (nine miles south-west of Pwllheli): SH226314

Ffynnon Fair at Bryncroes in 1988.

Ffynnon Gybi (St Cybi's Well), Llangybi

The surviving structures show this to have been a classic healing well, which was once visited by many pilgrims seeking cures for warts, lameness, blindness, scrofula, scurvy and rheumatism. By the eighteenth century there were three stone buildings whose walls still survive, plus a small separate building which acted as a latrine. The actual spring was in a small building behind the well chamber where the patients bathed. The well chamber was linked by a door to the adjoining cottage, where the patients rested during their treatment. Visitors also took away bottles of water for use at home.

Ffynnon Gybi at Llangybi in 1995: the well is in the left-hand building, the ruined cottage is to the right.

Since the well is dedicated to St Cybi, it is probable that this was originally a pilgrimage site and one of many where the healing function has overtaken the religious purpose. The well was also used for divination, with young people using it to foretell their futures. They would float a rag or feather on the water to find their lover's intentions. There was at one time a large eel living in the well, and patients were supposed to stand in the water with bare legs and if the eel coiled round their legs, they would be cured. When someone removed the eel, it was believed that the water had lost its curative powers.

The well can be found in the valley behind the church in Llangybi village five miles north-east of Pwllheli. Follow the path through the churchyard and across the field down into the valley where the group of ruined stone buildings will be seen below the wood. SH427413

MONMOUTHSHIRE

St Anne's Well (Virtuous Well), Trellech

This well has the merit of not only being a very good example of a well-maintained holy well, and easily accessible, but also it is only a short walk away from another major antiquity, the three dramatic standing stones known as Harold's Stones. The village also has a large Norman castle mound called Tump Terret, and all three historic features are depicted on an ancient sundial that is now kept in the church. So there are several good reasons for visiting Trellech, though for our purposes the holy well has to be first on the list. Steps lead down into the walled enclosure where a paved forecourt with a low bench leads to the actual well, in a small chamber in the rear wall. The water was once used medicinally to cure scurvy, colic, and other ailments, but later it degenerated into a wishing well. A wish was made when a pebble was dropped into the water, and if there was a good show of bubbles, it would be granted soon; a few bubbles meant a delay; none meant a failed wish. In

St Anne's Well at Trellech in 1976.

recent years visitors have started to attach rags to the branches of the hawthorn bushes behind the well, something which was not evident when I first visited it thirty years ago. The well can be found in a field beside a lane to Llandogo just to the south-east of the village. SO503051

St Tewdric's Well, Mathern

Tewdric, Tewdrig or Theodoric was a fifth or sixth century prince of Glamorgan who became a hermit at Tintern when he became old and had handed over his rule to his son. However when the Saxons invaded he led the defenders and was killed, being buried at Mathern. This name derives from the original name Merthyr Tewdric ('merthyr' being the Welsh form of the Latin *martyrium,* meaning 'a place with relics') and the church is dedicated to him. In the seventeenth century a stone coffin was found in the church containing St Tewdric's skeleton with a badly damaged skull. His well is said to be the place where he died, and he is supposed to have ordered that the church be built close by. Sadly this interesting corner of Wales is now blighted by the close proximity of the M48. The road to Mathern goes nowhere else: from the A48 at Pwllmeyric take the south-easterly lane to Newton Green and Mathern, passing under the M48, and the well is beside the road to your right, just to the north of the church (which is also worth visiting: the saint's burial place is beneath the chancel floor, with a large plaque on the north wall of the chancel commemorating its rediscovery in the early seventeenth century). ST523912

PEMBROKESHIRE

Bletherston Holy Well

This evocative well, from which water for baptisms used to be fetched, lies below the church: follow the path down to the pool and the well will be found tucked away in the corner beside the pool at the end of the path. SN070212

Bletherston holy well in 2007.

St Govan's chapel seen from the clifftop in 1989: the well is among the boulders to the left.

Burton Church Well

Several springs below the church provide water to fill the bath in this well-maintained structure which has been used as a baptistery, but there appears to be no other record of its use. Burton is five miles east of Milford Haven. SM985056

St Govan's Well, Bosherston

This well would most likely head the list of the most dramatically sited wells in Britain, being almost on the shore and at the foot of tall cliffs. Its access is unusual too: down a steep flight of stone steps and through the tiny chapel of St Govan. It was once visited to cure failing eyesight, lameness and rheumatism, and pilgrims would often make a poultice from the red clay near the well, applying this to their sick limbs and eyes and lying in the sun for several hours. Before the Reformation, the well was probably not the main reason why pilgrims came: they would be visiting the saint's burial place in the small shrine chapel. No one knows the identity of St Govan but he may have been a sixth-century hermit from Ireland; he is unlikely to have been Sir Gawain of the Arthurian legends, as has been suggested. The road from Bosherston to the clifftop is sometimes closed by the army, but assuming you are not impeded, you will reach a large car park from where it is a short walk to the top of the steps. On coming out of the chapel you can see the small stone well among the rocks below; sadly it is now dry. SR967929

*The holy well close to
Llanllawer church in 2000.*

Gumfreston Church Wells

Three springs rise close together in the churchyard to the south of the church, two of them being chalybeate and one of them said to be good for the eyes. Visitors to Tenby Spa would also 'take the waters' at Gumfreston, but fortunately a plan to develop the wells as a spa was never put into effect and only a few low stone walls surround the springs today. It was once the custom to throw crooked pins into the water on Easter Day, and in recent years the wells have also been dressed with flowers and plants at Easter. Gumfreston is just to the west of Tenby and the wells are easily found in the churchyard. SN109010

Llanllawer Holy Well

The name of this well is uncertain, one possibility being Ffynnon Gapan. The water was believed to be good for sore eyes, and offerings of coins and pins were left, the pin being bent if harm was intended towards anyone. Today modern offerings of flowers and ribbons are fastened to the well. Its heavy stone canopy, which creates a dark tunnel, has been recently restored. The well, which tends to dry up in summer, can be found in a field just outside the churchyard at Llanllawer two miles south-east of Fishguard, up a steep lane north from Llanychaer Bridge. SM987360

St Justinian's Well, St Justinian

Justinian was a sixth-century hermit who lived on Ramsey Island across the sea from the St Davids peninsula. His legend tells how he was beheaded by his servants and a spring flowed where his head fell. Justinian picked up his severed head and carried it across the sea to the mainland, to the place now called St Justinian. Here there is a well known as St Justinian's Well, very close to the chapel where he was buried. However there is no evidence that this was ever regarded as a holy well and it seems to have been a modern substitution for the saint's well on Ramsey Island which can

The back of the well at St Justinian in 1992, with Ramsey Island visible on the horizon.

no longer be identified. The ruined chapel can be seen from the well (though not visited as it is on private property), as also can Ramsey Island. From St Davids take the lane heading west to St Justinian; the well is on top of the bank on your left, opposite the ruined chapel, just before the road ends at the lifeboat station. SM724252

Margaret's Well, Templeton

It is not known whether this well is named for St Margaret or some other Margaret; in fact little is known about the well. To visit it, take West Lane at the north end of Templeton, park, and walk along single-track road to left of Sunnymead. Not far along, the footpath to the well is to the left beside the garden of a house called Margaret's Well. SN111168

St Non's Well, St Davids

This is a well that remains in the memory, and its wonderful location tends to draw one back for repeat visits. It is close to the ruins of St Non's Chapel in a field overlooking the sea; and also close to a modern chapel of ancient design which is open to visitors and where you will find stained-glass windows of several Celtic saints including St Non. She was the mother of St David, patron saint of Wales, whose cathedral is a short walk away in the small city of St Davids. An eleventh-century source tells us that she was a nun who was seduced by a prince, and David

Margaret's Well in Templeton. Photographed in 2007.

The beautiful St Non's Well above the cliffs at St Davids, much visited and rightly so. Photographed in 2007.

was their son, but this version may not be accurate, as she may have become a nun late in life. She also has strong links with Altarnon in Cornwall where she first settled, and with Brittany where she died (her tomb survives at Dirinon). According to folklore, the well began to flow at the birth of St David, which was said to have taken place on the cliff-top where the ruined chapel now stands. The well has been a focus for pilgrimage for hundreds of years, and its water was also believed to have healing qualities, especially for eye ailments and rheumatism. Babies were dipped in the well, and its water was used for holy water in the cathedral before the Reformation. The well has a rounded stone cover over a stone trough which holds the water. It is possible to drive to the well or walk there, as it is only half a mile south of St Davids above St Non's Bay (follow signs for Warpool Court Hotel, then follow lane past hotel). SM751243

POWYS

Ffynnon Fair (St Mary's Well), Llanfair Caereinion

This well was derelict when I first saw it, but thankfully it has since been restored and is now well worth visiting. It was once a healing well, the large bath showing it was

161

The restored Ffynnon Fair in its riverside location below Llanfair Caereinion church. Photographed in 2005.

used for bodily immersion at one time, to cure rheumatism and skin diseases. The water was also used in the church for baptisms, and it was said to protect against curses and witchcraft. The well can be found in the churchyard, downhill between the church and the river: on entering the churchyard, walk towards the church but go left around it. SJ104065

Ffynnon Fair (St Mary's Well), Pilleth

Located very close to the church, on the north side of the tower, with steps leading down to it. The water was once used to cure eye ailments, and in the Middle Ages

Ffynnon Fair in Pilleth churchyard. Photographed in 2005.

*A rustic shelter protects
Ffynnon Gynydd today.
Photographed in 2005.*

many pilgrims came to Pilleth to see Our Lady of Pilleth, a wooden effigy of St Mary kept in the church. This is now a very quiet rural location, and it's difficult to imagine what it was like in 1402 when the Battle of Pilleth was fought, where Owain Glyndwr's forces defeated the English, and also burnt the church down. The church is on the hillside above Pilleth (four miles north-west of Presteigne) and there is a footpath leading up to it. Alternatively you can drive all the way to the church along a track off the B4356 at SO254679. The well is at SO256683.

Ffynnon Gynydd (St Cynidr's Well), Glasbury

A timber-framed shelter was erected over this well around 1900, and the water is beneath an iron lid. It may not be the original well, though there has been a holy well around here for several centuries, a 'Finnon Kynid' being mentioned in 1653. Nothing more is known of its history. To locate it, follow a lane off the A438 north of Glasbury that is signposted to Maesyronnen Chapel, keep on past the chapel entrance for another mile until a cluster of buildings is reached, park at the road junction, and the well is beside the lane to your right. SO164413

St Issui's (Isho's/Ishow's) Well, Partrishow/Patrisio/Patricio

Remote yet well worth seeking out, Partrishow church should not be missed. It has a separate shrine chapel with an early stone altar, which may have been the location

*This self-effacing well could
easily be missed: St Issui's Well
below Partrishow church in
2004.*

St Myllin's Well is above Llanfyllin: behind the photographer is a fine view out over the town and surrounding hills. Photographed in 2005.

of the saint's cell and was the place where he was buried; and his well is close by, a short way downhill and off to the left on the bend when approached from the church (there is room to park nearby). It is up against a stone wall and set into the bank, a very simple yet evocative well with a small niche at the back into which people place natural offerings such as crosses made of twigs or grass, also coins and stones.

A nearby tree is decorated with rags, ribbons, jewellery and crosses. Partrishow is five miles north-west of Abergavenny, only accessible along rural lanes. Best approached from Llanfihangel Crucorney: follow the road towards Llanthony and at Stanton take a left turn and follow the signs to Partrishow. SO278224

Ffynnon Myllin (St Myllin's Well), Llanfyllin

St Myllin was possibly the Irish St Moling: both Myllin and Moling have the same feast day, 17th June. The saint is said to have baptised converts at this well in the sixth century, but this must be a late tradition because St Moling never visited Wales, though some of his disciples presumably did. It used to be customary to visit the well on Trinity Sunday for the purpose of drinking sugared water provided by the young girls who would then be offered cakes and ale by the young men at the public house! It was also visited by the sick who would tie rags to the bushes, and it was used for divination. The well is set into a steep hillside under a stone arch and a tree, and although a lane leads right to it, it is best not to drive all the way as there is nowhere to turn round. It is only a short walk from the town centre: follow one of the lanes from the central square in a westerly direction: the well is signposted en route. SJ138195

SOUTH WALES

St Cenydd's Well, Llangennith, Gower, Swansea

The well is now a modern spout beneath a square stone cover, but once it was roofed with a large stone carved with a cross. It is on the village green not far from the church. SS428914

St David's Well and St John's Well, Newton Nottage, Porthcawl

The parish of Newton Nottage is formed from the villages of Newton and Nottage on the outskirts of Porthcawl and the two wells are only a mile or so apart. St David is reputed to have rested at Nottage on his way from Llantwit Major. There was once a chapel near his well, which was in a valley called Dewiscumbe in the twelfth century. From the central crossroads (The Cross) in Nottage, take the road leading north down Cradocks Hill and halfway down turn left into Moor Lane. St David's Well is three hundred yards down on the left. Again from The Cross, take the road east for just over a mile to Newton church and St John's Well is on the village green below. It is also known as Stanford's Well, de Stanford being a Knight Hospitaller who built Newton church. St David's Well: SS821786; St John's Well: SS836773.

Ffynnon Deilo (St Teilo's Well), Llandaff, Cardiff

There is a story that when St Teilo saw some women washing butter at the well, he asked if they had a vessel he could drink the water from, but they had nothing but the butter. So he shaped a vessel from it and used that – afterwards it miraculously

The site of St Teilo's Well has been preserved even though the well itself is now dry. Photographed in 2005.

changed into a metal bell which is now preserved in Llandaff Cathedral. It was believed that touching the bell was curative, and the water from the well was also believed to have healing powers. Llandaff is to the west of Cardiff, and the site of the well can be found in a stone wall close to the cathedral, beside a lane leading uphill from the east end of the cathedral. The well is now dry, and hidden behind a grating. ST156781

Ffynnon Fair (St Mary's Well), Penrhys, Rhondda

One of the most interesting holy wells in South Wales, but sadly neglected the last time I visited it. This is still a pilgrimage site, and the gathering place is indicated by a large statue of Our Lady of Penrhys on the hill above the well, together with an amphitheatre. The statue was erected on the site of the medieval pilgrimage chapel, of which part of one wall remains beside the statue. The pilgrimages commemorate the miraculous appearance of a statue of the Virgin and Child in an oak tree, and until the Reformation it was the image and not the well which was the principal object of the pilgrimage. Many people came to the shrine seeking a cure in the Middle Ages: in the early sixteenth century the poet Lewis Morgannwg described how the dead were brought back to life, the blind regained their sight, the deaf could hear again, and cripples were able to run. At the Reformation the effigy of Our Lady was removed and taken to London where it was burned. But despite all the efforts of the Protestants, the Catholic pilgrims kept visiting Our Lady's Well, until the pilgrimage was officially restored in 1947 when four thousand pilgrims were present.

High above the Rhondda Valley, St Mary's Well at Penrhys rates highly for its scenic setting. Photographed in 2005.

More recently, in 1995, the pilgrimage from Llantarnam Abbey to Penrhys was reopened and each year the pilgrims spend three days walking the thirty-two miles to the shrine. The well is housed in a stone building which is the surviving part of the original well-chapel, but the area is plagued by vandalism and the well has not escaped, so it has an unloved air about it.

The well is close to the Penrhys housing estate about four miles north-west of Pontypridd and a mile south of Ferndale; the road to follow is the B4512 linking Tylorstown and Ystrad. There is a large roundabout by the Penrhys estate and a car park. From there walk past the tall statue of Our Lady of Penrhys downhill to the right of the amphitheatre towards the footpath sign. Follow the stony track downhill and take the first footpath to the right. The first part of the path down the hillside may be difficult for the less sure-footed, so an alternative route from the car park is to walk a short distance along the main road in a westerly direction and take the first left down to the foopath sign before turning right on to the grassy track down to the well. ST001945

Trinity Well, Ilston, Gower, Swansea

There was probably a pre-Reformation well-chapel dedicated to the Trinity, together with a holy well, at this site, but it was replaced in the mid seventeenth century by a

167

The Trinity Well is in the foreground; the ruined chapel can also be seen. Photographed in 1997.

Baptist chapel, the ruins of which can still be seen. The likely site of the well, whose water was used to cure sore eyes, can be seen a short distance away in the trees. Reached by footpath from the A4118 east of Parkmill (close to public house) which leads north into Ilston Cwm (south-west of Ilston village). SS553895

Scotland

Aberdeenshire – Angus – Argyll and Bute – Borders – Dumfries and Galloway – East Lothian – Edinburgh – Fife – Highland – Isle of Skye – Moray – North Lanarkshire – Perth and Kinross – Stirling

My personal exploration of Scottish holy wells has been patchy so far, and therefore I do not pretend to be able to offer an exhaustive guide to them. What follows is a listing of wells that I know do exist and are worth visiting, with map references (and more detailed directions where available to me). There are many more surviving wells in Scotland, and more information on where to find details of them is in given the *Sources.*

ABERDEENSHIRE

St Drostan's Well, New Aberdour

The well is on the shore, reached down a winding cliff road. Nearby are the ruins of an old church said to have been founded by St Columba and this is also the place where St Drostan landed from Caithness to christianise the area and found a monastery. A mile north of New Aberdour, six miles south-west of Fraserburgh. NJ887646

ANGUS

St Fergus's Well (Lady Well), Glamis

In woods below the church; signposted. NO386469

ARGYLL AND BUTE

St Columba's Well, Keil Point, Southend, Kintyre

At the place where St Columba is traditionally said to have first set foot in Scotland in the sixth century can be seen two carved footprints (only one genuinely old, and said to be St Columba's), a ruined chapel and cemetery, and the saint's well (twenty yards north-west of chapel). NR673077

Holy Well, Kilmory Oib, Tayvallich

Holy well close to a ninth-century cross at the site of the deserted village of Kilmory Oib. NR780902

St Ninian's Well (Tobar Ninian), Dervaig, Isle of Mull

Behind Kilninian parish church; a path between two walls leads to the well. NM357457

BORDERS

Cheese Well, Minchmoor

A spring beside the old drove road between Selkirk and Peebles, now the Southern Upland Way. Passers-by would leave offerings of cheese for the fairies. Reached by footpath from Traquair. NT357336

St Ronan's Well, Innerleithen

Originally the Doo (Pigeon) Wells, the name was changed in 1824 after the publication of Sir Walter Scott's novel *St Ronan's Well*. This was never a true holy well, but because of the mineral spring it became a popular spa. Today the spa building is well maintained and houses an interesting museum. The original well on the hillside above can be visited, and the water can be tasted. Signposted in the town. NT328373

Tamlane's Well, Carterhaugh

Tamlane was a local boy stolen by the Fairy Queen; his story is told in the ballad *Young Tam Lin*. He haunted Carterhaugh Wood until rescued by 'the fair Janet'. The well is in a wall beside a lane at Carterhaugh farm three miles south-west of Selkirk. NT438268

Right: *The Cheese Well,
Minchmoor. Photo: Hamish M.
Brown.*

Below: *The jaunty building at
St Ronan's Well, painted blue
and white when I visited in
2006.*

DUMFRIES AND GALLOWAY

Brow Well, Ruthwell

Possibly originally dedicated to St Mungo, this healing chalybeate well is famous for its Burns connection, as Robert Burns visited in the last weeks of his life in search of a cure for rheumatism. Beside B725 road west of Ruthwell; signposted. NY084675. (Also do not miss the unique eighteen feet tall seventh-century cross, carved with religious scenes, and Latin texts and runes, inside Ruthwell church.

Chipperdingan Well, near Port Logan

The strange name means Tiobar Dingan or Well of St Ninian, and it came into being when a boy being educated by the saint committed some offence and ran away, taking the saint's staff to comfort him. He took a boat, which would have sunk in the sea but for the divine power of the staff, and when it came to rest on land the boy planted the staff on the shore, asking God for proof of the miracle. Whereupon the staff turned into a living tree, and a spring burst forth among its roots, its water being 'health-giving to the sick because of the merits of the saint.' This well can be found close to the eastern shore of the Rhinns of Galloway at New England Bay: there is a car park at the entrance to the caravan site. From there, walk across the A716 road and the well will be seen across a field: the water flows into a tank. NX120418

St Finnan's Well, Chapel Finian, Mochrum

The well, now dry, can be found in the ruined chapel, close to the perimeter wall by the entrance. NX278490

St Medan's Well, Monreith

Medan (sometimes Medana) was an Irish princess who came to the Rhinns of Galloway and developed a Christian community; her well and cave-chapel are among the rocks just north of the Mull of Galloway (NX144317 but difficult of access). According to folklore, her former suitor tracked her down and so she fled on a stone 'boat' across Luce Bay to the Machars, landing at Monreith where she built a chapel. (Both parishes were called Kirkmaiden, meaning Medan's Church.) Her

Brow Well near Ruthwell in 2007.

suitor followed her there and told her that he could not live without her beautiful eyes; whereupon she plucked them out and threw them at his feet. A well sprang up where she washed her face and her sight was miraculously restored. The well later became known as Chincough or Kingcost Well, from its reputation for healing whooping cough. St Medan's stone 'boat' can still be seen on the shore below her chapel at Monreith Bay, as can her well, though again it is among rocks and difficult to reach. From the A747 east of Monreith, take the lane south signposted to St Medan's Golf Club and follow it right to the end where there is a car park. Walk back along the beach to Monreith Bay where you will see the chapel on the hillside, reached by steps. Further along the shore, start walking round the rocky headland (only accessible at low tide), looking up until you see a mossy patch: this is the location of the well. The water collects in a small pool in the cliff and drips down through the moss in a small but steady stream. NX364402

St Queran's Well, Islesteps, Dumfries

This atmospheric well in its quiet location is on my list of favourites, so comes highly recommended. A small circular stone basin with a picture of the saint's face inside contains clear fresh water. When it was cleaned out in 1870, hundreds of coins were found, some dating back to the reign of Elizabeth I. The water was once used for healing, and 'clouties' and other offerings are still fastened to the trees. Interestingly, we noticed that a powerful chalybeate spring was flowing from the stream bank near the bridge only yards away, and in the well's location as shown on the OS map, so

Assorted offerings hang on the branches around St Queran's Well in 2007.

perhaps this was once the true source of the healing water? The well is a couple of miles south of Dumfries: a signposted footpath leads from a lane half a mile west of Islesteps. NX956723

EAST LOTHIAN

St Baldred's Well, East Linton

St Baldred was a local saint in the eighth century; he spent some time as a hermit on the Bass Rock. After his death, each of his three churches wanted to have his body for burial, and so he caused his remains to be triplicated in order to satisfy them all. His simple well is a stone-lined pool beside the River Tyne, down steps from a path opposite the graveyard of Preston Kirk, one of the churches Baldred founded. NT593778

St Bay's Well, Dunbar

This well is on the seashore at Dunbar: it is a pool on the floor of Bay's Well Cave. The cave can be found in the cliffs to the west of the leisure pool: from the car park by the pool building head west past the pool and down the steps, keeping right down onto the rocky beach. The cave is immediately to the right, but great care should be taken as the rocks can be very slippery. NT675794

Rood Well, Stenton

The well-preserved stone well-house stands beside the road to the north-east of the village. NT624744

EDINBURGH

St Anthony's Well, Holyrood Park

This well takes the form of a small stone basin beneath a large boulder, on the hillside below St Anthony's Cave and the ruins of St Anthony's Chapel. It's by the footpath leading uphill from St Margaret's Loch towards the chapel: keep the chapel on your left as you walk from the loch, and when a short distance up the slope look for the large boulder. The water was once believed to have healing powers, and it was also customary on May Day to wash one's face in the dew on Arthur's Seat, then make a wish at the well. NT275736

Balm Well, Liberton

Also known as St Catherine's Well, because according to one version of St Catherine of Alexandria's legend, the saint's body was being carried by angels from Alexandria to Mount Sinai and they were flying over Scotland when a drop of oil distilled from

St Anthony's Well on the hillside above St Margaret's Loch in 2006.

her body fell into the Liberton Well. This is the origin of the oil or balm rising in the well. Healing oil was also said to flow from the saint's relics at her shrine in the Burning Bush Monastery at Mount Sinai, and a pilgrim brought back a phial of it for St Margaret of Scotland in the eleventh century. The well water is black and tarry from the bituminous shale beds the water flows through, and it has long had a

The apparent calm of the setting of the Balm Well contrasts with the constant traffic noise to be heard when you are there, just as the abandoned air of the well today contrasts with its former importance as a pilgrimage centre. Photographed in 2006.

St Margaret's Well at its new location in Holyrood Park, photographed in 2006.

reputation for healing sprains, burns, dislocations and skin complaints. The present well-house was first built in 1617, but now the structure and well have an abandoned air. There was once a chapel nearby, but this had gone before the construction of a house on the site in 1806. This is now the Balm Well Hotel, with the well sitting on the lawn in front; please request permission to view. The Balm Well is off the A701, Howdenhall Road, Liberton, southern Edinburgh – immediately opposite Mortonhall Crematorium. NT273683

St Margaret's Well, Holyrood Park

This well is to the west of St Anthony's Well and St Margaret's Loch, beside the road leading into the centre of Edinburgh. The well-house inside the Victorian structure dates from the late fifteenth century and originally stood near Restalrig church, but was removed when a railway depot was built, and rebuilt close to a natural spring in Holyrood Park. It is said to be a miniature copy of St Triduana's well-house at Restalrig. NT271737

St Mungo's Well, Currie

On the Water of Leith Walkway close to Currie Kirk; this small well with a stone surround may date from the time of the earliest church on this site. NT184677

St Triduana's Well, Restalrig

This is the finest well building surviving today, after St Winefride's Well, Holywell, Flintshire, and it stands adjacent to Restalrig church. The well is in the undercroft of a hexagonal chapel (now destroyed) dating from the fifteenth century, and a shrine in the chapel containing St Triduana's relics, and the well, were once a focus for pilgrimage. However this was not universally approved of, and in 1560 the General Assembly of the Presbyterian Church of Scotland decreed that the church was 'a monument of idolatrie' and should be destroyed, after which it stood for three hundred years as 'a bare, gaunt ruin'. The shrine was destroyed, with the upper chapel, but the well crypt survived because it was used for the burials of an aristocratic family. This building later became overgrown with turf and was not restored until the early twentieth century.

The large building to the right of Restalrig church now houses St Triduana's Well; steps lead down to an impressive chapel undercroft, the well is below the floor. Photographed in 2006.

St Triduana's Well was once visited by people wishing to restore their sight, or with other eye complaints. The well's connection with blindness stems from the legend of St Triduana (who lived a monastic life in Angus). A pagan prince admired her eyes, and sooner than marry him, she plucked them out, skewered them on a thorn and gave them to him. There is still plenty of water in the well under the floor: it has to be constantly pumped out or the chapel would flood. The water is still accessible for pilgrims to drink, at their own risk. The well building is kept locked and an appointment must be made to enter it (the exterior can be viewed from the churchyard) by contacting St Margaret's Parish Office in St Margaret's Apartments at 176 Restalrig Road South, EH7 6EA (Tel. 0131 554 7400) from where the key has to be obtained. The church is near the fire station in Restalrig (off Restalrig Road South) and there is on-street parking close by. NT284745

FIFE

St Fillan's Well, Pittenweem

St Fillan, an eighth-century abbot, lived at Pittenweem (which means 'town of the cave'), supposedly in St Fillan's Cave by the harbour. He was guided by a miraculous light which shone from his left arm, which later became a sacred relic carried at the Battle of Bannockburn. His well, a small pool, can still be found in the cave (far left

The holy well inside St Fillan's Cave. Photo: Hamish M. Brown.

side). It was rededicated for worship in 1935, and access is in Cove Wynd. NO550024

HIGHLAND

St Boniface's Well (Cloutie Well), Munlochy

Famous for the sheer quantity of clouties (rags) festooning the well surrounds, this former healing well is now a wishing well and the required ritual is to spill a little water on the ground three times, tie a rag on a tree, make the sign of the cross, and drink some of the well water. The rags are not cleared up because it is strongly believed that anyone interfering with them will take on himself the ill-health of the donors. The well consists of a pipe in the bank from which water flows into a small stone basin. It is beside a lay-by on the south side of the A832 north-west of Munlochy. NH641537

Just a small sample of the rags which always festoon the Cloutie Well. Photo: Dr Elmar R. Gruber.

Craigie Well complete with clouties. Photo: Hamish M. Brown.

St Bennet's Well (Craigie Well), Avoch

A few clouties adorn this spring flowing from between two boulders at the foot of a bank, fifty yards above the north shoreline of Munlochy Bay (east of sandstone quarry inlet). Said to be difficult of access and hard to find. Its water was once used to protect against disease, witchcraft and fairies, but to be effective it had to be drunk before the sun appeared on the first Sunday in May. NH679532

St Ignatius's Well, Glassburn

The stone well-house, reconstructed in 1880, is topped by a large cross and covered with names, dates, and inscriptions (see photograph overleaf). NH370344

St John the Baptist's Well, Fodderty

This well may once have been used as a healing well, especially for madness, and offerings of coloured threads and cloths were left on the bushes. It is up a hill south of Fodderty: from Dingwall, turn left before Fodderty church on a lane passing Fodderty Lodge, park at the end, and follow footpath from there. NH514588

St John the Baptist's Well, Helmsdale

The stone well-house is across the River Helmsdale from the site of St John the Baptist's chapel, alongside a path by the river. ND025156

Two plaques on St Ignatius's Well just above the spout. Photo: Tony Healy.

St Mary's Well, Culloden

This well has several other names, including Culloden (Wishing) Well, Tobar na Coille (well of the wood), Tobar na h-Oige (well of youth), and Tobar Ghorm (blue well). It is still much frequented, with coins thrown into the water as offerings, and rags hung on the trees. Traditionally, the water turns to wine for a short time on 1st

An old photograph (possibly forty years old, so the trees may now look different) of St Mary's Well, Culloden – note the clouties on the tree to the left. Photo: Hamish M. Brown.

180

The restored stone structure of St Ninian's Well. Photo: Andreas Trottmann.

May. The well is surrounded by an unroofed stone wall, and can be found in Forestry Commission woodland; access via Blackpark Farm from B9006, south-east of Inverness. NH723453

St Ninian's Well, Drumnadrochit

At the site of an ancient St Ninian's church, now replaced by a later one, this well was visited for healing purposes and the walls and trees used to be covered with rags left by pilgrims. A hoard of coins was found in the well when the main road was widened. Close to the church, this well is near the standing stone marking the site of a Knight's Templar house by Temple Pier. NH530300

Well of the Dead, Culloden

The chief of the Macgillivrays crawled here to die during the Battle of Culloden in 1746: it is at the eastern edge of the battlefield near Leanach Cottage, marked by an information board. NH745450

Well of the Heads (Tobar nan Ceann), Loch Oich

This loch-side well has a distinctive monument topped by a hand holding a dirk and seven severed heads. This refers to an event in the 1660s when seven men were beheaded in revenge for having murdered two young MacDonalds. The heads were washed at the spring as they were being taken for presentation to MacDonald of

The Well of the Dead marks a site of high drama in Scottish history. Photo: Andreas Trottmann.

The dramatic lochside memorial to the murdered MacDonalds which was erected above the Well of the Heads. Photographed in 1998.

Glengarry. An inscription on the memorial, erected in 1812, commemorates the event. The well is beside the A82 south of Invergarry; NN304993

ISLE OF SKYE

Tobar Ashik (St Maelrubha's Well), Broadford

Maelrubha was a seventh-eighth century Irish monk who founded a monastery at Applecross and from there evangelized Skye. It is thought that a chapel once stood close to this well, and a cross-marked stone has been found. The well is easily reached from a lane north of the A850 two miles north-east of Broadford. NG687242

MORAY

St Fumac's Well, Botriphnie

The well is to the east of the churchyard which has the ruins of an earlier chapel where a wooden image of the saint was once kept. This was washed 'with much formality' in the well every 3rd May, the saint's fair day, by an old woman who

One of Scotland's many saints is remembered at Tobar Ashik, a coastal well on Skye. Photographed in 1998.

looked after it. The water it had been washed in was considered to have healing properties. The carving also used to be carried round the parish on the saint's day. When the River Isla flooded in the late eighteenth century, the carving was washed away and later found at Banff, where the minister ordered it to be broken up and burned. The well, a circular stone-lined hole in the ground, is on the route of a wildlife walk in the area of Drummuir Castle and Loch Park. NJ376443

St Mary's Well (Well of Grace), Orton

This well is described as 'a gem for the serious well finder with a sense of adventure' by Betsy Gray; it is in a maze of lanes east of the B9015 and quite difficult to find, though at one time it was an important pilgrimage site. It is in the outer wall of a pre-Reformation chapel, and its basin may have been the chapel font. Pilgrims still came to the well after the Reformation seeking cures for whooping cough, and eye and joint diseases, but the Presbyterian Church authorities were not happy with this superstition and pilgrims were punished. This well may be the one associated with the white witch Dame Aliset, who cured a fairy child using the well water. The well is south of Inchberry and next to St Mary's farm, Orton. NJ323552

Pictish Well, Burghead

The rock-cut well chamber is below ground level, and reached by a flight of twenty steps, at the bottom of which is a deep tank or pool of water ten feet square and four feet deep with a narrow walkway around it, and steps leading down into the water. Two other unusual features are a submerged semicircular pedestal and a small sink. This ancient well is at the site of a Pictish fort, and may have had more than one use over the years: as a water supply for the fort, as a site of execution (the Picts favoured death by drowning) and as a Pictish Christian baptistery. There was an early church close by. The well may be locked for safety reasons, but details of the key-holder are on display. The well is close to Burghead promontory fort, at the end of King Street. NJ109692

NORTH LANARKSHIRE

Holy Well, Carfin Lourdes Grotto

This is an extraordinary sanctuary, little-known outside Scotland, where many shrines to Catholic saints have been constructed in a large garden since 1922. At the Lourdes grotto, which was the first of the shrines to be erected, a representation of the Vision of Our Lady seen by Bernadette at Lourdes in France in 1858 has been created, and there are also two holy water taps, the water from which has been blessed by contact with water from the real Lourdes, to create, in effect, a new holy well. In the grotto shop plastic bottles are on sale for use by pilgrims wishing to take some of the water away with them. This water source performs the same function as a traditional holy well, in that it supplies water impregnated with the numinous aura of the saint.

Carfin is the National Scottish Shrine of the Blessed Virgin Mary, and is thronged with pilgrims throughout the summer months, making this not only the most recent, but also the most visited of Scottish holy wells. The grotto is signposted in Carfin which is a mile to the north-east of Motherwell.

Collecting water from the 'holy well' at the Lourdes Grotto in Carfin in 2006.

PERTH AND KINROSS

St David's Well, Weem

Two springs flow into stone basins from a rock outcrop on a hill behind Weem church, reached by a footpath starting alongside the church. The name was originally St Cuthbert's Well: the local tradition is that he had a retreat in the cliffs when he was at Dull, and he is said to have brought the well into existence. He spent several hours at a time in a rock hollow filled with water, later known as St Cuthbert's Bath and visited by people seeking cures. The site was restored in the fifteenth century by Sir David Menzies, and the well took his name as the result of a mistake. The well later became a wishing well and people threw in offerings of pins, buttons and coins. Weem is nine miles south-west of Pitlochry. NN843501

Well at Scotlandwell

The village is named for the impressive well in its centre, which is fed by several springs. A pool six by four feet is covered by a wooden pavilion erected in 1858, and the water flows out from a pipe at the end, which is reached by two sets of steps. The well was much frequented in the Middle Ages by people seeking cures who came to the hospital of the Red Friars. It was said that Robert the Bruce was cured of his leprosy by application of the water. Scotlandwell is east of Loch Leven. NO185016

STIRLING

St Fillan's Well, Strathfillan

This 'well' is in fact a deep pool in the River Fillan. It was used to try and cure madness. The victims would be immersed in the pool and then taken to the nearby St Fillan's Chapel or Priory (where St Fillan was traditionally believed to have been buried) where they would be tied to a wooden frame with ropes and left overnight

The impressive structure surrounding the well in Scotlandwell shows how important it must once have been. Photographed in 1991.

The ancient font where the insane were left overnight can be seen in the corner of the ruined walls of St Fillan's Chapel. Photographed in 1998.

with the head in the font and the saint's bell on the head. If the ropes were found untied or loosened next day, there was believed to be the chance of a cure. This ritual was still taking place in the mid-nineteenth century, but the pool lost its healing power when a farmer tried to cure a mad bull. People with other ailments also used to immerse themselves, and bring stones out of the pool which they placed on cairns close by, following circling rituals. The pool is close to the A82 four miles north-west of Crianlarich; leave the main road at the sign to Auchtertyre Farm, park, and walk to the river. It is also possible to walk up the track to the farm and follow a footpath to the right which leads to the ruins of St Fillan's Chapel on Kirkton farm, where the font can still be seen. St Fillan's Bell is in the Royal Museum of Scotland in Edinburgh along with his crozier. NN350288

Sources

Websites

There are many online sources of information on holy wells and the following websites are probably the best ones to start with.

1. **Source** and **Living Spring** journals: http://people.bath.ac.uk/liskmj/holywell.htm.
2. **The Megalithic Portal** (over 600 wells listed): www.megalithic.co.uk. 'TMP' in the Sources indicates that an entry for the well can be found in The Megalithic Portal.
3. **Devon:** www.holywells.com is a thorough website primarily about wells in Devon but also has general information.
4. **Books:** www.antipope.org/feorag/wells/index.html has the texts of some interesting publications including Hope's book. Google Books includes some on holy wells: do a search for 'holy wells' at http://books.google.co.uk.
5. **James Rattue:** James Rattue is the author of *The Living Stream* and his website gives details of his favourite holy wells, and some useful books: www.geocities.com/jamesrattue/wells_home.html.
6. **The Modern Antiquarian:** Covers mostly ancient sites, but a number of wells are included: check the listings for the area you are especially interested in: www.themodernantiquarian.com/home/.
7. **Water Talk:** This is an e-mail discussion list for springs and spas enthusiasts; the archive of messages goes back to 1998: www.jiscmail.ac.uk/lists/WELLS-AND-SPAS.html.
8. **PastScape:** The information on the website www.pastscape.org comes from English Heritage's National Monuments Record database on the archaeology and buildings of England, and searches can be made for details of holy wells throughout England. Location details are provided by aerial photographs, maps and grid references.
9. **National Wells Index:** Can be accessed through its website at http://nwi.skyphos.co.uk. It aims to catalogue, research and preserve the surviving holy wells of Britain, and offers a free holy well discussion forum.

Sources used in this guidebook:

All the publications referred to in brief are listed with full details in the *Bibliography*. 'TMP' is The Megalithic Portal at www.megalithic.co.uk.

England: South-West
CORNWALL

St Anne's Well, Whitstone: Quiller-Couch 1894: 7; Straffon 2005: 14–15; TMP; PastScape. My latest visit June 2001.

St Cleer's Well, St Cleer: Lane-Davies 1970: 5–6; Meyrick 1982: 31–2; Orme 2000: 88–9; Quiller-Couch 1894: 36–41; Straffon 2005: 18; TMP; PastScape. My latest visit June 2001.

St Clether's Well, St Clether: 'At a Cornish Well-Chapel – Unique Ceremony', *Daily Mail*, 20 September 1899; Baring-Gould 1899 (1981: 32–3); Lane-Davies 1970: 25–6; Meyrick 1982: 32–3; Orme 2000: 89; Quiller-Couch 1894: 42–3; Straffon 2005: 16; Thompson 2004: 43–6; TMP; PastScape; www.peaeland.org.uk. My visit May 1990.

St Cuby's Well, Duloe: Quiller-Couch 1894: 52–3; Straffon 2005: 24–5; TMP. My visit May 1990.

Dupath Well, Callington: Quiller-Couch 1894: 63–5; Straffon 2005: 6; TMP; PastScape. My latest visit September 2004.

St Guron's Well, Bodmin: Quiller-Couch 1894: 80–3; Straffon 2005: 70–1; Betsy Gray (TMP) (Eye Well). My latest visit June 2000.

Jordan Well, Laneast: Quiller-Couch 1894: 115–17; Straffon 2005: 17; TMP; PastScape. My visit May 1990.

St Keyne's Well, St Keyne: Hunt 1871(1993: 292–3); Meyrick 1982: 68–9; Orme 2000: 162–3; Quiller-Couch 1894: 106–12; Straffon 2005: 24; TMP. My latest visit June 2001.

Madron Well: Hunt 1871(1993: 293–6); Meyrick 1982: 92–3; Orme 2000: 169–71; Quiller-Couch 1894: 125–38; Straffon 2005: 40–2; TMP. My latest visit May 1990.

St Michael's Well, Michaelstow: Quiller-Couch 1894: 11; Straffon 2005: 22. My visit November 1998.

St Neot's Well, St Neot: Doble 1997: 53–88; Meyrick 1982: 109–10; Orme 2000: 200–3; Quiller-Couch 1894: 167–70; Straffon 2005: 19; Thompson 2004: 48–51; TMP. There is a full-page colour photograph of the St Neot stained-glass window in Jenkins: 2000: 86. My latest visit June 1998.

St Sampson's Well, Golant: Doble 1970: 80–103; Orme 2000: 228–30; Quiller-Couch 1894: 73–4; Straffon 2005: 26; Thompson 2004: 39–40; TMP; PastScape. My latest visit June 2000.

St Swithin's Well, Launcells: Straffon 2005: 61. My latest visit June 2001.

More information on Cornish wells: Straffon 2005 (the best up-to-date guide). There are also more than 130 Cornish wells listed on the Megalithic Portal (TMP), and a large number on PastScape.

DEVON

St Brannoc's Well, Braunton: Faull 2004: 122–3; Hunt 1989: 3–4; Harte 2008; Angie Lake (TMP). My visit September 2004.

Fice's Well, Princetown: Faull 2004: 60–1; Hope 1893: 65–6; Hunt 1989: 9; Betsy Gray (TMP); Richard L. Pederick: www.bath.ac.uk/~prsrlp/kernunos/england/fices.htm; www.legendarydartmoor.co.uk/fice_well.htm

Fitz's Well, Okehampton: Faull 2004: 56; Hope 1893: 63; Hunt 1989: 8; Betsy Gray (TMP); Richard L. Pederick: www.bath.ac.uk/~prsrlp/kernunos/england/fitz.htm; www.legendarydartmoor.co.uk/fitz_well.htm

St Gudula's Well, Ashburton: Faull 2004: 84–5; Harte 2008; *Herald Express (Torbay),* 31 January 2007 and 6 June 2007; Betsy Gray (TMP); www.legendarydartmoor.co.uk/gudula_well.htm My visit November 1998.

Ladywell, Pilton: Faull 2004: 122; Hunt 1989: 9; Harte 2008.

Lady Well, Sticklepath: Faull 2004: 58; Hunt 1989: 10; Harte 2008; Betsy Gray (TMP).

Leechwell, Totnes: Faull 2004: 81–2; Betsy Gray and Angie Lake (TMP); PastScape.

St Leonard's Well, Sheepstor: Faull 2004: 71; Harte 2008; Betsy Gray (TMP). My visit June 2001.

St Nectan's Well, Stoke: Faull 2004: 34–5; Harte 2008; Notes by Jeremy Harte and Christine Buckley circulated to wells-and-spas@jiscmail.ac.uk in August 2006; Hunt 1989: 7; Farmer 1997: 361; Richard L. Pederick: www.bath.ac.uk/~prsrlp/kernunos/england/necstoke.htm; Betsy Gray (TMP). My visit September 2004.

St Nectan's Well, Welcombe: Faull 2004: 33; Harte 2008; Betsy Gray (TMP); PastScape. My visit September 2004.

St Urith's Well, Chittlehampton: Faull 2004: 119; Harte 2008; http://en.wikipedia.org/wiki/Urith; www.geocities.com/david_ryall2001/saint_teara.htm?200619

More information on Devon wells: Brown 1957: 205–15; Faull 2004; Hunt 1989: 3–13; Harte 2008; TMP; PastScape; www.holywells.com

ISLES OF SCILLY

St Warna's Well, St Agnes: Orme 2000: 67–8; Quiller-Couch 1894: 215; Straffon 2005: 44; Whitfeld 1852: 177–86; TMP; PastScape. Location details courtesy of Peter Griffin who saw the well in April 2007.

SOMERSET

St Agnes' Well, Cothelstone: Horne 1923: 46–7; Harte 2008; www.themodernantiquarian.com/site/8803; directions from entry in TMP.

St Aldhelm's Well, Doulting: Horne 1923: 26; Jordan and Pederick 2000; Thompson 2004: 87–91; Walters 1928: 99–100; Harte 2008; Betsy Gray (TMP). My visit July 2007.

St Andrew's Well, Stogursey: Horne 1923: 48; Harte 2008; letter from Rev. Peter Pengelley, 21 February 1984; TMP; PastScape.

St Andrew's Well, Wells: Horne 1923: 24–5; Harte 2008; www.bishopspalacewells.co.uk/outergardens.php; Betsy Gray (TMP). My visit September 2006.

St Anne's Well, Brislington: Horne 1923: 11–15; Lovegrove 1986: 11–13; Quinn 1999: 147–9; Walters 1928: 153–5; Harte 2008.

Chalice Well, Glastonbury: Mann and Glasson 2005; Rahtz 1993: 106–9, 129–31; Sharp 1997: 34, 156. My latest visit September 1989.

St Decuman's Well, Watchet: Farmer 1997: 133; Norman 1992: 7; Horne 1923: 49; Harte 2008. My visit September 2004.

Holy Well, Edington: Horne 1923: 41–2; Harte 2008; Account by A.A. Moon dated 1979 whose family once owned the well.

St Joseph's Well, Glastonbury: Farmer 1997: 275–6; Horne 1923: 39; Rahtz 1993: 84–7; Harte 2008; www.glastonburyabbey.com; Marion Benham (TMP).

King Arthur's Well and Queen Anne's Well, South Cadbury: Horne 1923: 33–4; James Rattue (TMP). My visit September 2006.

St Mary's Well, Charlcombe: Horne 1923: 17; Quinn 1999: 167–8; Harte 2008.

Sacred Spring, Bath: Bord 2006: 10–12; Cunliffe 1995; Quinn 1999: 73–85; Stewart 1981; Sharp 1997: 79–81.

More information on Somerset wells: Quinn 1999; Harte 1985b; Horne 1923; Rattue 1988; Harte 2008; PastScape (check Bristol as well as Somerset).

England: South

BERKSHIRE

St Anne's Well, Caversham: Rattue 1995: 75–7, 80, 103, 105; Kift 2004; Gillett 1957: 79–92; Verrill 1931: 135–6; Harte 2008; David C. Woods (TMP).

Ladywell, Speen: Bayley 1995: 5; Harte 2008; David C. Woods (TMP); PastScape.

More information on Berkshire wells: Rattue 1995: 173; Harte 2008.

DORSET

St Augustine's Well, Cerne Abbas: Harte 1985a: 3–4; Harte 2008; Legg 1997: 102–3; Thompson 2004: 84–7; PastScape. My latest visit September 206.

Holy Well, Hazelbury Bryan: Information supplied by Geraldine Hobson; Harte 2008.

Holy Well, Holwell: Rattue 1986: 19; Harte 1985a: 5; Harte 2008; Betsy Gray (TMP); written description by the rector, Rev. D.J. Hillier, dated October 1979.

Lady's Well, Hermitage: Rattue 1986: 19; Harte 1985a: 5; Harte 2008; Betsy Gray (TMP). My visit September 2006.

St Wite's Well, Morcombelake: Harte 1985a: 7; Harte 2008; Jenkins 2000: 163; Knight 1998: 112–15; Legg 1997: 133–5; Rattue 1986: 16–18; Waters 1980. My visit September 2006.

Wishing Well, Upwey: Harte 1985a: 6; Knight 1998: 112–13; http://dspace.dial.pipex.com/town/avenue/pd49/places/wells/upwey.html; www.dorset-opc.com/UpwayWishingWell.htm; TMP. My visit September 2006.

More information on Dorset wells: Harte 1985a: 3–8; Harte 2008; Knight 1998: 108–19; Rattue 1995: 174–5; Rattue 1986: 16–20.

HAMPSHIRE

Holy or Wishing Well, Binsted: Hampshire Treasures website (www.hants.gov.uk/hampshiretreasures/vol06/page052.html); Harte 2008; TMP.

Holy Well, Sopley: Rattue 1987a: 16; David C. Woods (TMP).

Holybourne Springs: Hope 1893: 76–7; Holybourne church guidebook and letter from rector in 1984; David C. Woods (TMP).

Iron's Well (Lepers' Well), Fritham: Hope 1893: 77; Rattue 1987b: 17; Jim Champion (TMP).

More information on Hampshire wells: Rattue 1995: 175; Rattue 1987a: 16–18; Rattue 1987b: 16–18; Harte 2008.

ISLE OF WIGHT

St Lawrence Well, St Lawrence: As White Well below.

White Well, Whitwell: *Holy Wells and Pilgrim Paths* leaflet; British History Online: www.british-history.ac.uk/report.asp?compid=42074 Information supplied by

Graham Bennett, Curator of the Ventnor Heritage Museum, and by the Reverend Sandra Lloyd. Visited July 2007 by Susan and Peris Sinnett-Jones, who kindly photographed the wells and information boards, and obtained the leaflet for me.

WILTSHIRE

Cat's Well, Bratton: Jordan 2000a: 26; Harte 2008; At the Edge archive: Black dogs folklore (www.indigogroup.co.uk/edge/bdemails.htm); TMP. My visit August 2006.

Daniel's Well, Malmesbury: Harte 2008; PastScape; www.davidforward.co.uk/riverwalk See also 'Immersion' in Bord 2006: 74. My visit August 2006.

Ladywell, Bradford on Avon: Jordan 2000a: 30–1; Harte 2008; TMP. My visit August 2006.

Monkswell, Edington: Jordan 2000a: 31–2; Harte 2008; TMP. My visit August 2006.

More information on Wiltshire wells: Jordan 1998; Jordan 2000a; Jordan 2000b; Rattue 1995: 178–9; Harte 2008.

England: South-East

GREATER LONDON

Caesar's Well, Keston: 'Source of the Ravensbourne', Hone 1838: 642; Hope 1893: 80; David C. Woods (TMP).

Caesar's Well, Wimbledon Common: Hughes 1989: 21; www.themodernantiquarian.com/site/2901

St Eloy's Well, Tottenham: Hope 1893: 90-1; Farmer 1997: 160-1; Harte 2008; David C. Woods (TMP).

St Mary's Well, Willesden: Schofield post-2002; Lionel Beer, 'Is the Holy Well in Willesden Overseen by a Black Madonna?', *TEMS News* no.31 (January 2003), 4-5; Harte 2008; Independent Catholic News: www.indcatholicnews.com; www.ourladyofwillesden.co.uk

More information on Greater London wells: Potter 1985; Harte 2008; David Furlong's website: www.kch42.dial.pipex.com/holywellslond.htm

KENT

The Black Prince's Well, Harbledown: Rattue 2003b: 16; Kent Resources (www.digiserve.com/peter/harbledown-pow.htm); Rev. Canon Derek Ingram Hill, *Medieval Hospitals in Canterbury: St Nicolas, Harbledown* (leaflet); Dorothy Gardiner, *The Hospital of St. Nicholas, Harbledown – The Early History* (leaflet); David C. Woods (TMP).

St Edith's Well, Kemsing: Rattue 2003b: 19; letter from Victor Bowden of Kemsing dated 23 October 1979; Farmer 1997: 150; Harte 2008; David C. Woods (TMP).

St Ethelburga's Well, Lyminge: Rattue 2003b: 22; Harte 2008; David C. Woods (TMP).

St Leonard's Well, West Malling: Rattue 2003b: 34; Harte 2008; David C. Woods (TMP).

St Margaret's Well, Broomfield: Rattue 2003b: 8; Harte 2008; David C. Woods (TMP).
More information on Kent wells: Martin 1985: 27–8; Rattue 1995: 176; Rattue 2003b; Harte 2008.

SURREY
St Anne's Well, Chertsey: Baker 1982–3: 187 (1985: 26); Harte 2008; Lionel Beer in *TEMS News* no.15 (March 1997) p. 2; David C. Woods (TMP).
St Anne's Well, Stanwell: Lionel Beer in *TEMS News* no.13 (May 1996) p.2; Information from James Rattue; David C. Woods (TMP).
Anne Boleyn's Well, Carshalton: Baker 1982–3: 189–90 (1985: 28–9); David C. Woods (TMP).
St Catherine's Spring, Artington: Baker 1982–3: 187 (1985: 26); Harte 2008; Lionel Beer in *TEMS News* no. 12 (December 1995) p.4; David C. Woods (TMP) (under the name Artington Spring).
St Edward's Well, Sutton Park: Lionel Beer in TEMS News no.23 (December 1995) p.4; Harte 2008; information supplied in 1984 by Father John Stapleton, and in 2006 by Father Brian Taylor.
St John the Baptist's Well, Bisley: Baker 1982–3: 186–7 (1985: 25); Harte 2008; David C. Woods (TMP); PastScape.
Mag's Well, Mugswell: Baker 1982–3: 189 (1985: 28); David C. Woods (TMP).
St Mary the Virgin's Well, Dunsfold: Baker 1982–3: 187 (1985: 26); Lionel Beer in *TEMS News* no.23 (December 1995) p.4; Jenkins 2000: 673–5; Harte 2008; David C. Woods (TMP).
More information on Surrey wells: Baker 1982–3: 186–92 (1985: 25–30); Harte 2008.

EAST AND WEST SUSSEX
Bone Well, Willingdon: Osborne 1995: 14–15.
Ludwell Spring, Horsted Keynes: www.horstedkeynes.com/ludwell.html
St Peter's Well, Lodsworth: David C. Woods (TMP).
Spring at Fulking: Osborne 1998: 33–4. My visit 1974.
More information on Sussex wells: Harte 2008; Osborne 1994/1995/1998.

England: South Midlands
BEDFORDSHIRE
Holy Well, Stevington: Elliott 1933: 21–2; Stevington Genealogy Data online: www.cb5.co.uk/1851censusstevington.htm and www.genuki.org.uk/big/eng/BDF/Stevington/. Rattue 1995: 130; Harte 2008; David C. Woods (TMP). My visit October 1984.
More information on Bedfordshire wells: Elliott 1933; Harte 2008.

BUCKINGHAMSHIRE
St Osyth's Well, Bierton: Farmer 1997: 377; Rattue 2003a: 31–2; Harte 2008; www.strangebritain.co.uk/holywells/osyth.html; www.biertonvillage.org.uk; David C. Woods (TMP).

St Rumbold's Well, Buckingham: Farmer 1997: 435; Rattue 2003a: 8; Leigh 2000; Love 1996: cxl–clxxxvii, 91–115; Harte 2008; PastScape; www.buckingham.ac.uk/life/buck/bucktown/rumbold.html; David C. Woods (TMP). My visit August 2006.

Schorne Well, North Marston: Bond 1914: 196–8; Hope 1893: 3–5; Hole 1954: 51–3; Jenkins 2000: 34–5; Rattue 2003a: 24–5; Harte 2008; David C. Woods (TMP); restoration information: www.buckinghamtoday.co.uk/ViewArticle2.aspx?sectionid=717andarticleid=99 3185

More information on Buckinghamshire wells: Valentine 1985: 22–6; Rattue 2003a; Harte 2008; TMP.

GLOUCESTERSHIRE

St Anthony's Well, Forest of Dean: H.G. Nicholls, *The Forest of Dean* (1858); Samuel Rudder, *A New History of Gloucestershire* (1779 and 1977); T.A. Ryder, *Portrait of Gloucestershire* (1966); Tony Oldham, *Caves of the Forest of Dean* (2002); Palmer 1994: 28; Simpson 1976: 100; Simpson 2003: 104–5; Walters 1928: 75–80; Harte 2008; TMP. My visit September 2006.

St Bride's Well, St Briavels: Walters 1928: 138–9; PastScape.

Calmsden Cross Well: Hunt 1994: 17; Walters 1928: 40–1; PastScape. My visit October 2004. (For information on Condicote cross well see www.condicote.freeserve.co.uk/cross.htm)

St Kenelm's Well, Winchcombe: Walters 1928: 6–12; Stewart: 2005; Hole 1966: 88–90, 94–5; Farmer 1997: 285–6; Love 1996: lxxxix–cxxxix, 49–89; Harte 2008. My visit September 2006.

Our Lady's Well, Hempsted: Walters 1928: 63–5; Hunt 1994: 18; Harte 2008; PastScape. My visit September 2006.

Our Lady's Well, Lower Swell: Walters 1928: 24–5; Hunt 1994: 19; Harte 2008; PastScape. My visit October 2004.

Seven Wells, Bisley: Walters 1928: 37–8; Hunt 1994: 17; www.bisley-glos.net/places/ My visit October 2004.

More information on Gloucestershire wells: Walters 1928; Hunt 1994; Harte 2008; PastScape.

HEREFORDSHIRE

St Ann's Well and Lady Well, Aconbury: Leather 1912 (1970: 11); Sant 1994: 16–17; Harte 2008; TMP.

St Clodock's Well, Clodock: Sant 1994: 28–9; Farmer 1997: 108; Harte 2008. My visit September 2004.

St Edith's Well, Stoke Edith: Sant 1994: 58–9; Leather 1912 (1970: 12); Harte 2008; TMP. My latest visit October 2004.

St Ethelbert's Well, Hereford: Sant 1994: 37–8; Leather 1912 (1970: 12); Farmer 1997: 168; Harte 2008. My visit July 1983.

Holy Well, Garway: Sant 1994: 34–5; Zaluckyj 2006: 270–1; Harte 2008; TMP.

Holy Well, Luston: Sant 1994: 49; information from Shirley Campbell in Luston. My visit August 2007.

St Peter's Wells, Peterchurch: Sant 1994: 54–5; Leather 1912 (1970: 13); Zaluckyj 2006: 296–7; Harte 2008.
More information on Herefordshire wells: Sant 1994; Harte 2008.

HERTFORDSHIRE
Amwell, Great Amwell: Letter from David Perman of The Ware Society, 14 February 1984; TMP.
Chadwell Spring, Ware: Letter from David Perman of The Ware Society, 14 February 1984; TMP.
Holy well, St Albans: Rattue 1995: 44; Hope 1893: 78–9; Farmer 1997: 10–11; Haynes 1986; Harte 2008; David C. Woods (TMP).
More information on Hertfordshire wells: Harte 2008.

NORTHAMPTONSHIRE
Becket's Well, Northampton: Valentine 1984: 9; Thompson (1911–15) vol.XVII no.136 December 1913: 76–7; Harte 2008; TMP.
St John's Spring, Boughton Green: Valentine 1984: 4; Thompson (1911–15) vol. XVII no.136 December 1913: 71–2; Harte 2008; David C. Woods (TMP). My first visit (when I actually saw the well) Spring 1972; my latest visit (when it was overgrown with nettles) August 2006.
St Rumbold's Well, King's Sutton: Denbigh 1981: 26–30; Buckley 1998: 21–4; Harte 2008; Valentine 1984: 7–8; Leigh 2000; Love 1996: cxl–clxxxvii, 91–115; Thompson (1911–15) vol.XVII no.136 December 1913: 85–91. My visit July 2006.
More information on Northamptonshire wells: Thompson 1911–15; Valentine 1984; Harte 2008.

OXFORDSHIRE
Fair Rosamond's Well, Woodstock: Walters 1928: 162; Westwood 1985: 231–4. My visit October 2004.
Lady Well, Wilcote: Letters from Mrs M. Rogers dated 11 March 1984 and from J.C.S. Nias dated 21 February 1984; Harte 2008; David C. Woods (TMP). My visit October 2004.
St Margaret's Well, Binsey: Walters 1928: 93–4; Hope 1893: 124–6; Thompson 2004: 83–4; Morgan 1986: 1–5; Farmer 1997: 195–6; Harte 2008. My latest visit October 2004.
More information on Oxfordshire wells: Rattue 1990; Stone 1998; Harte 2008.

WARWICKSHIRE
Berks Well, Berkswell: www.whitedragon.org.uk/gazette/gazwest.htm; Ekwall 1960: 39; Thompson 2004: 102–3; James Rattue (TMP); Harte 2008. My visit April 1984.
Holy Well, Burton Dassett: Nikolaus Pevsner and Alexandra Wedgwood, *The Buildings of England: Warwickshire* (Penguin Books, 1966): 221–2; Harte 2008. My latest visit June 2006.
Holy Well, Southam: Patchell 1987: 14; Darley 1995: 22–3; Morrell 1991: 1–3; Harte 2008; *The Leamington Observer*, 7 March 2007; PastScape; http://warkcom.net/live/cme2272.htm; Jenny Frith of Southam. My visit July 2007.

Rowton's Well, Sutton Park: Patchell 1987: 10;
  http://en.wikipedia.org/w/index.php?title=Sutton_Park.
More information on Warwickshire wells: Patchell 1987; Bates 1993–4; Harte
  2008.

WORCESTERSHIRE
St Ann's Well, and Holy Well, Malvern Hills: Weaver and Osborne 1994: 91–101,
  115–28; Weaver and Osborne 2006; Denbigh 1981: 174–83; Harte 2008;
  www.malvern-hills.co.uk/water.html. My visit October 1983.
St Katherine's Well, Bredon Hill: Stewart 2005: 53; Hoggard 1999: 31–2; Harte
  2008; www.whitedragon.org.uk/gazette/gazworc.htm;
  www.themodernantiquarian.com/site/2501.
St Kenelm's Well, Romsley: Walters 1928: 11–14; Farmer 1997: 285–6; Smith and
  Taylor 1995; Love 1996: lxxxix–cxxxix, 49–89; Saint Kenelm's Church
  guidebook; Stewart 2005; Harte 2008. My latest visit October 2004.
More information on Worcestershire wells: Harte 2008.

England: East
CAMBRIDGESHIRE
Holy Well, Holywell: Pennick 1985: 11–12; Harte 2008; TMP. My visit April 1974.
Holy Well, Longstanton: Well-dressing: *Source* 5 (1986/7): 27, and *Source* 7
  (1987): 18 (Phyllis Brown); Harte 2008;
  www.druidic.org/camchurch/churches/longstantonmichael.htm; TMP.
Holy Well, Longthorpe: Parish 2002; Thompson (1911–15) vol.XVII no.135
  September 1913: 59–63; PastScape.
Red Well, Knapwell: Ekwall 1960: 281; TMP;
  www.wildlifetrust.org.uk/bcnp/camres/Cambs.htm. My visit June 1977.
More information on Cambridgeshire wells: Pennick 1985: 9–12; Harte 2008.

ESSEX
St Cedd's Well, North Ockendon: Harte 2008; Emails from Pam and Maurice Day;
  David C. Woods (TMP).
St Peter's Well, West Mersea: TMP.
The Running Well, Runwell: Ekwall 1960: 397; Collins 1983 (both); Rattue 1995:
  140, 147; David C. Woods (TMP).
More information on Essex wells: Harte 2008.

LINCOLNSHIRE
Holy Well, Sempringham: Thompson 1999: 33; Harte 2008;
  http://homepages.which.net/~rex/bourne/sempringham.htm My visit March
  2006.
St John's Well, Bottesford: Thompson 1999: 17; Harte 2008.
Kell Well, Alkborough: Thompson 1999: 11; www.geograph.org.uk/photo/10477
Lud's Well, Stainton-le-Vale: Thompson 1999: 36.
Spring Wells, Billingborough: Thompson 1999: 16–17. My visit March 2006.
More information on Lincolnshire wells: Thompson 1999; Harte 2008.

NORFOLK

Walsingham wells: Yelton 2006; Hope 1893: 92–3; Porter 1974: 117–20; Warner 1995: 27–8; Harte 2008; www.walsinghamanglican.org.uk; www.walsingham.org.uk/romancatholic/ My latest visit March 2006.

St Walstan's Well, Bawburgh: Twinch 1989, 1995 and 2004; Jones 1999: 179–87; Farmer 1997: 500; Porter 1974: 115–16; Harte 2008; www.bawburghnews.freeserve.co.uk/saint_walstan_legend.htm; TMP. My latest visit March 2006.

St Withburga's Well, Dereham: Hope 1893: 93–5; Farmer 1997: 515; Harte 2008; 'The Return of St Withburga?' in *Source* 1 (1985) p.19; Cook 1987: 19; TMP. My latest visit March 2006.

More information on Norfolk wells: Harte 2008; Hidden East Anglia web-site: www.hiddenea.com/

SUFFOLK

The Lady's Well, Blythburgh: www.hiddenea.com/suffolkb.htm; Harte 2008; TMP.

More information on Suffolk wells: Harte 2008; Hidden East Anglia web-site: www.hiddenea.com/

England: North Midlands

CHESHIRE

Three Wells on Alderley Edge: Thompson 2004: 145–8; Sharp 1997: 140–1; Harte 2008; www.alderleyedge.org/the_wells.htm; TMP. My latest visit April 2006.

St Chad's Well, Chadkirk: Harte 2008; TMP; www.stockport.gov.uk/content/leisureculture/tourism/placestovisit/chadkirkchapel/; www.virtual-knutsford.co.uk/archaeology/i_chad2.htm; www.marple-uk.com/chadkirkchapel.htm. My visit April 2006.

St Patrick's Well, Bromborough: Hole 1937 (1970: 64); Harte 2008; Tim Prevett (TMP). My visit February 2007.

St Plegmund's Well, Plemstall: Background information and details of archaeological survey: http://archaeology.kmatthews.net/cheshire/st_plegmund/index.php; Harte 2008; Tim Prevett (TMP); PastScape. My visit September 2005.

Whistlebitch, Utkinton: Gray Hulse 1994a: 21–4; Hole 1937 (1970: 65–6); Harte 2008. My visit 2003.

More information on Cheshire wells: Harte 2008.

DERBYSHIRE

St Alkmund's Well, Derby: Thompson 2004: 104–6; Hope 1893: 55–7; Harte 2008; TMP.

St Anne's Well, Buxton: Thompson 2004: 160–2; Denbigh 1981: 37–46; Hope 1893: 50–2; Morrell 1994: 21–2; Sharp 1997: 26–7; Harte 2008. My visit April 2006.

Holy well, King's Newton: Usher 1986; Harte 2008; TMP.

Mompesson's Well, Eyam: Kightly 1986: 189; TMP. My latest visit April 2006.

Roman Baths, Stoney Middleton: Cowen 1910; Porteous 1949: 106–14; Harte 2008; notice-board at baths; TMP. My visit April 2006.

Tissington wells: Kightly 1986: 231–3; Porteous 1949: 43–55; Thompson 2004: 167–70; Sharp 1997: 177; TMP. My visit April 2006.
More information on Derbyshire wells: Harte 2008.

LEICESTERSHIRE
Holy Well, Ab Kettleby: Trubshaw 1990: 5; Trubshaw 2002. My visit August 2006.
Holy Well, Beeby: Trubshaw 1990: 7–9; Trubshaw 2002. My visit August 2006.
King Richard's Well, Bosworth Battlefield: Trubshaw 2002. My visit April 1984.
More information on Leicestershire wells: Trubshaw 1990; Trubshaw 2002; Rattue 1993; Potter 1985; Harte 2008.

NOTTINGHAMSHIRE
St Catherine's Well, Newark: Morrell 1988: 9–10; Hope 1893: 116; Harte 2008; www.nottshistory.org.uk/blagg1910/modern.htm.
St Catherine's Well, Southwell: Morrell 1988: 20–21; Harte 2008; TMP.
More information on Nottinghamshire wells: Harte 2008.

RUTLAND
Wishing well, Ashwell: Ekwall 1960: 16; Harte 2008; Trubshaw 1990: 6; Trubshaw 2002. My visit August 2004.
More information on Rutland wells: Harte 2008.

SHROPSHIRE
St Cuthbert's Well, Donington: Pamphlet 'William the Conqueror, 1066–1087, and Donington (Albrighton) Church'; letter from Revd C.W. Woods, 2 February 1984; Harte 2008; Tim Prevett (TMP); PastScape. My visit May 1984.
St Julian's Well, Ludlow: PastScape; Tim Prevett (TMP).
St Milburga's Well and St Owen's Well, Much Wenlock: Palmer 2004: 63; Brown 1990; Hope 1893: 140; Harte 2008; www.muchwenlockguide.info/much_wenlock_tour; Tim Prevett (TMP). My visit July 1982.
St Milburga's Well, Stoke St Milborough: Farmer 1997: 349–50; Palmer 2004: 60–3; Brown 1990; Burne 1883 (1974: 416–19); Hope 1893: 140–1; Harte 2008; Tim Prevett (TMP); PastScape. My visit August 2007.
St Oswald's Well, Oswestry: Farmer 1997: 379–80; Palmer 2004: 59–60; Burne 1883 (1974: 423–9); Hope 1893: 143–5; Thompson 2004: 72–4; Harte 2008; Betsy Gray (TMP). My latest visit June 2005.
St Winifred's Well, Woolston: Palmer 2004: 60; Burne 1883 (1974: 429–31); Thompson 2004: 76–7; Harte 2008; Tim Prevett (TMP). My latest visit June 2005.
More information on Shropshire wells: Burne 1883 (1974: 412–34); Palmer 2004: 59–66; Otter 1985–8; Hope 1893: 128–48; Harte 2008; PastScape.

STAFFORDSHIRE
St Bertram's Wells, Ilam: Thompson 2004: 98–101; Pickford 1994: 64–9; Hackwood 1924 (1974: 142); Harte 2008; James Rattue and Tim Prevett (TMP). My visit April 2006.

St Chad's Well, Stowe: Morrell 1992: 3–5; Hackwood 1924 (1974: 142); Farmer 1997: 97–8; Thompson 2004: 79–81; Walters 1928: 47; Harte 2008. My visit April 1984.

Egg Well, Bradnop: Hackwood 1924 (1974: 143); www.british-history.ac.uk/report.asp?compid=22912. My visit April 2006.

St Helen's Well, Rushton Spencer: Hope 1893: 156; Hackwood 1924 (1974: 144); Tim Prevett (TMP).

Holy Well, Sandwell Valley: Hackwood 1924 (1974: 141); Colloby 1992: 29–31; www.whitedragon.org.uk/gazette/gazwest.htm.

Wulfruna's Well, Wolverhampton: Hackwood 1924 (1974: 140); www.localhistory.scit.wlv.ac.uk/listed/wulfrunwell.htm; my correspondence with Wolverhampton Civic Society in August 1983.

More information on Staffordshire wells: Hackwood 1924; Harte 2008; PastScape.

England: North
CUMBRIA

St Andrew's Well, Kirkandrews-on-Eden: Page 1990: 25; Harte 2008. My visit April 2007.

St Cuthbert's Well, Colton: Taylor 1999: 54; Taylor 2007: 39; Harte 2008; Enid Barwell, *Holy Trinity Church, Colton*: 6–7 (undated booklet on sale in Colton church). My visit April 2007.

St Helen's Well, Great Asby: Page 1990: 24; Harte 2008. My visit April 2007.

St Kentigern's Well, Aspatria: Page 1990: 19; Harte 2008. My visit April 2007.

St Kentigern's Well, Caldbeck: Page 1990: 12, 21; Harte 2008. My visit April 2007.

St Mungo's Well, Bromfield: Page 1990: 14, 21; McIntire 1944: 6; Harte 2008. My visit April 2007.

St Ninian's Well, Brisco: Page 1990: 21; McIntire 1944: 15; Harte 2008. My visit April 2007.

St Oswald's Well, Kirkoswald: Page 1990: 15, 26; Thompson 2004: 77–9; Harte 2008; guide to Kirkoswald church on sale at the church. My visit April 2007.

St Patrick's Well, Patterdale: Page 1990: 12, 27; Harte 2008. My visit April 2007.

Stanger Well, Embleton: Page 1990: 23; McIntire 1944: 9; David Raven (TMP) quoting from Bulmer's *History and Directory of Cumberland* (1901). My visit April 2007.

More information on Cumbria wells: Page 1990; McIntire 1944; Park 1987; Harte 2008; PastScape.

DURHAM

St Cuthbert's Well, Durham: Hunt 1987: 10–22; Harte 2008; Betsy Gray (TMP). My visit April 1993.

Holy Well, Wolsingham: Hunt 1987: 15; Harte 2008; www.durham.gov.uk/durhamcc/ – search for 'Wolsingham'.

St Mary's Well, Gainford: Hunt 1987: 13; *Wood and Water* No.4 (Spring 1980) p.14.

St Oswald's Well, Durham: Hunt 1987: 11; Harte 2008.

More information on Durham wells: Hunt 1987: 8–15; Binnall and Dodds 1897–
1904; Harte 2008; www.durham.gov.uk/ – a search for 'holy well' will locate a
list of 50 sites in Durham and Northumberland.

ISLE OF MAN
Well of the Baptism, Patrick: Gill 1929: Ch.I; Cubbon 1967: 39.
St Catherine's Well, Port Erin: Gill 1929: Ch.I; Bruce 1968: 55.
St Mary's Well, Ramsey: Gill 1929: Ch.I; Fraser 1948: 92; www.ramsey-
heritage.iofm.net/TownCentreWalk.htm.
St Maughold's Well, Maughold: Gill 1929: Ch.I; Moore 1894: 220–4; Paton 1941:
187–8; Cubbon 1967: 40; Cubbon 1973: 26–7.
St Patrick's Well, Lonan: Gill 1929: Ch.I; Kermode 1930; Fraser 1948: 60.
St Patrick's Well, Peel: Gill 1929: Ch.I; Kermode 1930; Moore 1894: 225.
More information on Isle of Man wells: Gill 1929; Moore 1894; Paton 1941;
PastScape.

LANCASHIRE
Holy Well, Hollinshead Hall: Taylor 2004: 15; Crawshaw 1994: 31; Harte 2008;
PastScape; www.tockholes.org.uk/walks.htm. My visit April 2007.
Ladyewell, Fernyhalgh Lane, Fulwood: Thompson 2004: 128–33; Darwen 1988:
28–30; Harte 2008; James Rattue (TMP); *Ladyewell Past and Present*: booklet
available at Ladyewell. My latest visit April 2007.
St Oswald's Well, Winwick: Taylor 2006: 81; Hope 1893: 84–5; Harte 2008.
St Patrick's Well, Heysham: Taylor 1999: 9, 20; Taylor 2004: 89; Harte 2008;
www.slyne-with-hest.org.uk/description.htm. My visit April 2007.
St Thomas's Well, Windle: Taylor 2006: 48; Harte 2008.
More information on Lancashire wells: Darwen 1988: 25–30; Taylor 1999, 2002,
2004, 2005, 2006, 2007; Harte 2008.

NORTHUMBERLAND
St Cuthbert's Well, Bellingham: Hope 1893: 104–5; Harte 2008; church guidebook
by Robert Allen; Betsy Gray (TMP). My visit April 1993.
Lady Well, Holystone: Binnall and Dodds 1897–1904: 34; Hope 1893: 111–12;
Thompson 2004: 124–6; Harte 2008; Sharp 1997: 82–3; Betsy Gray (TMP). My
latest visit April 1998.
Pin Well, Wooler: Binnall and Dodds 1897–1904: 72–3; Thompson 2004: 156–7;
PastScape; www.themodernantiquarian.com/site/6541. My visit October 2006.
St Mary's Well, Jesmond Dene, Newcastle: Hope 1893: 100; Binnall and Dodds:
35; Harte 2008; www.jesmonddene.org.uk/HistoryTrail.htm. My visit April
1993.
St Mungo's Well, Holystone: Binnall and Dodds: 34; Harte 2008; Betsy Gray
(TMP).
More information on Northumberland wells: Binnall and Dodds 1897–1904; Harte
2008; PastScape; www.durham.gov.uk/ – a search for 'holy well' will produce a
list of 50 well sites in Durham and Northumberland.

YORKSHIRE: EAST

Drummer's Well, Harpham: Hope 1893: 197–8; Whelan and Taylor 1989: 64–5. My visit November 2005.

St Helen's Well, Goodmanham: Whelan and Taylor 1989: 69; Thompson 2004: 135–6; Harte 2008.

St John's Well, Harpham: Hope 1893: 196–7; Whelan and Taylor 1989: 64; Hopkins 1999: 42; Farmer 1997: 265; Harte 2008. My visit November 2005.

More information on East Yorkshire wells: Whelan and Taylor 1989: 63–74; Harte 2008; www.halikeld.f9.co.uk/holywells/

YORKSHIRE: NORTH

St Cedd's, St Chad's and St Ovin's Wells, Lastingham: Jenkins 2000: 778; Whelan and Taylor 1989: 12–13; Harte 2008; PastScape; www.halikeld.f9.co.uk/holywells/. My visit November 2005.

Dropping Well and Wishing Well, Knaresborough: Publications available at the Dropping Well; TMP. My visit April 1993.

Ebbing and Flowing Well (and Bank Well), Giggleswick: Whelan and Taylor 1989: 56–7; TMP. My visit November 2005.

St Helen's Well, Farnhill: Shepherd 2002: 40; Harte 2008.

St Helen's Well, Kirkby Overblow: Whelan and Taylor 1989: 46–7; Shepherd 2002: 41; Harte 2008.

St Hilda's Well, Hinderwell: Whelan and Taylor 1989: 24; Harte 2008; TMP; PastScape. My visit November 2005.

Our Lady's Well, Threshfield: Whelan and Taylor 1989: 54; Shepherd 2002: 44–5; Harte 2008.

Mary Magdalene Well, Spaunton: Whelan and Taylor 1989: 11; Harte 2008. My visit November 2005.

Old Wives' Well, Stape: Whelan and Taylor 1989: 14; www.themodernantiquarian.com/site/6683. My visit November 2005.

More information on North Yorkshire wells: Whelan and Taylor 1989; Harte 2008; www.halikeld.f9.co.uk/holywells/.

YORKSHIRE: SOUTH AND WEST

St James's Well, Midhopestones: Wilson 1991: 10–11, 25; Harte 2008.

Lady Well, Hartshead: Shepherd 1994: 62–3; Shepherd 2002: 35; Harte 2008.

Peace Well, Dore: Wilson 1991: 24–5.

Town's Well, Hampole: Thompson 2004: 122–3.

White Wells, Ilkley: Thompson 2004: 162–4; Bord 2004: 98; Denbigh 1981: 184–7; Shepherd 1994: 74–8; www.ilkley.org/iguide/ramblerumble.htm.

More information on South and West Yorkshire wells: Wilson 1991; Shepherd 1994; Shepherd 2002; Whelan and Taylor 1989; Harte 2008.

Wales

More information on Welsh wells: Jones 1954; Doughty 2001; Davis 2003; Thomas 2004.

ANGLESEY
Ffynnon Cerrigceinwen, Cerrigceinwen: Jones 1954: 141; Thomas 2004: 55. My latest visit November 2004.
Ffynnon Seiriol, Penmon: Jones 1954: 142–3; Thomas 2004: 185–7; Davis 2003: 105–7; Edwards 1994: 9, 10; Thompson 2004: 40–2. My latest visit November 2004.
Ffynnon Wenfaen, Rhoscolyn: Jones 1954: 143; Thomas 2004: 116–18; Sharp 1997: 145; Davis 2003: 108. My latest visit November 2004.

CARMARTHENSHIRE
St Anthony's Well, Llansteffan: Jones 1954: 163; Davis 2003: 35; Thomas 2004: 36–7. My visit April 1997.
Ffynnon Deilo, Llandeilo: Jones 1954: 164; Dearden 1989; www.llandeilofawr.org.uk/history.htm. My visit October 2007.
Ffynnon Gwyddfaen, Llandyfan: Jones 1954: 60–1, 115–16, 167; Davis 2003: 32; www.terrynorm.ic24.net/llandyfan%20church.htm. My visit October 2007.
More information on Carmarthenshire wells: Buckley 1995: 6–9.

CEREDIGION
Ffynnon Gybi, Llangybi: Jones 1954: 15, 159; Thomas 2004: 67–8; Davis 2003: 67. My latest visit October 2007.
Ffynnon Llawddog, Cenarth: Thomas 2004: 145. My latest visit October 2007.

CONWY
Ffynnon Gelynin, Llangelynin: Jones 1954: 101, 150; Thomas 2004: 56–8; Davis 2003: 97–8. My latest visit July 2006.
Ffynnon Drillo, Llandrillo-yn-Rhos: Jones 1954: 152;. Gray Hulse 1995: 31–42; Thomas 2004: 209–12; Davis 2003: 86; Thompson 2004: 62–3. My latest visit May 2005.

DENBIGHSHIRE
Ffynnon Beuno, Tremeirchion: Jones 1954: 178; Thomas 2004: 45–6; Davis 2003: 87; TMP. My latest visit July 2007.
Ffynnon Ddyfnog, Llanrhaeadr: Jones 1954: 35, 50, 62, 70, 173; Davis 2003: 84; TMP. My latest visit July 2007.
Ffynnon Degla, Llandegla: Jones 1954: 104, 173. My latest visit August 2007.
Ffynnon Fair, Cefn Meiriadog: Jones 1954: 174; Davis 2003: 91–91; Thomas 2004: 156–9; Wright 1968. My latest visit July 2004.
Ffynnon Sara, Derwen: Jones 1954: 177; Davis 2003: 73; Thomas 2004: 183–4; Betsy Gray (TMP). My latest visit February 2007.

FLINTSHIRE
Ffynnon Wenfrewy, Holywell: Jones 1954: 38, 39, 49–50, 59, 62, 64, 65, 66, 70, 72, 77, 82, 102, 113; Davis 2003: 76–9; Thomas 2004: 219–23; Gray Hulse 1994b: 11–17; Bord 2006: 71–3 (and see index); www.saintwinefrideswell.com; Betsy Gray and Tim Prevett (TMP). My latest visit June 2006.

GWYNEDD

Ffynnon Beuno, Clynnog Fawr: Jones 1954: 16, 148; Davis 2003: 100; Thomas 2004: 43–5; TMP. My latest visit March 2007.

Ffynnon Beris, Nant Peris: Jones 1954: 72, 109, 147–8; Davis 2003: 93–4; Thomas 2004: 175–6; Thompson 2004: 31–2; Betsy Gray (TMP). My latest visit September 2006.

Ffynnon Fair, Bryncroes: Jones 1954: 150; Davis 2003: 103; Thomas 2004: 151; TMP. My visit September 1988.

Ffynnon Gybi, Llangybi: Jones 1954: 27, 74, 110, 111, 151; Davis 2003: 101–3; Thomas 2004: 68–72; Thompson 2004: 51–3; Welsh Office guidebook (1982); TMP. My latest visit May 1996.

MONMOUTHSHIRE

St Anne's Well, Trellech: Jones 1954: 95, 196; Davis 2003: 60–1; Thomas 2004: 33–5; Sharp 1997: 142–3; Poultner 2000; Zaluckyj 2006: 391; Betsy Gray (TMP). My latest visit May 1996.

St Tewdric's Well, Mathern: Jones 1954: 195; Davis 2003: 49–50; Thomas 2004: 204–5; Farmer 1997: 462; Zaluckyj 2006: 375. My latest visit September 2005.

More information on Monmouthshire wells: The Wellsprings Fellowship 2000.

PEMBROKESHIRE

Bletherston Holy Well: Jones 1954: 210; Thomas 2004: 47–8; Trier 2004. My visit October 2007.

Burton Church Well: Jones 1954: 210; Davis 2003: 26; Thomas 2004: 51–2; Trier 2004.

St Govan's Well, Bosherston: Jones 1954: 66, 79, 100, 208; Davis 2003: 25; Thomas 2004: 109–11; TMP. My latest visit April 1997.

Gumfreston Church Wells: Jones 1954: 90, 211; Davis 2003: 30; Thomas 2004: 114–16; Silverman 1995: 20–2; Trier 2004. My latest visit April 1997.

Llanllawer Holy Well: Jones 1954: 211; Davis 2003: 33–4; Thomas 2004: 142–3; Trier 2004; TMP. My latest visit October 2007.

St Justinian's Well, St Justinian: Rees 1992: 30–1; Jones 1954: 36–7, 209; Davis 2003: 39; Thomas 2004: 133–6. My latest visit September 2003.

Margaret's Well, Templeton: Thomas 2004: 148; Davis 2003: 41; Trier 2004. My latest visit October 2007.

St Non's Well, St Davids: Rees 1992: 15–16; Trier 1998: 29–31; Jones 1954: 27, 42, 69, 79, 210; Davis 2003: 39–40; Thomas 2004: 168–72; Thompson 2004: 53–5; TMP. My latest visit October 2007.

More information on Pembrokeshire wells: Trier 1995: 17–22; Trier 1998: 28–31; Trier 2004.

POWYS

Ffynnon Fair, Llanfair Caereinion: Jones 1954: 197–8; Davis 2003: 66; Zaluckyj 2006: 84–5; Tim Prevett (TMP). My latest visit April 2005.

Ffynnon Fair, Pilleth: Jones 1954: 217; Davis 2003: 68; Thomas 2004: 151–2. My visit September 2005.

Ffynnon Gynydd, Glasbury: Jones 1954: 217; Davis 2003: 44–5; Thomas 2004: 72–4; Zaluckyj 2006: 161. My visit September 2005.

St Issui's Well, Partrishow: Jones 1954: 145; Davis 2003: 51–2; Thomas 2004: 129–31; Zaluckyj 2006: 245–6. My latest visit September 2004.

Ffynnon Myllin, Llanfyllin: Jones 1954: 198–9; Davis 2003: 66; Thomas 2004: 162–3; Zaluckyj 2006: 86–7; TMP. My latest visit April 2005.

SOUTH WALES

St Cenydd's Well, Llangennith: Jones 1954: 184; Davis 2003: 28–9; Thomas 2004: 59–60.

St David's Well and St John's Well, Newton Nottage: Jones 1954: 89, 181, 183; Davis 2003: 55–6; Thomas 2004: 131–3.

Ffynnon Deilo, Llandaff: Jones 1954: 181. My visit September 2005.

Ffynnon Fair, Penrhys: Jones 1954: 19, 47, 60, 93–4, 182; Davis 2003: 53–4; Gray 1996. My latest visit September 2005.

Trinity Well, Ilston: Jones 1954: 26; Davis 2003: 28. My visit April 1997.

Scotland

More information on Scottish wells: Mackinlay (1893) is indispensable for Scottish holy well folklore; a five-page list of wells in all regions is given in Barrett (1914). The best modern sources are Morris (1982) and Miller (2000 and 2004). Smith (1997) is a useful short guide to Scotland's saints and sacred places, with numerous holy wells mentioned. Also check the Megalithic Portal online.

ABERDEENSHIRE

St Drostan's Well, New Aberdour: Morris 1982: 36–8.

ANGUS

St Fergus's Well, Glamis: Miller 2004: 124; Morris 1982: 46; www.bath.ac.uk/~prsrlp/kernunos/scotland/wellglam.htm; Betsy Gray (TMP).

More information on Angus wells: A long list of wells, but with no indication of their present status, can be found at www.fife.50megs.com/scots-folklore-magic-wells.htm.

ARGYLL AND BUTE

St Columba's Well, Keil Point: Betsy Gray (TMP).

Holy Well, Kilmory Oib: Betsy Gray (TMP: consult entry for full location details).

St Ninian's Well, Dervaig: Betsy Gray (TMP).

BORDERS

Cheese Well, Minchmoor: Morris 1982: 152; Miller 2000: 71; Miller 2004: 116–17; www.ancient-stones.co.uk/borders/021/023/details.htm.

St Ronan's Well, Innerleithen: Morris 1982: 151. My visit October 2006.

Tamlane's Well, Carterhaugh: Morris 1982: 175. My visit October 2006.

DUMFRIES AND GALLOWAY

Brow Well, Ruthwell: Morris 1982: 84; Dinwiddie 1999: 47. My latest visit April 2007.

Chipperdingan Well, Port Logan: Morris 1982: 183; MacQueen 2005: 117–19. My visit September 2007.

St Finnan's Well, Chapel Finian: Morris 1982: 183. My latest visit September 2007.

St Medan's Well, Monreith: Morris 1982: 180–1; www.gallowaygazette.co.uk/galloway-past?articleid=3085061. (St Medan's Well at Mull of Galloway: Morris 1982: 182; Mackinlay 1893: 92–4.) My visit September 2007.

St Queran's Well, Islesteps: Morris 1982: 134–5; Mackinlay 1893: 196–7; Miller 2000: 100; Miller 2004: 145. My visit April 2007.

EAST LOTHIAN

St Baldred's Well, East Linton: Morris 1982: 140. My visit October 2006.

St Bay's Well, Dunbar: Morris 1982: 140. My visit October 2006.

Rood Well, Stenton: Morris 1982: 142. My latest visit October 2006.

EDINBURGH

St Anthony's Well, Holyrood Park: www.ancient-stones.co.uk/lothian/041/045/details.htm; Morris 1982: 94; Black 1884: 174–5; TMP. My visit October 2006.

Balm Well, Liberton: Williams 2000; Morris 1982: 95–6; Miller 2000: 88; Miller 2004: 138; Betsy Gray (TMP). My visit October 2006.

St Margaret's Well, Holyrood Park: www.cyberscotia.com/ancient-lothian/pages/holyrood-st-margarets-well.html; Morris 1982: 94–5; Betsy Gray (TMP). My visit October 2006.

St Mungo's Well, Currie: Betsy Gray (TMP).

St Triduana's Well, Restalrig: Farmer 1997: 480; Miller 2004: 146; Morris 1982: 96–8; Notman 1985; Betsy Gray (TMP). My visit October 2006.

FIFE

St Fillan's Well, Pittenweem: Morris 1982: 106; Miller 2000: 91; Betsy Gray (TMP).

HIGHLAND

St Bennet's Well, Avoch: Morris 1982: 165–6; Vaux 1902: 365–7; Sharp 1997: 172–3.

St Boniface's Well, Munlochy: Morris 1982: 169; Miller 2004: 133–4; Thompson 2004: 141–3; Sharp 1997: 174–5.

St Ignatius's Well, Glassburn: Morris 1982: 114; Betsy Gray (TMP).

St John the Baptist's Well, Fodderty: Miller 2000: 92; Miller 2004: 140; Betsy Gray (TMP).

St John the Baptist's Well, Helmsdale: Betsy Gray (TMP).

St Mary's Well, Culloden: Morris 1982: 112; Miller 2000: 96; Miller 2004: 142; Thompson 2004: 143–4; Sharp 1997: 175; Betsy Gray (TMP).

St Ninian's Well, Drumnadrochit: Morris 1982: 118; Betsy Gray (TMP).

Well of the Dead, Culloden: Morris 1982: 112; Tim Prevett (TMP); www.highlanderweb.co.uk/bloody/culloden/bloody3.htm.

Well of the Heads, Loch Oich: Morris 1982: 115; Sharp 1997: 167. My visit September 1998.

ISLE OF SKYE

Tobar Ashik, Broadford: Forbes 1923: 425; Betsy Gray (TMP). My visit September 1998.

More information on Skye wells: *Place-Names of Skye* contains 6 pages of Tobar names, referring to wells which once existed on Skye, but their present condition is uncertain.

MORAY

St Fumac's Well, Botriphnie: Morris 1982: 68; www.botriphnie.org.uk/wildlife_walks.htm; Betsy Gray (TMP).

St Mary's Well, Orton: Morris 1982: 150; Thompson 2004: 120–1; www.bath.ac.uk/~prsrlp/kernunos/scotland/maryorto.htm; Betsy Gray (TMP).

Pictish Well, Burghead: Miller 2004: 114; Morris 1982: 147; Mackinlay 1893: 98–100; Thompson 2004: 91–4; Sharp 1997: 95; Betsy Gray (TMP).

NORTH LANARKSHIRE

Holy Well, Carfin Lourdes Grotto: www.carfin.org.uk. My visit October 2006.

PERTH AND KINROSS

St David's Well, Weem: Thompson 2004: 64–7; Morris 1982: 164.

Well at Scotlandwell: Morris 1982: 124–5; Thompson 2004: 127–8. My visit June 1991.

STIRLING

St Fillan's Well, Strathfillan: Morris 1982: 162; Sharp 1997: 146–7; Mackinlay 1893: 123–6; Betsy Gray (TMP). My visit September 1998.

Bibliography

Many of the articles that first appeared in *Source* magazine can now be found online on the *Living Spring* website (http://people.bath.ac.uk/liskmj/living-spring/sourcearchive/front.htm), as can the two issues of the online journal *Living Spring* (http://people.bath.ac.uk/liskmj/living-spring/journal/home.htm).

There are numerous other websites where information on holy wells can be found: see the listings at the beginning of the Sources.

Alderson, Frederick, 1973, *The Inland Resorts and Spas of Britain,* David and Charles.

Baker, Rowland G.M., 1982–3, 'Holy Wells and Magical Waters of Surrey', *Surrey History,* vol.2 no.4, reprinted in *Source* 1 (March 1985) and available online: www.moleseyhistory.co.uk/books/surrey/holywells/index.html

Baring-Gould, S., 1899, *Book of the West: Cornwall,* Methuen; reprinted by Wildwood House 1981.

Barrett, Michael, 1914, *Footprints of the Ancient Scottish Church,* Sands and Co.

Bates, A.W., 1993–4, 'Healing Waters: Holy Wells and Spas of Warwickshire', *Warwickshire History,* vol.9 no.2 (Winter).

Bayley, Michael, 1994, 'Rebecca's Well on Crazies Hill', *Source,* New Series 2 (Winter).

— 1995, 'The Ladywell at Speen', *Source,* New Series 3 (Spring).

Binnall, P.B.G. and M. Hope Dodds, 1897– 1904, 'Holy Wells in Northumberland and Durham', *Proceedings of the Society of Antiquaries of Newcastle-upon-Tyne,* vols 9–11.

Black, William George, 1884, 'Holy Wells in Scotland', *Folklore Journal,* vol. 2 no. 6, 173-175.

Bond, Francis, 1914, *Dedications and Patron Saints of English Churches,* Oxford University Press.

Bord, Janet, 2004, *The Traveller's Guide to Fairy Sites,* Gothic Image Publications.

— 2006, *Cures and Curses: Ritual and Cult at Holy Wells,* Heart of Albion.

Bord, Janet and Colin, 1985, *Sacred Waters: Holy Wells and Water Lore in Britain and Ireland,* Granada Publishing.

Broadhurst, Paul, 1988, *Secret Shrines: In Search of the Old Holy Wells of Cornwall,* Paul Broadhurst.

Brown, Mary Gifford, 1990, *An Illuminated Chronicle: Some Light on the Dark Ages of Saint Milburga's Lifetime*, Bath University Press.

Brown, Theo, 1957, 'Holy and Notable Wells of Devon', *Transactions of the Devonshire Association for the Advancement of Science, Literature and Art*, vol.89.

Bruce, J.R., 1968, *The Manx Archaeological Survey, Sixth Report 1966: Keeills and Burial Grounds in the Sheading of Rushen*, The Manx Museum and National Trust.

Buckley, Kemmis, 1994, 'The Well and the Skull', *Source*, New Series 2 (Winter).

— 1995, 'Some Holy Wells of South Carmarthenshire', *Source*, New Series 3 (Spring).

— 1988, 'St. Rumbold and His Well', *Source*, New Series 6 (Summer).

Burne, Charlotte S., 1883, *Shropshire Folk-Lore*, Trübner and Co.; reprinted by EP Publishing, 1974.

Collins, Andrew, 1983, *The Running Well Mystery*, The Supernaturalist.

— 1983, 'Runwell Update – The Good News and the Bad!', *Earthquest News* 6 (Spring).

Colloby, Christine, 1992, 'Sandwell Priory', *Mercian Mysteries* 10 (February).

Cook, Mildred M., 1987, 'Saint Withburga and Her Well at East Dereham', *Source* 6; online at *Living Spring* website.

Cope, Phil, 2005, *Well Kept Secrets: New Photographs of the Holy Wells of Wales*, Culture and Democracy.

Cowen, Thomas E., 1910, *History of the Village of Stoney Middleton*, Wilfred Edmunds; online at www.genuki.org.uk/big/eng/DBY/StoneyMiddleton/Cowen/index.html

Crawshaw, John, 1994, 'Hollinshead Hall Holy Well', *Source*, New Series 2 (Winter).

Cubbon, A.M., 1967, *The Ancient and Historic Monuments of the Isle of Man: A General Guide including a selected list with notes*, 3rd edition, The Manx Museum and National Trust.

— (editor), 1973, *Prehistoric Sites in the Isle of Man: A Selection Visited by Members of the Prehistoric Society, April, 1971*, The Manx Museum and National Trust.

Cunliffe, Barry, 1995, *Roman Bath* (revised edn), B.T. Batsford/English Heritage.

Darley, Lois and John, 1995, 'Southam wells "revisited"', *Mercian Mysteries* 22 (February).

Darwen, Norman, 1988, 'Some Holy Wells In and Around Preston', *Source* 8.

Davis, Paul, 2003, *Sacred Springs: In Search of the Holy Wells and Spas of Wales*, Blorenge Books.

Dearden, Linda, 1989, 'St Teilo and Two Wells in West Wales', *Source* 9 (Spring).

Denbigh, Kathleen, 1981, *A Hundred British Spas*, Spa Publications.

Dinwiddie, J.L., 1999, *The Ruthwell Cross* (8th edn), privately printed.

Doble, Gilbert H., 1970, *The Saints of Cornwall: Part Five: Saints of Mid-Cornwall*, Dean and Chapter of Truro Cathedral.
— 1977, *The Saints of Cornwall: Part Six: Saints of North Cornwall*, Llanerch Publishers, for the Dean and Chapter of Truro Cathedral.
Doughty, Audrey, 2001, *Spas and Springs of Wales*, Gwasg Carreg Gwalch.

Edwards, Nancy, 1994, 'Holy Wells in Wales and Early Christian Archaeology', *Source,* New Series 1 (Autumn)
Ekwall, Eilert, 1960, *The Concise Oxford Dictionary of English Place-Names* (4th edn), Oxford University Press.
Elliott, J. Steele, 1933, 'Bygone Water Supplies', *Survey of Ancient Buildings Volume II*, The Bedfordshire Historical Record Society.

Farmer, David, 1997, *The Oxford Dictionary of Saints* (4th edn), Oxford University Press.
Faull, 2004, Terry, *Secrets of the Hidden Source: In Search of Devon's Ancient and Holy Wells,* Halsgrove.
Forbes, Alexander Robert, 1923, *Place-Names of Skye and Adjacent Islands: With Lore, Mythical, Traditional and Historical,* Alexander Gardner.
Fraser, Maxwell, 1948, *In Praise of Manxland* (2nd edn), Methuen.

Gill, W. Walter, 1929, *A Manx Scrapbook,* J.W. Arrowsmith; see also www.isle-of-man.com/manxnotebook/fulltext/scrap1/index.htm
Gillett, H.M., 1957, *Shrines of Our Lady in England and Wales,* Samuel Walker.
Gray, Madeleine, 1996, 'Penrhys: The Archaeology of a Pilgrimage', *Morgannwg* (Journal of the Glamorgan History Society), vol. 40; online at http://cistercian-way.newport.ac.uk/Penrhys/reconstruction.html
Gray Hulse, Tristan, 1994a, 'The Whistlebitch Well, Utkinton, Cheshire', *Source,* New Series 1 (Autumn).
— 1994b, 'Holywell – Clwyd', *Source,* New Series 1 (Autumn).
— 1994c, 'St Teilo and the Head Cult', *Source,* New Series 2 (Winter).
— 1995, 'A Modern Votive Deposit at a North Welsh Holy Well, *Folklore* 106.
— 1998, 'Three Saints, Two Wells and a Welsh Parish', *Source,* New Series 6 (Summer).
— 2002, 'The Documentation of Ffynnon Ddeier: Some Problems Reconsidered', *Living Spring* 2 (November).
Green, Miranda, 1994, 'The Religious Symbolism of Llyn Cerrig Bach and Other Early Sacred Water Sites', *Source* New Series 1 (Autumn).

Hackwood, Frederick William, 1924, *Staffordshire Customs, Superstitions and Folklore,* The Mercury Press; reprinted 1974 EP Publishing.
Harte, Jeremy, 1985a, 'Dorset Holy Wells', *Source* 1 (March).
— 1985b, 'The Holy Wells of Somerset', *Source* 2 (July) .

— 2000, 'Holy Wells and Other Holy Places', *Living Spring* 1 (May).

— 2008, *The Holy Wells of England: A Sourcebook,* Heart of Albion.

Haynes, Tony, 1986, 'Well-Wishing in St Albans', *Source* 6 (Winter).

Hoggard, Brian, 1999, *Bredon Hill: A Guide to its Archaeology, History, Folklore and Villages,* Logaston Press.

Hole, Christina, 1937, *Traditions and Customs of Cheshire,* Williams and Norgate; reprinted 1970 by S.R. Publishers)

— 1954, *English Shrines and Sanctuaries,* B.T. Batsford.

— 1966, *Saints in Folklore,* G. Bell and Sons.

Hone, William, 1838, *The Every-Day and Table Book,* Thomas Tegg.

Hope, Robert Charles, 1893, *The Legendary Lore of the Holy Wells of England,* Elliot Stock; reprinted: Singing Tree Press 1968; online at: www.antipope.org/feorag/wells/hope/contents.html

Hopkins, Pamela, 1999, *St John of Beverley,* Hallgarth Publishing.

Horne, Ethelbert, 1923, *Somerset Holy Wells and Other Named Wells,* Somerset Folk Press.

Hughes, John L., 1989, 'Caesar's Well, Wimbledon Common', *Source* 9 (Spring).

Hunt, Laurence, 1985, 'The Holy Wells of West Penwith, Cornwall', *Source* 3.

— 1987, 'Ancient, Healing and Holy Wells of County Durham', *Source* 7.

— 1989, 'Some Ancient and Holy Wells of Devon', *Source* 9 (Spring).

— 1994, 'Some Ancient Wells, Springs and Holy Wells of the Cotswolds', *Source,* New Series 2 (Winter).

Hunt, Robert, 1871, *The Drolls, Traditions, and Superstitions of Old Cornwall: Second Series* (original title: *Popular Romances of the West of England*); facsimile of 3rd edn. 1881 printed Llanerch Publishers 1993.

Jenkins, Simon, 2000, *England's Thousand Best Churches,* Penguin Books.

Jones, Francis, 1954, *The Holy Wells of Wales,* University of Wales Press; facsimile reissue 1992.

Jones, Trefor, 1999, *The English Saints: East Anglia,* The Canterbury Press.

Jordan, Katherine M., 1998, 'Seven Wiltshire Wells and Their Folklore', *Source,* New Series 6 (Summer).

Jordan, Katy, 2000a, *The Haunted Landscape: Folklore, Ghosts and Legends of Wiltshire,* Ex Libris Press.

— 2000b, 'Wiltshire Healing Wells and the Strange Case of Purton Spa', *Living Spring* 1 (May).

Jordan, Katy, and Rich Pederick, 2000, 'St Aldhelm's Well, Doulting, Somerset', *Living Spring* 1 (May)

Kift, Mary, 2004, *Life in Old Caversham* (2nd edn), published in collaboration with John and Lindsey Mullaney of the Caversham Bookshop.

Kightly, Charles, 1986, *The Customs and Ceremonies of Britain: An Encyclopaedia of Living Traditions,* Thames and Hudson.

Knight, Peter, 1998, *Sacred Dorset,* Capall Bann.

Lane-Davies, A., 1970, *Holy Wells of Cornwall: A Guide,* Federation of Old Cornwall Societies.

Leather, Ella Mary, 1912, *The Folk-Lore of Herefordshire,* Jakeman and Carver, 1912; reprinted S.R. Publishers 1970.

Legg, Rodney, 1997, *Mysterious Dorset,* Dorset Publishing Company.

Leigh, Rumwold, 2000, *In Search of Saint Rumwold,* Sveti Ivan Rilski Press.

Love, Rosalind C. (editor and translator), 1996, *Three Eleventh-Century Anglo-Latin Saints' Lives,* Clarendon Press.

Lovegrove, Chris, 1986, 'St Anne in the Wood, Brislington', *Source* 4.

McIntire, W.T., 1944, 'The Holy Wells of Cumberland', *Transactions of the Cumberland and Westmorland Antiquarian and Archaeological Society,* vol.44.

Mackinlay, James M., 1893, *Folklore of Scottish Lochs and Springs,* William Hodge and Co.; facsimile reprint by Llanerch Publishers 1993.

MacLeod, Finlay, 2000, *The Healing Wells of the Western Isles,* Acair.

MacQueen, John, 2005, *St Nynia,* Birlinn.

Mann, Nicholas R., and Philippa Glasson, 2005, *Avalon's Red and White Springs: A Guide to the Healing Waters at Glastonbury,* Green Magic.

Martin, Valerie, 1985, 'Some Holy Wells in Kent', *Source* 2 (July).

Meyrick, J., 1982, *Holy Wells: A Pilgrim's Guide to the Holy Wells of Cornwall and Their Saints,* J. Meyrick.

Miller, Joyce, 2000, *Myth and Magic: Scotland's Ancient Beliefs and Sacred Places,* Goblinshead.

— 2004, *Magic and Witchcraft in Scotland,* Goblinshead.

Moore, A.W., 1894, 'Water and Well-Worship in Man', *Folklore* vol.5.

Morgan, Chris (editor), 1986, *Strange Oxford,* Oxford Golden Dawn Publishing.

Morrell, R.W., 1988, *Nottinghamshire Holy Wells and Springs,* APRA Press.

— 1991, 'Southam Holy Well', *Mercian Mysteries* 9 (November).

— 1992, 'The Stowe Bandstand or What Not To Do With a Holy Well', *Mercian Mysteries* 13 (November).

— 1994, 'Some Notes on St Anne's Well at Buxton', *Mercian Mysteries* 18 (February); online at www.indigogroup.co.uk/edge/Buxton.htm

— 1995, 'Some Observations on the Earliest Spring Called After Robin Hood', *Source,* New Series 4 (Summer).

Morris, Ruth and Frank, 1982, *Scottish Healing Wells: Healing, holy, wishing and fairy wells of the mainland of Scotland,* The Alethea Press.

Notman, Robert Black, 1985, *Restalrig Parish Church: A Short Account of its History and Traditions* (4th edn), The Society of Friends of Restalrig Parish Church.

O'Malley, B.B., 2005, *The Holy Wells of Pembrokeshire and Their Associated Native Saints (excluding St David);* unpublished thesis, University of Wales (Lampeter).

Orme, Nicholas, 2000, *The Saints of Cornwall,* Oxford University Press.

Osborne, Bruce, 1994, 'The Springs and Wells of the South Downs': part 1 in *Source*, New Series 2 (Winter)
— 1995, 'The Springs and Wells of the South Downs': part 2 in *Source*, New Series 3 (Spring).
— 1998, 'The Springs and Wells of the South Downs': part 3 in *Source*, New Series 6 (Summer)

Otter, Laurens, 1985, 'Notes Towards a Survey of Shropshire Holy Wells': part 1 in *Source* 3 (November).
— 1986a, 'Notes Towards a Survey of Shropshire Holy Wells': part 2 in *Source* 4 (March).
— 1986b, 'Notes Towards a Survey of Shropshire Holy Wells': part 3 in *Source* 6 (Winter).
— 1987, 'Notes Towards a Survey of Shropshire Holy Wells': part 4 in *Source* 7 (May).
— 1988, 'Notes Towards a Survey of Shropshire Holy Wells': part 5 in *Source* 8 (Autumn)

Owen, Elias, 1893, 'The Holy Wells of North Wales', *Collections Historical and Archaeological Relating to Montgomeryshire,* vol.27, Powysland Club.

Page, Jim Taylor, 1990, *Cumbrian Holy Wells,* North West Catholic History Society.

Palmer, Roy, 1994, *The Folklore of Gloucestershire*, Westcountry Books.
— 2004, *The Folklore of Shropshire,* Logaston Press.

Parish, R.B., 2002, 'The Holy Well, or St Cloud's Well, at Longthorpe Park near Peterborough', *Living Spring* 2 (November).

Park, Lesley, 1987, 'Cumbrian Well Waking', *Source* 6.

Patchell, P.M. and E.M., 1987, 'The Wells of Old Warwickshire', *Source* 6.

Paton, Cyril I., 1941, 'Manx Calendar Customs: Wells', *Folklore* 52.

Pennick, Nigel, 1985, 'Cambridgeshire Wells', *Source* 1 (March).

Pickford, Doug, 1994, *Staffordshire: Its Magic and Mystery,* Sigma Leisure.

Porteous, Crichton, 1949, *The Beauty and Mystery of Well-dressing,* Pilgrim Press.

Porter, Enid, 1974, *The Folklore of East Anglia*, B.T. Batsford.

Potter, Chesca, 1985, 'The River of Wells', *Source* 1 (March).

Potter, Clive, 1985, 'The Holy Wells of Leics and Rutland', *Source* 1 (March).

Poultner, Stephanie, 2000, 'Wells and Springs Around Trellech', *Living Spring* 1 (May).

Quiller-Couch, M. and L., 1894, *Ancient and Holy Wells of Cornwall,* Chas. J. Clark.

Quinn, Phil, 1999, *The Holy Wells of Bath and Bristol Region,* Logaston Press.

Rahtz, Philip, 1993, *English Heritage Book of Glastonbury*, B.T. Batsford/English Heritage.

Rattue, James, 1986, 'Some Wells in the South and West', part 1, *Source* 5.
— 1987a, 'Some Wells in the South and West', part 2, *Source* 6.
— 1987b, 'Some Wells in the South and West', part 3, *Source* 7.
— 1988, 'Some Wells in the South and West', part 4, *Source* 8.
— 1989, 'Some Wells in the South and West', part 5, *Source* 9.
— 1990, 'An Inventory of Ancient and Holy Wells in Oxfordshire', *Oxoniensia*, vol.55.
— 1993, 'An Inventory of Ancient, Holy and Healing Wells in Leicestershire', *Transactions of Leicestershire Archaeological and Historical Society*, vol.67.
— 1995, *The Living Stream: Holy Wells in Historical Context,* The Boydell Press.
— 2003a, *The Holy Wells of Buckinghamshire,* Umbra Press.
— 2003b, *The Holy Wells of Kent,* Umbra Press.
Rees, Nona, 1992, *St David of Dewisland,* Gomer Press.

Sant, Jonathan, 1994, *The Healing Wells of Herefordshire,* Moondial.
Schofield, Nicholas, post-2002, *Our Lady of Willesden: A Brief History of the Shrine and Parish,* no publisher named.
Sharp, Mick, 1997, *Holy Places of Celtic Britain,* Blandford.
Shepherd, Val, 1994, *Historic Wells In and Around Bradford,* Heart of Albion.
— 2002, *Holy Wells of West Yorkshire and the Dales,* Lepus Press.
Silverman, Gina, 1995, 'Gumfreston Wells', *Source*, New Series 3 (Spring).
Simpson, Jacqueline, 1976, *The Folklore of the Welsh Border,* B.T. Batsford; revised edn Tempus Publishing 2003.
Smith, Donald, 1997, *Celtic Travellers: Scotland in the Age of the Saints,* The Stationery Office.
Smith, Mike, and David Taylor, 1995; 'The Crown and the Well', *Mercian Mysteries* 22 (February); online at www.indigogroup.co.uk/edge/Stkenelm.htm
Smith, W., 1923, *The Ancient Springs and Streams of the East Riding of Yorkshire,* A. Brown and Son.
Stéphan, John, 1968, *St Brannoc's Chapel and Well, Braunton, N. Devon* (2nd edn); no publisher named.
Stewart, Bob, 1981, *The Waters of the Gap: The Mythology of Aquae Sulis,* Bath City Council.
Stewart, Gerry, 2005, *St Kenelm's Way: From Clent to Cotswold,* Countryside Matters.
Stone, David, 1998, 'The Holy Wells of Holywell, Oxford, part 1: The Well of Saints Winifred and Margaret', *Source,* New Series 6 (Summer).
Straffon, Cheryl, 2005, *Fentynyow Kernow: In Search of Cornwall's Holy Wells* (2nd edn),Meyn Mamvro Publications.

Taylor, Henry, 1999, *The Ancient Crosses and Wells of Lancashire: A Revised Version (Vol. 1 Lonsdale Hundred),* North West Catholic History Society.
— 2002, *The Ancient Crosses and Wells of Lancashire: A Revised Version (Vol. 2 Amounderness Hundred),* North West Catholic History Society.

— 2004, *The Ancient Crosses and Wells of Lancashire: A Revised Version (Vol. 3 Blackburn Hundred)*, North West Catholic History Society.

— 2005, *The Ancient Crosses and Wells of Lancashire: A Revised Version (Vol 4 Salford Hundred)*, North West Catholic History Society.

— 2006, *The Ancient Crosses and Wells of Lancashire: A Revised Version (Vol 5 West Derby Hundred)*, North West Catholic History Society.

— 2007, *The Ancient Crosses and Wells of Lancashire: A Revised Version (Vol 6 Leyland Hundred)*, North West Catholic History Society.

Thomas, Charles, 1994, 'Holy Wells of Camborne', *Source,* New Series 2 (Winter).

Thomas, Chris J., 2004, *Sacred Welsh Waters,* Capall Bann.

Thompson, Beeby, 1911–15, 'Peculiarities of Waters and Wells', *Journal of the Northamptonshire Natural History Society and Field Club,* vol.16 no.128 to vol.18 no.142.

Thompson, Ian, 1999, *Lincolnshire Springs and Wells: A Descriptive Catalogue,* Bluestone Books.

Thompson, Ian and Frances, 2004, *The Water of Life: Springs and Wells of Mainland Britain,* Llanerch Press.

Trier, Julie, 1995, 'The Sacred Springs and Holy Wells of the St Davids Peninsula': part 1, *Source,* New Series 4 (Summer).

— 1998, 'The Sacred Springs and Holy Wells of the St Davids Peninsula': part 2, *Source,* New Series 5 (Spring).

— 2004, *A Study of Holy Wells in Pembrokeshire Including Those of Our Lady and of St David and Their Possible Association with Pilgrimage Routes to St Davids*; unpublished thesis, University of Wales (Lampeter).

Trubshaw, Bob, 1990, *Holy Wells and Springs of Leicestershire and Rutland,* Heart of Albion.

— 2002, *Interactive Little-Known Leicestershire and Rutland* (CD-ROM),Heart of Albion.

Twinch, Carol (ed.), 1989, *Walstan of Bawburgh: Norfolk's Patron Saint of Agriculture,* Media Associates.

— 1995, *In Search of St Walstan: East Anglia's Enduring Legend,* Media Associates.

— 2004, *Saint With the Silver Shoes: The Continuing Search for St Walstan,* Media Associates.

Usher, Howard, 1986, 'The Holy Well at King's Newton, Derbyshire', *Source* 4.

Valentine, Mark, 1984, *The Holy Wells of Northamptonshire,* The Hundreds Press.

— 1985, 'Buckinghamshire Wells', *Source* 2.

Varner, Gary R., 2002, *Sacred Wells: A Study in the History, Meaning, and Mythology of Holy Wells and Waters,* PublishAmerica.

Vaux, J. Edward, 1902, *Church Folk Lore,* Skeffington and Son.

Verrill, A. Hyatt, 1931, *Secret Treasure: Hidden Riches of the British Isles,* D. Appleton and Co.

Walters, R.C. Skyring, 1928, *The Ancient Wells, Springs, and Holy Wells of Gloucestershire: Their Legends, History, and Topography*, The St. Stephen's Press.

Warner, Martin, 1995, 'The Holy Well in the Shrine of Our Lady of Walsingham', *Source,* New Series 3 (Spring).

Waters, Christine, 1980, *Who Was St. Wite? The Saint of Whitchurch Canonicorum*, published by author.

Weaver, Cora, and Bruce Osborne, 1994, *Aquae Malvernensis: A History and Topography of the Springs, Spouts, Fountains and Wells of the Malverns and the Development of a Public Water Supply,* published by Cora Weaver.

— 2006, *The Illumination of St Werstan the Martyr,* published by Cora Weaver.

Wellsprings Fellowship, The, 2000, 'A Gazetteer of Monmouthshire Wellsites', *Living Spring* 1 (May)

Westwood, Jennifer, 1985, *Albion: A Guide to Legendary Britain,* Granada Publishing.

Whelan, Edna, 1985, 'Holy Wells in Yorkshire': part 1, *Source* 3.

— 1986a, 'Holy Wells in Yorkshire': part 2, *Source* 4.

— 1986b, 'Holy Wells in Yorkshire': part 3, *Source* 5.

— 1987a, 'Holy Wells in Yorkshire': part 4, *Source* 6.

— 1987b, 'Holy Wells in Yorkshire': part 5, *Source* 7.

— 1988, 'Holy Wells in Yorkshire': part 6, *Source* 8.

— 1989, 'Holy Wells in Yorkshire': part 7, *Source* 9.

— 2001, *The Magic and Mystery of Holy Wells*, Capall Bann.

Whelan, Edna, and Ian Taylor, 1989, *Yorkshire Holy Wells and Sacred Springs,* Northern Lights.

Whitfeld, H.J., 1852, *Scilly and Its Legends*; facsimile reprint Llanerch 1992.

Williams, Helen, 2000, 'Is There a Healing Well in Liberton?', *Living Spring* 1 (May).

Wilson, Rob, 1991, *Holy Wells and Spas of South Yorkshire,* Northern Arts Publishing.

Wright, Cecil F., 1968, 'Capel Ffynnon Fair: The Chapel of St Mary's Well, near Cefn, Denbighshire', *Transactions of the Ancient Monuments Society*, vol. 15.

Yelton, Michael, 2006, *Alfred Hope Patten and the Shrine of Our Lady of Walsingham,* Canterbury Press.

Zaluckyj, Sarah and John, 2006, *The Celtic Christian Sites of the Central and Southern Marches,* Logaston Press.

Index

Ab Kettleby holy well 105
Aberdeenshire 169
Aconbury 63
Agnes, St 22: Cothelstone well 22
Alban, St 68: St Albans well 68
Alderley Edge 95–6: holy well 95–6;
    wishing well 95–6
Aldhelm, St 22: Doulting well 22
Alice in Wonderland (Carroll) 75
Alkborough 87–8
Alkmund, St 100: Derby well 100
Altarnon 161
Amwell (Great Amwell) 67
Andrew, St 22–3, 116: Kirkandrews-
    on-Eden well 116; Stogursey well,
    22–3; Wells well 23
Anglesey 141–3
Angus 169, 177
Ann, St 63, 79: Aconbury well 63;
    Malvern well 79
Anna, King 92, 94
Anna, St 4, 121
Anne Boleyn's Well (Carshalton) 47
Anne, St 3, 23, 27, 29, 47, 100–1, 156:
    Brislington well 23–4; Buxton well
    100–1; Cadbury Castle well 27;
    Carshalton well 47; Caversham
    well 29–30; St Anne's Hill well
    47; Stanwell well 47; Trellech
    well 156–7; Whitstone well 3–4
Anthony, St 55–7, 143, 174: Forest of
    Dean well 55–7; Holyrood Park
    well 174, 175; Llansteffan well
    143
Antiquity of Glastonbury (William of
    Malmesbury) 27
Antony, St 57
Aquae Malvernensis (Weaver and
    Osborne) 79

Argyll and Bute 170
Arnemetia 100
Arthur, King 24, 27, 95
Arthur's Seat 174
Artington 48
Ashburton 16
Ashwell wishing well 107
Aspatria 117
Astrop: Spa 71; Well 71
Aubrey, John 47
Augustine, St 31–3: Cerne Abbas well
    31–3
Avoch 179
Aylesbury 53

Baker, Rowland G.M. 49
Baldred, St 174: East Linton well 174
Balm Well (Liberton) 174–5
Bank Well (Giggleswick) 136
Baring-Gould, Sabine 5–6
Bass Rock 174
Bath 28, 100: Roman spring 28
Bawburgh 91–2
Bay, St 174: Dunbar well 174
Bazille-Corbin, Revd John Edward 86
Becket, St Thomas 37, 44, 68–9:
    Canterbury well 68; Northampton
    well 68–9
Bede 127, 135
Bedfordshire 52–3
Beeby holy well 106
Bellingham 129
Bennet, St 179: Avoch well 179
Berks Well (Berkswell) 76
Berkshire 29–31
Berkswell 76
Bertram, St 112: Ilam wells 112–13;
    St Bertram's Ash 112
Bettelin 112
Beuno, St 149, 152, 153: Clynnog
    Fawr well 153–4; Holywell well
    152; Tremeirchion well 149
Bevercotes, Sir Everard 106
Beverley Minster 133
Bierton 53–4
Billingborough 87, 88
Binsey 74–5

Binsted holy well 36–7
Bisley: (Surrey) 48–9;
    (Gloucestershire) 62–3
Black Prince, The 43–4, 53
Black Prince's Well, The (Harbledown)
    43–4
Blenheim Palace and Park 72–3
Blessed Virgin Mary *see* Ladywell;
    Mary, St; Our Lady
Blessed Well (Peel) 124
Bletherston holy well 157
Blood Spring (Glastonbury) 24
Blythburgh 94
Bodmin 6–8
Boiling Well (Bromborough) 97
Bone Well (Willingdon) 50
Boniface, St 178: Munlochy well 178
Book of Old Ballads, A (Brock) 72
Borders 170–1
Borlase, William 10, 11
Bosherston 158
Bosworth Battlefield 106
Botriphnie 182–3
Bottesford 87
Bottomless Well (Wells) 23
Boughton Green 69–70
bowssening 4–5
Brackley 70
Bradford on Avon 40–1
Bradnop 114–15
Bradwell-on-Sea 85
Brannoc, St 15: Braunton well 15–16
Bratton 39
Braunton 15–16
Bredon Hill 80
Bride, St 58: St Briavels well 58
Bridget, St 73
Brisco 119
Bristol 23–4
Brittany 13, 23, 61, 161
Broadford 182–3
Brock, H.M. 72
Bromborough 97
Bromfield 118
Brow Well (Ruthwell) 172
Bruce, Robert the 185
Brychan 5, 8, 63

Brynach 15
Bryncroes 154–5
Buckingham 53–4, 70
Buckinghamshire 53–5, 70
Bulcamp 94
Burghead 184
Burne, Charlotte 111
Burns, Robert 172
Burton Church Well 158
Burton Dassett holy well 76–7
Butterfield, William 140
Buxton 100–1

Cadbury Castle 27–8
Caesar's Camp 42
Caesar's Well: Keston 42; Wimbledon
    Common 42
Caldbeck 117, 118
Callington 6, 7
Calmsden cross well 58
Cambridgeshire 83–5
Candida, St 34
Canterbury Cathedral 37, 68
Canute, King 67
Capel Ffynnon Drillo 148
Capel Ffynnon Fair 150–1
Cardiff 165–6
Carew, Richard 8
Carfin Lourdes Grotto well 184
Carmarthenshire 143–5
Caroe, W.D. 50
Carroll, Lewis 75
Carshalton 47
Carterhaugh 170
Cat's Well (Bratton) 39
Catherine of Aragon 75
Catherine, St 32, 39, 48, 74, 106, 123,
    174–5: Artington well 48; Bratton
    well 39; Liberton well 174–5;
    Newark well 106; Port Erin well
    123; Southwell well 106
Caversham 29–30
Cecilia, St 74
Cedd, St 85, 12, 134–5: Lastingham
    well 134–5; North Ockendon well
    85
Cefn Meiriadog 150–1

Ceinwen, St 141
Celynin, St 147–8: Llangelynin well
    147–8
Cenarth 146
Cenydd, St 165: Llangennith well 165
Ceredigion 146
Cerne Abbas 31–3; Giant 32
Cerrigceinwen 141
Chad, St 67, 96–7, 112–14, 134–5:
    Chadkirk well 96–7; Lastingham
    well 134–5;   Stowe well 112–14;
    Ware well 67
Chadkirk 96–7
Chadwell Spring (Ware) 67
Chalice Well (Glastonbury) 24–5, 26
Chapel Finian well 172
Charlcombe 28
Charles I 115
Cheese Well (Minchmoor) 170, 171
Chertsey 47
Cheshire 95–100
Chibbyr Catreeney 123
Chibbyr Noo Pherick 124
Chibbyr Pherick 124
Chibbyr Sheeant 124
Chibbyr y Chrink 123
Chibbyr y Vashtee 122–3
Chibbyr y Woirrey 123
Chibbyr yn Argid 124
Chincough Well (Monreith) 173
Chipperdingan Well (Port Logan) 172
Chittlehampton 20
Church Well (Heysham) 128
Cinderford 57
Clair (Clare/Clarus), St 4
Cleer, St 4: St Cleer well 4–5
Clent Hills 60, 80–2
Clether, St 5: St Clether well 5–6
Clifford, Rosamond 72
Clodock 63–4
Clodock, St 63–4: Clodock well 63–4
Cloud, St 84: Longthorpe well 84
Cloutie Well (Munlochy) 178
Clydawg, St 63–4
Clydog, St 63–4
Clynnog Fawr 153–4
Coenwulf, King 58

Coker, Revd Mr 34
Collinson, John, 26
Colton 116
Columba, St 169, 170: Keil Point well
    170
Condicote cross well 58
Conwy 147–8
Cornwall 3–14, 161
Corrin's Hill 124
Costessey 91
Cothelstone 22
Coventry, Francis 10
Craigie Well (Avoch) 179
Cromwell, Thomas 100
Cropton Forest 139
Cuby, St 6: Duloe well 6, 7
Cuddy's Well (Bellingham) 129
Culloden wells 180–1
Cumbria 116–21
Cuthbert, St 108, 109, 116, 121, 122,
    129, 185: Bellingham well 129;
    Colton well 116; Donington well
    108; Durham well 121; Weem
    well 185
Cybi, St 146, 155–6: Llangybi
    (Ceredigion) well 146; Llangybi
    (Gwynedd) well 155–6
Cynidr, St 163: Glasbury well 163

Daniel's Well (Malmesbury) 39–40
David, St 160–1, 165, 185: Newton
    Nottage well 165; Weem well 185
Decuman, St 25: Watchet well 25
Denbighshire 111, 149–52
Derby 100
Derbyshire 100–5
Dereham 92–3
Dervaig 170
Derwen 151–2
Devon 15–20, 187
Domesday Book 67, 83, 84, 86
Donington 108
Doo Wells (Innerleithen) 170, 171
Dore 139
Dorset 22, 31–6
Dorstone 66
Doulting 22

Dropping Well (Knaresborough) 135–6
Drostan, St 169: New Aberdour well
    169
Druid's Well (Sutton Park) 78–9
Drummer's Well (Harpham) 132–3
drumming wells 133
Drumnadrochit 181
Dull 185
Duloe 6, 7
Dumfries and Galloway 172–4
Dunbar 174
Dunsfold 49–50
Dunstan, St 26: Glastonbury well 26
Dupath Well (Callington) 6, 7
Durham 109, 121–2; Cathedral 121
Dyfnog, St 149: Llanrhaeadr well
    149–50

East Dereham 92–3
East Linton 174
Ebbing and Flowing Well (Giggleswick)
    136
Edgar, King 45
Edinburgh 174–7
Edington: (Somerset) holy well 26;
    (Wiltshire) 41
Edith, St 45–6, 64: Kemsing well 45–6;
    Stoke Edith well 64
Edmund, St 31, 48
Edward, St 34, 48: Sutton Park well 48
Edward the Confessor, King 48
Edwold, St 31–2, 33: Stockwood well
    32, 33
eels, *see* fishes
Egbert, King 139
Egg Well (Bradnop) 114–15
Eleanor, Queen 72
Eligius, St 42: Tottenham well 42
Eloy, St 42: Tottenham well 42
Ely 135; Cathedral 92–3
Embleton 121
Emma's Well (Great Amwell) 67
Erasmus 44
Essex 85–6
Ethelbert, St 65: Hereford well 65–6;
    Marden well 65
Ethelburga, St 46: Lyminge well 46

Etheldreda, Queen 135
Everswell (Woodstock) 72
Exeter 20
Eyam 102, 103
Eye Well (Bodmin) 8

Fair Rosamond's Well (Woodstock)
    72–3
Fairfax, Michael 82
Farnhill 137
Faull, Terry 15, 17
Faverches, Richeldis de 88
Fentynyow Kernow (Straffon) 3
Fergus, St 169: Glamis well 169
Fernyhalgh 126–7
Ffynnon Beris (Nant Peris) 154
Ffynnon Beuno: Holywell 152;
    Tremeirchion 149
Ffynnon Cerrigceinwen (Cerrigceinwen)
    141
Ffynnon Ddyfnog (Llanrhaeadr) 149–50
Ffynnon Degla (Llandegla) 150
Ffynnon Deilo: Llandaff 165–6;
    Llandeilo 143–4
Ffynnon Drillo (Llandrillo-yn-Rhos) 148
Ffynnon Fair: Bryncroes 154–5; Cefn
    Meiriadog 150–1; Llanfair
    Caereinion 161–2; Llansteffan 143;
    Penrhys 166–7; Pilleth 162–3
Ffynnon Gapan (Llanllawer) 159
Ffynnon Gelynin (Llangelynin) 147–8
Ffynnon Gwyddfaen (Llandyfan) 144–5
Ffynnon Gybi: Llangybi (Ceredigion)
    146; Llangybi (Gwynedd) 155–6
Ffynnon Gynydd (Glasbury) 163
Ffynnon Llawddog (Cenarth) 146
Ffynnon Myllin (Llanfyllin) 164, 165
Ffynnon Sara (Derwen) 151–2
Ffynnon Seiriol (Penmon) 141–2
Ffynnon Wen (Llangybi) 146
Ffynnon Wenfaen (Rhoscolyn) 142–3
Ffynnon Wenfrewy (Holywell) 152–3
Fice's Well (Princetown) 16
Fiennes, Celia 100–1
Fife 177–8
Fillan, St 177, 185–6: Pittenweem well
    177–8; Strathfillan well 185–6

Finnan, St 172: Chapel Finian well 172
Fisher, Parzianus, 30
fishes in wells 12, 13, 19, 66, 67, 154, 156
Fitz, Sir John 16
Fitz's Well (Okehampton) 16
Flaxley Abbey 56, 57
Flintshire 150, 152–3
Fodderty 179
Foley, Lady Emily 64
Forest of Dean 55–7
Fremund, St 77
Frideswide, St 74–5
Fritham 38
Fulking spring 50–1
Fulwood 126–7
Fumac, St 182–3: Botriphnie well 182–3

Gainford 122; Spa 122
Galloway 172
Garner, Alan and Robert 95
Garway holy well 66
George, St 48
Giggleswick 136
Gill, W. Walter 122, 123
Glamis 169
Glasbury 163
Glassburn 179, 180
Glastonbury 12, 24–5, 26–7
Glen Roy 124
Gloucester 61
Gloucestershire 55–63, 80, 81
Godstow nunnery 72
Golant 13–14
Golden Well (Dorstone) 66
Goodmanham 133
Goscelin 31, 32, 109
Govan, St 158: Bosherston well 158
Gower 165, 167–8
Gray, Betsy 183
Great Amwell 67
Great Asby 117
Great Malvern 79–80
Greater London 42–3
Gudula, St 16: Ashburton well 16
Guildford 48

Gumfreston Church Wells 159
Guron, St 6: Bodmin well 6–8
Guthred, St 106
Gwenfaen, St 142–3: Rhoscolyn well 142–3
Gwenfrewy, St 152–3: Holywell well 152–3
Gwenllian 87
Gwynedd 153–6
Gwytherin 111

Hall Well (Tissington) 103, 104, 105
Hall, Joseph 9
Hals, William 4
Hampole 139–40
Hampshire 36–8
Hands Well (Tissington) 104, 105
Harbledown 43–4
Harbury 77
Harpham 132–3, 133–4
Harrison, Revd S.N. 123
Hartland 18
Hartshead 139
Hazelbury Bryan holy well 33
head-carrying saints 18, 20, 25, 77, 122
heads at wells 4, 6, 7, 77–8, 140, 149, 181–2
Helen, St 115, 117, 133, 137: Farnhill well 137; Goodmanham well 133; Great Asby well 117; Rushton Spencer well 115; Tissington well 104
Helly Well (Bromfield) 118
Helmsdale 179
Hempsted 60–1
Henry II, King 68, 72
Henry VII, King 23
Henry VIII, King 47, 75, 100
Hereford 65–6
Herefordshire 63–7
Hermitage 34
Hertfordshire 67–8
Hewson, Tom 132–3
Heysham 128
Highland 178–82
Hilda, St 137: Hinderwell well 137
Hinderwell 137

Hollinshead Hall holy well 125–6
Holwell holy well 33–4
Holy Grail 24, 26
Holy House of Nazareth, replica at
    Walsingham 88–90
Holy Wells of Bath and Bristol Region,
    The (Quinn) 22
Holybourne springs 37
Holyrood Park 174, 176
Holystone 130, 132
Holywell: (Cambridgeshire) holy well
    83; (Flintshire) 152–3
Hope, Robert Charles 187
Horne, Dom Ethelbert 22, 23, 24, 27
Horsted Keynes 50
Houghton St Giles 90
Hunt, Laurence 61, 122
Hunt, Robert 11

Ignatius, St 179: Glassburn well 179,
    180
Ilam 112–13
Ilkley 140
Ilston 167–8
immersion 13, 39, 149
incubation 11, 146, 154
Innerleithen 170, 171
Iron's Well (Fritham) 38
Isho(w), St 163–4: Partrishow well
    163–5
Islesteps 173–4
Issui, St 163–4: Partrishow well 163–5
Itinerary (Leland) 23

James, St 139: Midhopestones well
    139
Jesmond Dene 131–2
Jocelin of Furness 123
John of Beverley, St 133–4: Harpham
    well 133–4
John the Baptist, St 48–9, 179: Bisley
    well 48–9; Fodderty well 179;
    Helmsdale well 179
John, St 69, 87, 165: Bottesford well
    87; Boughton Green well 69–70;
    Newton Nottage well 165
Jordan Well (Laneast) 8

Joseph of Arimathea, St 24, 26, 27, 60:
    Glastonbury well 26
Julian, St 108: Ludlow well 108
Justinian, St 159–60: St Justinian well
    159–60

Katherine, St 80: Bredon Hill well 80
Kayne, St 8
Keble, Revd Thomas 62
Keeper's Well (Sutton Park) 79
Keil Point 170
Kein(wen), St 8
Kell Well (Alkborough) 87–8
Kemsing 45–6
Kenelm, St 58–60, 80–2: Romsley well
    80–2; Winchcombe well 58–60
Kent 43–7
Kentigern, St 117, 118: Aspatria well
    117; Bromfield well 118;
    Caldbeck well 117, 118
Keston 42
Keyne, St 8: St Keyne well 8–9
Kilmory Oib holy well 170
King Arthur's Well (Cadbury Castle)
    27–8
King Richard's Well (Bosworth
    Battlefield) 106
King's Newton holy well 101–2
King's Sutton 54, 70–1
Kingcost Well (Monreith) 173
Kings Lynn 89
Kintyre 170
Kirkandrews-on-Eden 116
Kirkby Overblow 137
Kirkmaiden 172
Kirkoswald 119–20
Knapwell 84–5
Knaresborough wells 135–6

Lady Well: (Aconbury) 63; (Glamis)
    169; (Goodmanham) 133;
    (Hartshead) 139; (Holystone) 130;
    (Southwell Minster) 106;
    (Sticklepath) 17; (Threshfield)
    137–8; (Wilcote) 73–4: *see also*
    Lady's Well; Ladyewell; Ladywell;
    Mary, St; Our Lady

Lady Wulfruna's Well (Wolverhampton) 115

Lady's Fountain, The (Blythburgh) 94

Lady's Well (Hermitage) 34

Lady's Well, The (Blythburgh) 94

Ladyewell (Fernyhalgh) 126–7

Ladywell: (Bradford on Avon) 40–1; (Pilton) 17; (Speen) 30–1

Lanarkshire, North 184

Lancashire 125–9

Laneast 8

Lanfranc, Archbishop 44

Lastingham 112, 134–5

Launcells 14

Lawrence, St 38, 40: St Lawrence well 38

Leechwell (Totnes) 17

Leicestershire 105–6

Leland, John 23, 27

Leonard, St 18, 46: Sheepstor well 18; West Malling well 46

Lepers' Well (Fritham) 38

Lhuyd, Edward 144, 146, 149, 151

Liberton 174–5

Lichfield 112–14, 135

Lincolnshire 86–8

Lindisfarne, 109, 122

Little Walsingham 88–91

Living Spring 187, 206

Llandaff 165–6

Llandegla 150

Llandeilo 143–4

Llandrillo-yn-Rhos 148

Llandyfan 144–5

Llanfair Caereinion 161–2

Llanfyllin 164, 165

Llangelynin 147–8

Llangennith 165

Llangybi: (Ceredigion) 146; (Gwynedd) 155–6

Llanlawer holy well 159

Llanrhaeadr-yng-Nghinmeirch 149–50

Llansteffan 143

Llawddog, St 146: Cenarth well 146

Llech Gybi 146

Lodsworth 50

Lonan 124

London 42–3, 67

Long Itchington 77

Longstanton holy well 84

Longthorpe holy well 84

Lothian, East 174

Lourdes, Our Lady of 15

Loveday, John 29

Lower Swell 61–2

Loy, St 42: Tottenham well 42

Lud's Well (Stainton-le-Vale) 88

Ludlow 108

Ludwell Spring (Horsted Keynes) 50

Luston holy well 66

Lyminge 46

Mad(d)ern(us), St 10, 11

Madron, St 11: Madron well 9–11

Maelrubha, St 182: Broadford well 182–3

Mag's Well (Mugswell) 49

Maguire, Fergus 126

Maiden Well (Wooler) 131

Malmesbury 22, 39–40

Malmesbury, William of 27, 39, 74, 134

Maltwood, Katharine 24

Malvern Hills 79–80

Malvern Wells holy well 80

Man, Isle of 122–4

Manx Scrapbook (Gill) 122

Marden 65

Margaret, St 47, 49, 74, 176: Binsey well 74–5; Broomfield well 47; Holyrood Park well 176; Mugswell well 49

Margaret's Well (Templeton) 160

marriage 8

Martin, St 103: Stoney Middleton well 103

Mary, St 26, 28, 43, 88, 122, 123, 131, 143, 150, 154, 162, 162, 166–7, 180, 183, 184: Bryncroes well 154–5; Charlcombe well 28; Cefn Meiriadog well 150–1; Culloden well 180–1; Gainford well 122; Glastonbury well 26; Jesmond well 131–2; Llanfair Caereinion well 161–2; Llansteffan well 143;

Orton well 183; Penrhys well
166–7; Pilleth well 162–3;
Ramsey well 123; Sutton Park well
79; Willesden well 43; *see also*
Ladywell; Our Lady
Mary, St: wells dedicated to her in all
variations of her name: 17, 26, 28,
30, 34, 40, 43, 50, 60, 61, 63, 73,
94, 122, 123, 126, 130, 131, 133,
137, 139, 143, 150, 154, 161,
162, 166, 169, 180, 183
Mary Magdalene Well (Spaunton) 138
Mary the Virgin, St 50: Dunsfold well
49–50
Maserfield, Battle of 109
Mathern 157
Maughold, St 123–4: Maughold well
123–4
Medan, St 172–3: Monreith well
172–3; Mull of Galloway well 172
Meg's Well (Mugswell) 49
Megalithic Portal 3, 187
Merewald, King 109
Merlin 95
Michael, St 11, 15, 37: Michaelstow
well 11; Sopley well 37
Michaelstow 11
Midhopestones 139
Milburga, St 108, 109: Much Wenlock
well 108; Stoke St Milborough
well 109
Minchmoor 170, 171
Miracles of St Cuthbert (Reginald of
Durham) 129
Mochrum 172
Modern Antiquarian, The 187
Moling, St 165
Mompesson, William 103
Mompesson's Well (Eyam) 102, 103
Monkswell (Edington) 41
Monmouthshire 156–7
Monreith 172–3
Moray 182–4
Morgannwg, Lewis 166
Much Wenlock 108
Mugswell 49
Mull, Isle of 170

Mungo, St 118, 132, 172, 176:
Bromfield well 118; Caldbeck well
118; Currie well 176; Holystone
well 132
Munlochy 178
Myddelton, Sir Hugh 67
Myllin, St 165: Llanfyllin well 164, 165

Nant Peris 154
National Wells Index 187
Nectan, St 18–19, 20: Stoke well
18–19; Welcombe well 19–20
Neddy Well (Kirkandrews-on-Eden) 116
Neot, St 12–13, 22: St Neot well 12–13
Nevern 15
New Aberdour 169
New Found Well (Utkinton) 99–100
Newark 106
Newcastle 131–2
Newton Nottage 165
Nias, Revd J.C.S. 73
Ninian, St 119, 130, 170, 172, 181:
Brisco well 119; Dervaig well 170;
Drumnadrochit well 181;
Holystone well 130; Port Logan
well 172
Non, St 160–1: St Davids well 160–1;
St Non's Chapel 160
Norfolk 88–93
North Marston 54–5
North Ockendon 85
Northampton 68–9
Northamptonshire 54, 68–71
Northumberland 129–32
Norwich 92
Nottinghamshire 106
Nun's Well (St Anne's Hill) 47

Offa, King 65
Oich, Loch 181–2
Okehampton 16
Old Wives' Well (Stape) 138–9
Orton 183
Osborne, Bruce 79
Oswald, St 109–10, 119–20, 122, 127:
Durham well 122; Kirkoswald well
119–20; Oswestry well 109–10;

Winwick well 127–8
Oswestry 109–10, 127
Osyth, St 53: Bierton well 53–4
Our Lady 60–1: Hempsted well 60–1;
    Lower Swell well 61–2;
    Threshfield 137–8; *see also*
    Ladywell; Mary, St
Our Lady: at the Well 90; of
    Caversham 29; of Lourdes 15;
    of Penrhys 166–7; of Pilleth 163;
    of the Running Well 86;
    of Walsingham 88–91;
    of Wellesdone (Willesden) 43
Ovin, St 134–5: Lastingham well
    134–5
Owen, St 108: Much Wenlock well
    108
Oxford 74
Oxfordshire 72–6

Palm Sunday 73
Paralipomena Philosophica (Coventry)
    10
Parish, R.B. 84
Partrishow 163–5
PastScape 187
Patricio 163–5
Patrick 122–3
Patrick, St 97, 120–1, 123, 124, 128:
    Bromborough well 97–8;
    Heysham well 128; Lonan well
    124; Patterdale well 120–1; Peel
    well 124; Slyne well 128
Patrisio 163–5
Patten, Revd Alfred Hope 89
Patterdale 120–1
Paulinus, St 130: Holystone well 130
Peace Well (Dore) 139
Peel 124
Pembrokeshire 157–61
Penda, King 70, 109
Penmon 141–2
Pennell, Joseph 35
Penrhys 166–7
Peregrinatio religionis ergo (Erasmus)
    44
Peris, St 154: Nant Peris well 154

Perth and Kinross 185
Peter, St 50, 66–7, 85: Lodsworth well
    50; Peterchurch wells 66–7; West
    Mersea well 85
Peterborough Cathedral 84
Peterchurch 66–7
Petrifying Well (Knaresborough) 135–6
Petroc, St 6
Pevsner, Nikolaus 76
Pictish Well (Burghead) 184
Pilgrim's Way 37, 45, 48
Pilleth 162–3
Pilton 17
Pin Well (Wooler) 131
Pio, Padre 127
Pittenweem 177–8
Plegmund, St 98: Plemstall well 98–9
Plemstall 98–9
Port Erin 123
Port Logan 172
Porteous, Crichton 104
Porthcawl 165
Potter's Well (Midhopestones) 139
Powys 161–5
Preston 126–7
Preston Kirk 174
Prevett, Tim 112
Princetown 16
Prout, Revd 75
Pryme, Abraham de la 87
Pyrford 49

Queen Anne's Well: (Blythburgh) 94;
    (Cadbury Castle) 27–8;
    (Carshalton) 47
Queen Anne's Wishing Well (Cadbury
    Castle) 27–8
Quendreda, Princess 60, 80
Queran, St 173: Islesteps well 173–4
Quiller-Couch, Thomas 4, 8, 11
Quinn, Phil 22, 23

Radford Semele 77
Rahtz, Philip 27
Ramsey (Isle of Man) 123
Ramsey Island 159–60
Rattue, James 187

Red Spring (Glastonbury) 24
Red Well (Knapwell) 84–5
Reginald of Durham 129
Restalrig 176–7
Rhadegund, St 38
Rhondda 166–7
Rhoscolyn 142–3
Rhos-on-Sea 148
Richard III, King106
Rob Roy (Scott) 132
Rogers, Margaret 73
Rolle, Richard 139–40
Roman Baths (Stoney Middleton) 103
Romiley 96–7
Romsley 60, 80–2
Ronan, St 170: Innerleithen well 170, 171
Rood Well (Stenton) 174
Rosamond, Fair 72
Roscarrock, Nicholas 9
Rowton's Well (Sutton Park) 78–9
Rudder, Samuel 56
Rumbold/Rumbald/Rumwold/Rumwald, St 53, 54, 70–1: Buckingham well 53–4; King's Sutton well 70–1; font 71
Running Well, The (Runwell) 86
Runwell 86
Rushton Spencer 115
Ruskin, John 51
Ruthwell 172
Rutland 107
Ryder, T.A. 56

saints: see individual saints' names; saints' wells are listed under name of saint
Sampson, St 13–14: Golant well 13–14
Sandwell Valley holy well 115
Sant, Jonathan 66
Saucimer, Sir Guy 106
Schorne, Sir John 54–5: North Marston well 54–5
Scilly, Isles of 21
Scotlandwell well 185
Scott, Sir Walter 132, 170
Scunthorpe 87

Seckworth 75
Secrets of the Hidden Source (Faull) 15
Seiriol, St 141: Penmon well 141–2
Sempringham holy well 86–7
Seven Wells (Bisley) 62–3
Sheepstor 18
Sherborne 22
Sheridan, Henry Brinsley 38
Shipton, Mother 135–6
Shod's Well (Spital) 97
Shrewsbury 111
Shropshire 108–12, 127
Sidwell, St 20
Silver Well (Cerne Abbas) 31–2, 33
Skye, Isle of 182–3
Somerset 22–8
Sopley holy well 37
Source 187, 206
Sourozh, Metropolitan Anthony of 17
South Cadbury 27–8
Southam holy well 77–8
Southey, Robert 8
Southwell 106; Minster holy well 106
Spaunton 138
Speen 30–1
Spital 97
Spring Wells (Billingborough) 87, 88
St Agnes 21
St Albans holy well 68
St Anne's Hill 47
St Bertram's Ash 112
St Briavels 58
St Cleer 4–5
St Clether 5–6
St Davids 159–61
St Decumans 25
St Fillan's: Cave 177; Chapel 185–6
St Justinian 159–60
St Keyne 8–9
St Lawrence 38
St Lawrence's Well – A Fragmentary Legend (Sheridan) 38
St Maddern's Bed 10, 11
St Neot 12–13
St Ronan's Well (Scott) 170
Staffordshire 112–15
Stainton-le-Vale 88

Stanger Spa 121
Stanwell 47
Stape 138–9
Stenton 174
Stephen, St: Utkinton well 99
Stevington holy well 52–3
Stewart, Gerry 60, 81
Sticklepath 17
Stirling 185–6
Stockwell (Beeby) 106
Stockwood, 32, 33
Stogursey 22–3
Stoke (Devon) 18–19
Stoke Edith 64
Stoke St Milborough 109
Stoney Middleton 103
Stowe 112–14
Straffon, Cheryl 3
Strathfillan 185–6
Sudeley Hill 60
Suffolk 94
Surrey 47–50
Survey of Dorsetshire (Coker) 34
Susanna's Well (Embleton) 121
Sussex, East and West 50–1
Sutton Coldfield 78–9
Sutton Park (Guildford) 48
Sutton Park (Sutton Coldfield) 78–9
Swansea 165, 167–8
Swithin, St 14: Launcells well 14

Taddy Well (Chittlehampton) 20
Tamlane's Well (Carterhaugh) 170
Tavistock 16
Tayvallich 170
Teara, St 20: Chittlehampton well 20
Tegla, St 150: Llandegla well 150
Teilo, St 143–4, 165–6: Llandaff well 165–6; Llandeilo well 143–4
Templeton 160
Tewdric/g, St 157: Mathern well 157
Theodoric, St 157: Mathern well 157
Thomas, St 128: Windle well 128–9
Thomas Becket, St 37, 68–9: Canterbury well 68; Northampton well 68–9
Thompson, Ian 86

Threshfield 137–8
Tiobar Dingan (Port Logan) 172
Tissington wells 103–5
Tobar Ashik (Broadford) 182–3
Tobar Ghorm (Culloden) 180–1
Tobar na Coille (Culloden) 180–1
Tobar na h-Oige (Culloden) 180–1
Tobar nan Ceann (Loch Oich) 181–2
Tobar Ninian (Dervaig) 170
Tockholes 125–6
Totnes 17
Tottenham 42
Town's Well (Hampole) 139–40
Treffynon 152–3
Trelille, John 9
Trellech 156–7
Tremeirchion 149
Triduana, St 176–7: Restalrig well 176–7
Trillo, St 148: Llandrillo-yn-Rhos well 148
Trinity Well (Ilston) 167–8
Trubshaw, Bob 105

Uptown Well (Bierton) 53
Upwey wishing well 35–6
Urith, St 20: Chittlehampton well 20
Utkinton 99–100

Virtuous Well (Trellech) 156–7

Wade's Causeway 139
Walsingham 88–91
Walstan, St 91–2: Bawburgh well 91–2
Walters, R.C. Skyring 61, 113
Ware 67
Warna, St 21: St Agnes well 21
Warwickshire 76–9
Watchet 25
Water Talk 187
Weaver, Cora 79
Weem 185
Welcombe 19–20
Well of Grace (Orton) 183
Well of St Keyne, The (Southey) 8
Well of the Baptism 122–3
Well of the Dead (Culloden) 181

Well of the Heads (Loch Oich) 181–2
Well of the Silver (Peel) 124
well-dressing 83, 84, 103, 104, 108,
    115, 139
Wells Cathedral 23, 60
Wenlock Priory 109
Werstan, St 79
West Bromwich 115
West Malling 46
West Mersea 85
Westhorpe 106
Westminster Abbey 34
Weymouth 35
Whistlebitch Well (Utkinton) 99–100
Whitchurch Canonicorum 34–5
White Well (Whitwell) 38
White Wells (Ilkley) 140
Whitstone 3–4
Whitwell 38
Wight, Isle of 38
Wilcote 73–4
Willesden 43
Willingdon 50
Wilton 64
Wiltshire 22, 39–41, 64
Wimbledon Common 42
Winchcombe 80, 81
Winchester 37

Windle 128–9
Winefride/Winifred, St 111, 152–3 :
    Holywell well 150, 152–3;
    Woolston well 111–12
Winwick 127–8
wishing wells 27, 32, 35–6, 88, 94,
    95–6, 107, 110, 114, 131, 135,
    180
Wite, St 34–5: Morcombelake well
    34–5
Withburga, St 92–3: Dereham well
    92–3
Wizard's Well (Alderley Edge) 95–6
Wolsingham holy well 121–2
Wolverhampton 115
Woodstock 72
Wooler 131
Woolston 111–12
Worcestershire 60, 79–82
Wulfruna, Lady 115
Wulfruna's Well (Wolverhampton) 115
Wulfwine 80

Yorkshire: East 132–4; North 112,
    134–9; South 139–40; West
    139–40
Young Tam Lin 170

Also from Heart of Albion Press

Cures and curses

Ritual and cult at holy wells

Janet Bord

Understanding the mysteries of sacred springs

Why are some wells said to be miraculously created by saints? Why are the rituals associated with them sometimes about divination or cursing? What evidence is there for the water curing illnesses? Do the wells have guardians? If so, are they humans, fairies, or even dragons? Is there treasure hidden there? What should be left there – rags, pins, coins, pebbles or even votive offerings?

Until recently the answers had been almost entirely forgotten. However a revival of interest in holy wells started in 1985 with the publication of Janet and Colin Bord's book *Sacred Waters* and in recent years research has gathered pace. In this entirely new book Janet brings together the latest understanding of such lore as 75 topic-by-topic descriptions, including their links to pre-Christian practices. There is also a list of 25 recommended wells to visit. The 135 illustrations include historic photographs of wells and rituals.

Cures and Curses provides an enticing overview for those looking for an introduction to holy wells and a source of reliable but little- known information for those already seduced by the allure of sacred springs.

Janet Bord lives in North Wales, where she and her husband Colin run the Fortean Picture Library. They have written more than 20 books on folklore and mysteries since their first successful joint venture, *Mysterious Britain* (1972).

> 'The book contains not only a plethora of illustrations, but also a very full bibliography, referring to many unusual items. But Janet Bord's style is blessedly unacademic. All in all, like the author's other books, this is a synthesis of imagination, poetry and scholarship, a must-have-read for all interested in the ancient traditions of these islands.' **Peter Costello** *Irish Catholic*

ISBN 978-1-872883-953. 2006. 245 x 175 mm, 191+ viii, 100 b&w photographs, 35 line drawings, paperback. **£14.95**

The Enchanted Land

Myths and Legends of Britain's Landscape

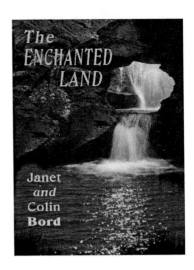

Revised, fully illustrated edition

Janet and Colin Bord

Britain's landscape is overlain by a magic carpet of folklore and folktales, myths and legends. Enchantment and legend still lurk in places as diverse as hills and mountains, rivers and streams, caves and hollows, springs and wells, cliffs and coasts, pools and lakes, and rocks and stones.

The dramatic stories woven around these places tell of sleeping knights, beheaded saints, giants, dragons and monsters, ghosts, King Arthur, mermaids, witches, hidden treasure, drowned towns, giant missiles, mysterious footprints, visits to Fairyland, underground passages, human sacrifices, and much more.

The 'Places to Visit' section locates and describes in detail more than 50 sites.

This revised edition is fully illustrated, with around 130 photographs and illustrations.

Janet and Colin Bord live in North Wales, where they run the Fortean Picture Library. They have written more than 20 books since their first successful joint venture, *Mysterious Britain* in 1972.

From reviews of the first edition:

'Janet's own enthusiasm for a number of the sites is conveyed vividly and lends credibility to the notion that Britain is still an enchanted land.' *Mercian Mysteries*

ISBN 1 872883 91 5. 2006. 245 x 175 mm, over 200 illustrations, paperback **£16.95**

Also from Heart of Albion Press

Footprints in Stone

The significance of foot- and hand-prints and other imprints left by early men, giants, heroes, devils, saints, animals, ghosts, witches, fairies and monsters

Janet Bord

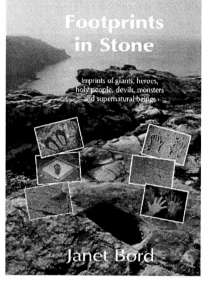

'A delightful exploration of a truly mysterious subject. 9 out of 10'
Bob Rickard *Fortean Times*

'Fascinating stuff and highly recommended.' Mike Howard *The Cauldron*

'... a good and wide-ranging first step into investigating the significance of the foot imprint.' John Billingsley *Northern Earth*

From the earliest humans to the present day, there has always been a compulsion to 'leave one's mark': early cave art includes thousands of hand outlines, while many churches in Britain have foot outlines inscribed in lead and stone. These two extremes span almost 30,000 years during which time all kinds of persons, real and legendary, have left visible traces of themselves. But 30,000 years ago seems almost recent, when compared with the finding of some (admittedly controversial) fossilized human footprints in rocks apparently contemporary with dinosaur footprints that are tens of millions of years old.

Most of the footprints – and hand-prints, knee-prints, and impressions of other body parts – are clearly not real, having allegedly been impressed into rocks around the world by such high-profile figures as the Buddha, Vishnu, Jesus Christ, and the Virgin Mary, as well as a vast panoply of saints, whose footprint traces and associated stories occupy two chapters. Their horses also left hoof-prints, and other animals are represented too. Not surprisingly, the ubiquitous Devil has a whole chapter to himself – but giants, villains and heroes, such as King Arthur, also feature strongly. Witches, fairies, ghosts and assorted spirits have made their mark: there are many modern instances of phantom hand- and foot-prints, the latter often bloodstained and indelible.

Hundreds of imprints are described in this book, which concludes with location details for more than 100 imprint sites all around the world.

ISBN 1 872883 73 7. 2004. 245 x 175 mm, 263 + x pages, 112 b&w photos, 26 line drawings, paperback. **£14.95**

English Holy Wells

A sourcebook

Jeremy Harte

What happens if you track down the earliest known reference to every holy well in England? The vivid traditions of these sites, many of them hitherto unknown, cast a new light on whether holy wells were taken over from pagan precursors, and what the Reformation meant for sacred landscapes. Colourful tales of saints, sprites and charlatans reveal the lively side of medieval popular religion.

With this book the study of English holy wells moves out of the realms of romanticism and myth-making into the light of history. Jeremy Harte draws on maps, miracles, legends and landscapes to present his detailed discussions in a readable and often witty manner.

Jeremy Harte is a folklorist with a particular interest in sacred places and supernatural encounters. His other books include *Explore Fairy Traditions, Cuckoo Pounds and Singing Barrows, The Green Man, Research in Geomancy* and *Alternative Approaches to Folklore.* He is curator of Bourne Hall Museum in Surrey.

'... an invaluable source of information and a damn good read. 9/10'
Janet Bord *Fortean Times*

'Very highly recommended' Mike Howard *The Cauldron*

'Highly recommended' Jerry Bird *Merry Meet*

English Holy Wells comprises three volumes. Volume One is supplied with a CD-ROM of Volumes Two and Three to make the complete work available at an affordable price.

Volume One (includes CD-ROM of Volumes Two and Three):
ISBN 978-1-905646-10-4, 245 x 175 mm, 168 + xvi pages, 24 b&w line drawings, paperback, 2008. **£14.95**

Singing Up The Country

The songlines of Avebury and beyond

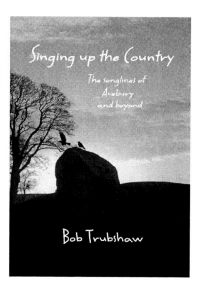

Bob Trubshaw

Singing Up the Country reveals that Bob Trubshaw has been researching a surprising variety of different topics since his last book six years ago. From Anglo-Saxon place-names to early Greek philosophy – and much in between – he creates an interwoven approach to the prehistoric landscape, creating a 'mindscape' that someone in Neolithic Britain might just recognise. This is a mindscape where sound, swans and rivers help us to understand the megalithic monuments.

Continuing from where scholarship usually stops and using instead the approaches of storytelling, the final chapter weaves this wide variety of ideas together as a 'songline' for the Avebury landscape. This re-mythologising of the land follows two 'dreamtime' ancestors along the Kennet valley to the precursors of Avebury henge and Silbury Hill.

Few writers have Bob Trubshaw's breadth of knowledge combined with a mythopoetic ability to construct a modern day story that re-enchants the landscape. *Singing Up the Country* will be an inspiration to all those interested in prehistory, mythology or the Neolithic monuments of the World Heritage Site at Avebury.

> 'This is a book with enormous appeal for anyone with an interest in prehistory, megalithic sites, mythology and folklore, and indeed for anyone who enjoys the countryside, and who can recognise the mystery and magic it holds in its secret past. Highly recommended' Jerry Bird *Merry Meet*

> 'Trubshaw writes with practised and confident ease. His entertaining and sometimes jocular style makes for very easy reading; the experience is rather like sitting in a comfortable pub with a pint, listening to a seasoned storyteller.' Steve Marshall *Fortean Times*

ISBN 978-1-905646-21-0 2011. 245 x 175 mm, 189 + xiv pages, 64 b&w photos, 29 line drawings, paperback. **£14.95**

Sacred Places
Prehistory and popular imagination
Bob Trubshaw

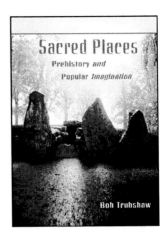

Sacred Places asks why certain types of prehistoric places are thought of as sacred, and explores how the physical presence of such sacred sites is less important than what these places signify. So this is not another guide book to sacred places but instead provides a unique and thought-provoking guide to the mental worlds – the mindscapes – in which we have created the idea of prehistoric sacred places.

Recurring throughout this book is the idea that we continually create and re-create our ideas about the past, about landscapes, and the places within those landscapes that we regard as sacred. For example, although such concepts as 'nature', 'landscape', 'countryside', 'rural' and the contrast between profane and sacred are all part of our everyday thinking, in this book Bob Trubshaw shows they are all modern cultural constructions which act as the 'unseen' foundations on which we construct more complex myths about places.

Key chapters look at how earth mysteries, modern paganism and other alternative approaches to sacred places developed in recent decades, and also outline the recent dramatic changes within academic archaeology. Is there now a 'middle way' between academic and alternative approaches which recognises that what we know about the past is far less significant than what we believe about the past?

Bob Trubshaw has been actively involved with academic and alternative approaches to archaeology for most of the last twenty years. In 1996 he founded *At the Edge* magazine to popularise new interpretations of past and place.

> '*Sacred Places*... is a very valuable addition to the small body of thoughtful work on the spiritual landscapes of Great Britain and therefore recommended reading.' Nigel Pennick *Silver Wheel*

> 'One of the best books in the field I have ever read.'
> D J Tyrer *Monomyth Supplement*

ISBN 1 872883 67 2. 2005. 245 x 175 mm, 203 + xiv pages, 43 b&w illustrations and 7 line drawings, paperback. **£16.95**

Stonehenge:
Celebration and Subversion

Andy Worthington

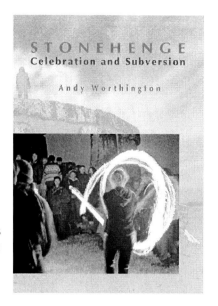

This innovative social history looks in detail at how the summer solstice celebrations at Stonehenge have brought together different aspects of British counter-culture to make the monument a 'living temple' and an icon of alternative Britain. The history of the celebrants and counter-cultural leaders is interwoven with the viewpoints of the land-owners, custodians and archaeologists who have generally attempted to impose order on the shifting patterns of these modern-day mythologies.

The story of the Stonehenge summer solstice celebrations begins with the Druid revival of the 18th century and the earliest public gatherings of the 19th and early 20th centuries. In the social upheavals of the 1960s and early 70s, these trailblazers were superseded by the Stonehenge Free Festival. This evolved from a small gathering to an anarchic free state the size of a small city, before its brutal suppression at the Battle of the Beanfield in 1985.

In the aftermath of the Beanfield, the author examines how the political and spiritual aspirations of the free festivals evolved into both the rave scene and the road protest movement, and how the prevailing trends in the counter-culture provided a fertile breeding ground for the development of new Druid groups, the growth of paganism in general, and the adoption of other sacred sites, in particular Stonehenge's gargantuan neighbour at Avebury.

The account is brought up to date with the reopening of Stonehenge on the summer solstice in 2000, the unprecedented crowds drawn by the new access arrangements, and the latest source of conflict, centred on a bitterly-contested road improvement scheme.

> '*Stonehenge Celebration and Subversion* contains an extraordinary story. Anyone who imagines Stonehenge to be nothing but an old fossil should read this and worry. [This book is] ... the most complete, well-illustrated analysis of Stonehenge's mysterious world of Druids, travellers, pagans and party-goers'. Mike Pitts *History Today*

ISBN 1 872883 76 1. 2004. Perfect bound, 245 x 175 mm, 281 + xviii pages, 147 b&w photos, **£14.95**

*Winner of the Folklore Society
Katharine Briggs Award 2005*

Explore Fairy Traditions

Jeremy Harte

We are not alone. In the shadows of our countryside there lives a fairy race, older than humans, and not necessarily friendly to them. For hundreds of years, men and women have told stories about the strange people, beautiful as starlight, fierce as wolves, and heartless as ice. These are not tales for children. They reveal the fairies as a passionate, proud, brutal people.

Explore Fairy Traditions draws on legends, ballads and testimony from throughout Britain and Ireland to reveal what the fairies were really like. It looks at changelings, brownies, demon lovers, the fairy host, and abduction into the Otherworld. Stories and motifs are followed down the centuries to reveal the changing nature of fairy lore, as it was told to famous figures like W.B. Yeats and Sir Walter Scott. All the research is based on primary sources and many errors about fairy tradition are laid to rest.

Jeremy Harte combines folklore scholarship with a lively style to show what the presence of fairies meant to people's lives. Like their human counterparts, the secret people could kill as well as heal. They knew marriage, seduction, rape and divorce; they adored some children and rejected others. If we are frightened of the fairies, it may be because their world offers an uncomfortable mirror of our own.

> '... this is the best and most insightful book on fairies generally available... ' John Billingsley *Northern Earth*

> '*Explore Fairy Traditions* is an excellent introduction to the folklore of fairies, and I would highly recommend it.' Paul Mason *Silver Wheel*

ISBN 1 872883 61 3. 2004. Demy 8vo (215 x 138 mm), 171 + vi pages, 6 line drawings, paperback. **£9.95**

Also from Heart of Albion Press

'Highly recommended'
Folklore Society Katharine Briggs
Award 2003

Explore Folklore

Bob Trubshaw

'A howling success, which plugs
a big and obvious gap'
Professor Ronald Hutton

There have been fascinating developments in the study of folklore in the last twenty-or-so years, but few books about British folklore and folk customs reflect these exciting new approaches. As a result there is a huge gap between scholarly approaches to folklore studies and 'popular beliefs' about the character and history of British folklore. *Explore Folklore* is the first book to bridge that gap, and to show how much 'folklore' there is in modern day Britain.

Explore Folklore shows there is much more to folklore than morris dancing and fifty-something folksingers! The rituals of 'what we do on our holidays', funerals, stag nights and 'lingerie parties' are all full of 'unselfconscious' folk customs. Indeed, folklore is something that is integral to all our lives – it is so intrinsic we do not think of it as being 'folklore'.

The implicit ideas underlying folk lore and customs are also explored. There might appear to be little in common between people who touch wood for luck (a 'tradition' invented in the last 200 years) and legends about people who believe they have been abducted and subjected to intimate body examinations by aliens. Yet, in their varying ways, these and other 'folk beliefs' reflect the wide spectrum of belief and disbelief in what is easily dismissed as 'superstition'.

Explore Folklore provides a lively introduction to the study of most genres of British folklore, presenting the more contentious and profound ideas in a readily accessible manner.

ISBN 1 872883 60 5. 2002. Demy 8vo (215x138 mm), 200 pages, illustrated, paperback **£9.95**

Heart of Albion

Publishing folklore, mythology and
local history since 1989

Further details of all Heart of Albion titles online at
www.hoap.co.uk

All titles available direct from Heart of Albion Press.

Heart of Albion Press

113 High Street, Avebury
Marlborough, SN8 1RF

Phone: 01672 539077
email: albion@indigogroup.co.uk
Web site: www.hoap.co.uk